Encyclopedia of
Victorian Colored Pattern Glass
Book 5
U. S. Glass From A to Z

by
william heacock & fred bickenheuser

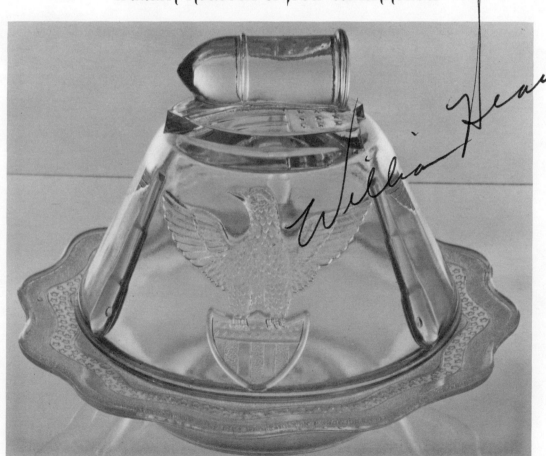

Bullet pattern covered butter dish, introduced in 1898 by U.S.G.C.

Color Photography by
RICHARDSON PRINTING CORPORATION
Marietta, Ohio

To Lisa Tobin & Ruth Bickenheuser

Published & Distributed by:

Antique Publications
P.O. Box 655
Marietta, Ohio 45750

TABLE OF CONTENTS

INTRODUCTION
by WILLIAM HEACOCK

Without doubt, this volume in my pattern glass series was the most difficult to produce. As it goes to press, it still seems incomplete — a mere surface study of the primary output of the largest table glass company in the history of this nation.

The idea for this book first came to existence in the mind of my co-author, Fred Bickenheuser. Fred was one of those all-too-important chance meetings which led to my career as a pattern glass historian. He showed me some material he had located while researching his proposed book on the United States Glass Company. He even shared the location of this material for my own efforts at preparing the first book in this series. As I leafed through this priceless stash of old journals, it became clear to me that what I found needed to be documented, and I initiated my column in the "Antique Trader." I can never thank Fred enough for opening the door for me, and I consider it a priviledge to share the credit for this book with him.

In 1976, Mr. Bickenheuser located a number of rare old U.S. Glass Company catalogues which again he unselfishly showed to me. He even granted permission to reprint small portions in my Book 3. At this time I suggested the possibility of a collaboration, with his knowledge of the history of the company and my knowledge of pattern glass. It took two years from conception to actual publication, and it's been a rough go all the way.

As we finalized our efforts for the presses, additional catalogues surfaced in new York, which necessitated additional travel, considerable revision, more additions and a last minute update. This volume contains literally thousands of pieces of information, and it would be a virtual impossibility to present it with **no** mistakes and **no** omissions. I have listed all colors I know about, but without doubt a few have escaped our attention. No attempt has been made to list the items made in each pattern, as this often proves too time-consuming and easy prey for many omissions. I trust my readers are now aware that the validity of my books is a primary concern of mine. However, often an important bit of data is somehow overlooked during production. I offer here the best of which I am capable, and I hope I have not disappointed you.

INTRODUCTION
by FRED BICKENHEUSER

Our first piece of United States pattern glass, a large brilliant green bowl with a fluted rim, was discovered in an old barn in Holland, Massachusetts.

At that time Ruth and I did not know it was a United States Glass piece, as it wasn't marked in any way. We showed this piece to quite a number of antique dealers, and took it to many flea markets and antique shows in quest of information. We searched for over two years. It was finally identified as the "Colorado" pattern, one of the States patterns produced by the United States Glass Company about 1898. Our curiosity was not satisfied as we wanted to know more about these State patterns. Looking for additional information, we quickly realized that there was very little in print about the States patterns and even less about the United States Glass Company.

I began to research old periodicals of that era, and to write to public libraries in the towns where the U.S.G.C. had at one time located their factories. Most of my inquiries came back with very little information, other than "the old records of the United States Glass Company were destroyed by fires and floods". I then started to write to glassware companies, hoping they would help us with our research. Our inquiries included one to Tiffin Glass, Tiffin, Ohio, which was one of the last factories that operated under the U.S.G.C. About this time I discovered a number of old glass periodicals in one of the local libraries, and became engrossed in studying these.

A year had gone by, and my original inquiry to Tiffin Glass had gone unanswered. Just on a hunch I telephoned Mr. C. W. Carlson, Jr., Vice President of Tiffin Glass. He advised that he had not received my inquiry, asking me to write another and mark it personal. It was about ten days after I had written my second inquiry, that I received the good news. I received a letter from Mr. Carl Assenheimer, Director of Customer Relations, advising Mr. Carlson's permission to use "any old records that were available", so that the United States Glass Company could be documented. Upon my arrival at the Tiffin, Ohio plant the next day, Mr. Assenheimer guided me to one of the older buildings of the factory, up a number of time-worn wooden steps, into a pitch black loft, and back in time many years. It is the opinion of this researcher that this loft had been considered years ago a safe depository for the permanent records of the U.S.G.C., when their home office was moved from Pittsburgh, Pennsylvania in 1937. There were tons of dusty records, ledgers, receipts, letters, minutes of meetings; the documents of the largest glass company of its time.

Without these records, and Mr. C. W. Carlson, Jr.'s permission to use them, this book could not have been so completely documented.

HOW TO USE THIS BOOK

Organization of this book has been kept as simple as possible. A brief history of the United States Glass Company is offered, but our primary concern was to document as many of their patterns as possible, all colors which are known, and to clear up confusion where it exists.

The pattern listing is arranged in alphabetical order, with all pertinent information available at a glance. Included in this listing are a number of "possible U.S. Glass patterns, such as *Double Dahlia with Lens* and *Medallion*. I have also included patterns known made by member factories before the 1891 merger, but I suspect were continued after this date or were possible reissued by the conglomerate at a later date. I hope you will not find this speculative practice too objectionable.

It is virtually impossible to pinpoint production dates of patterns made by the U.S.G.C. Inventory records show many patterns were kept active for several decades. The dates provided are an estimate of the earliest production date as produced by U.S.G.C., even though they may have been *produced earlier* by the factory which joined the merger. Special note is made of those patterns which had an especially lengthy production life.

A color listing is provided, even though I am certain there will be dozens of rare limited items in colors not listed since they have not been seen by Mr. Bickenheuser and myself to date. These rare colors will be added to later editions as they are seen or are properly reported to us (with documentive photo's).

Often a pattern is known only in crystal, and yet a rare item will turn up in ruby-stain. It should be remembered that often an independent decorating firm would buy huge lots of discontinued U.S.G.C. product, to be decorated or souvenired and sold as their own product. Some of these items are scarce today and it would be considerably difficult to accumulate a "set". In such cases where colored production is so limited, special notation is made. For example, the *Amazon* pattern is known primarily in crystal; however the cruet (Fig. 231) is known in color. This does not necessarily mean the table set was made in color, even though it is possible it can be found in extremely limited quantities.

Due to the massive volume of output by the United States Glass Company, it would be very difficult to illustrate here all items and patterns produced by this firm. As impressive as the catalogue reprint in this book is, it could have been five times larger. We have tried to be very selective in our presentation. In some cases, we were unable to locate an example to photograph, so the Pattern Guide offers a cross-reference where the "best illustration" or the most complete illustration of the pattern can be found. Not all readers of this book will have these other references at their disposal. However, I am presenting this pattern guide on the assumption that it will be an aide to all serious glass collectors and amateur historians, most of whom already have the primary glass references referred to in the guide. The important patterns are illustrated in this book, so there should be little sense of loss that it is not a **complete** U.S. Glass pattern reference. Already a sequel is being planned to include those important items from early catalogues which had to be left out due to space limitations.

ACKNOWLEDGEMENTS

As difficult as it was to produce this book, it amazed us how easy it was to accumulate the glass shown in this book in color. Two major collectors from the Midwest wish to remain nameless, but we must single them out for their continued support of this series and their unselfish trust.

Other dealers and collectors who we wish to express our deepest gratitude to are Jack Burk, John Bennington, Penny Sulley, Robert Bickenheuser, Robert and Pat Costa, Ted and Ruth Heischman, John and Eva Gordon, Richard and Pat Olson, Tom Neale, Mary Jane Hastings, Mrs. Edward Fishman, Herbert and Betty Ward (Stage Coach Antiques), and Mary, Lyle and Lynn Welker.

A very special word of thanks must be extended to the most helpful staff and personnel at the Tiffin Glass Company (Division of Interpace Corporation), especially the previously mentioned Mr. C. W. Carlson, Jr. and Carl Assenheimer, as well as Ms. Martha Ziegler, who was never too busy to spare us a few minutes of unselfish help or advise.

For information found in early U.S. Glass catalogues, we wish to thank the staff of the Carnegie Institute, the Ohio State University Library, the Toledo and Cincinnati Public Libraries, and the New York Metropolitan Museum of Art.

We wish to thank Harry Kuhlman and Roy Williams for providing Information on the History of the U.S. Glass Company.

It is seldom that we have an opportunity to pinpoint the production staff of Richardson Printing Corp., so we wish to do so here. We are especially grateful to the art department who worked so hard designing and pasting up this book, a major undertaking in itself. Our deepest thanks to Robert A. Reid, Ronda Stephens, Robert Hall and Roderick Hook.

For consistent quality color photography, for endless amounts of patience and talent, we want to thank Dale Brown.

A final thank you to Lisa Tobin, Bobbi Kuenz, Sue Tresenrider and Julia Walls for their typing skills in helping prepare this book.

GLASS BY UNITED STATES GLASS COMPANY
Is It Collectible?

This is the fifth volume of a continuing series on pattern glass of the Victorian era. To date, each volume has concentrated on a type of or specific shape in glass. Book 1 covered a specific item, toothpick holders, which are very collectible in their own right. Book 2 dealt with a type of glass, opalescent, which is undergoing an astronomical rise in popularity. Book 3 again dealt with items originally used as part of a "seasoning service"—syrups, sugar shakers and cruets. Needless to say, collectors of these shapes are witnessing a considerable rise in values. Book 4 reverts back again to a type of glass, custard glass, which amazingly has gone up in value even more than I thought possible.

However, Book 5 is distinctly different from the others inasmuch as it concentrates on glass by a specific company, not a shape or a type. This book attempts to cover the earliest production of the largest table glass company in the history of this country. With the possible exception of my co-author, I can honestly say I have never heard of a true collector of glass made by the United States Glass Company. Bear in mind that this company was, in the beginning, a merger of seventeen independent companies. To attempt such a collection involving more than 325 patterns from 19 locations would take a considerable bank account, and endless amounts of patience. So where does the popularity, and thus collectibility, of the glass covered by this book begin?

The answer can only be broken down into four major factors. First, for reasons known only to the individual collector, glass is sought after for it's pattern. Many of those made by U.S. Glass are popular today, including Broken Column, King's Crown, Coin and Wildflower. We must also consider the popularity of the "States" series. Many collectors from all over this country today are trying to piece together a complete service of the pattern named after their home state. The most popular among these would probably be Delaware, Dakota, Kansas, Pennsylvania and Virginia (the latter because of the unfortunate "Portland Glass" misconceptions).

Second, glass is desirable because of it's color. While the vast majority of U.S. Glass was made in crystal, and in fact is much desired by many in this clear glass we witness as well a wide range of color output to please even the most discriminating among us. Many collectors today search for sets of ruby-stained glass. A wide number of the patterns issued by U.S. Glass in clear glass were also sent to their decorating shop to be stained red. Other popular colors which are collectible include custard (Vermont), purple slag (Stylized Flower), milk glass (the fowl-covered dishes), and even opalescent and carnival glass (Palm Beach).

Third, many collectors search for items made in their home town or at a particular factory. I know of several people who search diligently for glass made by Hobbs, virtually impervious to the fact that it was Factory "H" of the U.S.G.C. The same is true for Wheeling, Greentown, Albany, Findlay or even Pittsburgh glass. The fact that a local factory merged into a big corporation is of little importance to many collectors—only the location of manufacture concerns them.

Finally we have collectors of various shapes. There are many hundreds of collectors of toothpick holders, and almost as many who accumulate salt shakers. Other popular items are tumblers, cruets, syrup pitchers, and even complete four-piece table sets (creamer, sugar, spooner and butter dish). Since the United States Glass Company virtually dominated the market for pressed glass tableware at the turn of the century, it is hard to imagine a collection of the above shapes not including many pieces of this company's glass.

Broken down we can see that much of this U.S. Glass is in demand, but as an entity I suppose I have to say it is not. In it's heyday, this huge company was far too big with a tremendous product output. Collectors today have been "spoon-fed" so little authoritative data concerning the U.S.G.C. and it's patterns, that most have turned to other areas where the ground is more familiar. Perhaps now, with this publication, the quality glass produced by this major contributor of Victorian tableware will come out of the shadows and into the limelight.

An early history of The United States Glass Company 1891-1910

By
Fred Bickenheuser

First President of U.S. Glass Company, Daniel C. Ripley.

Rare commemorative paperweight produced by U.S. Glass in 1908 honoring the 150th anniversary of the founding of Pittsburgh, Pa.

On Thursday, December 16, 1890, in the city of Pittsburgh, Pennsylvania, very close to the hour of 3:00 in the afternoon, Mr. Daniel C. Ripley made his way to the Bank of Commerce Building, Room #704, for the purpose of meeting with his peers.

Those present at that first meeting were: James B. Lyon, O'Hara Glass Co., Ltd., Pittsburgh, Pa.; William C. King, King Glass Co., Pittsburgh, Pa.; Daniel C. Ripley, Ripley Glass Co., Pittsburgh, Pa.; Andrew Bryce, Bryce Brothers Glass Co., Pittsburgh, Pa.; A. A. Adams, Adams & Co., Pittsburgh, Pa.; J. D. Wilson, Richards & Hartley Glass Co., Tarentum, Pa.; William P. Shinn, well known as a careful and efficient organizer who had introduced the system of accounts so successfully used by the Pennsylvania Co. and the Edger Thopson Steel Works.

This was the first of five meetings that would be held in that room for the purpose of setting up a charter for what would be later known as the United States Glass Company.

The second, third, and fourth meetings were held, pursuant to forming committees, and setting up the organization of the corporation.

One of the most important committees was "The Natural Gas & Fuel Committee", which investigated the sources of supply of fuel for the different factories which had expressed their desire to become a part of the company. In many cases, natural gas wells were located on the factory's property, from which they received their fuel. Others held gas contracts with the local gas companies, which the company had signed over the the United States Glass Co. after they joined.

Another committee investigated patents of which there were thousands; design patents for glassware and those pertaining to the production of glassware. Other committees would investigate molds and glass patterns currently in production, reporting to the executive committee which patterns to continue to produce and which to discontinue. Others would examine real estate and the locations of the factories.

The members of these committees were the owners, managers, and department heads of the factories, men with experience who knew what they were doing. These monumental tasks took six months to complete.

On Saturday, June 27, 1891 at 10:00 A.M. a meeting of the Incorporators of the U.S.G.C. was held, again in Room #704 of the Bank of Commerce Building, in the city of Pittsburgh, Pa. This meeting was called for the explicit purpose of incorporating the U.S.G.C. According to the bylaws, the number of directors was set at eleven, and the following persons were to constitute the first Board of Directors: James B. Lyon, representing O'Hara Glass Co., Ltd., Pittsburgh, Pa.; William C. King, representing King Glass Co., Pittsburgh, Pa.; Daniel C. Ripley, representing Ripley & Co., Pittsburgh, Pa.; A. A. Adams, representing Adams & Co., Pittsburgh, Pa.; Andrew H. Bryce, representing Bryce Brothers, Pittsburgh, Pa.; Hanson E. Waddell, representing Hobbs Glass Co., Wheeling, West V.; D. C. Jenkins, representing Columbia Glass Co., Findlay, Ohio; A. H. Heisey, representing George Duncan & Sons, Pittsburgh, Pa.; A. J. Smith, representing Nickel Plate Glass Co., Fostoria, Ohio; James D. Wilson, representing Richards & Hartley Glass Co., Tarentum, Pa., and William P. Shinn, who was contracted for the purpose of setting up the record and bookkeeping systems of the corporation.

William P. Shinn presented letters of patent dated February 12, 1891, granted by the state of Pennsylvania, incorporating the U.S.G.C. Upon motion, duly seconded, the letters were accepted and it was resolved that the application for the Charter, together with all endorsements, be at once recorded in the Recorder's Office of Allegheny Co., Pennsylvania, as required by law. On a motion, it was resolved that the organization of the U.S.G.C. date from July 1, 1891. Thus, the largest glass company in the world was formed.

This was the era of consolidation, and the aim and expectation of the newly organized U.S.G.C. was to make larger profits, by the use of a thorough purchasing system, increased economy in the production and sale of its glassware, the consolidation of it's offices at home and abroad, and to give special attention to new foreign markets. It was evident that these objectives could not have been accomplished to any great extent by individual or small companies. The newly formed company did not contemplate increasing it's profits by any excessive raise in selling prices.

The official organization was as follows: President—Daniel C. Ripley; Vice President—William C. King; Secretary—Andrew H. Bryce; and Treasurer —John Stevenson.

Operating Officers

Accounting Department—James D. Wilson (Auditor); William J. Farley (Asst. Auditor); Commercial Department—A. H. Heisey (Manager); Manufacturing Department—Joseph Anderson (General Manager); J. McD. Bryce (Asst. Manager); Supply Department—William A. Gorby (Purchasing Agent).

A prospectus letter dated September 1, 1891 advised: "The undersigned glass manufacturers desire to inform their patrons and friends that they have associated themselves together in the formation of the United States Glass Company.

	Which will be known as factory:
Adams & Company, Pittsburgh, Pa.	A
Bryce Brothers, Pittsburgh, Pa.	B
Bellaire Goblet Co., Findlay, Ohio	M
Central Glass Co., Wheeling, West Va.	O
Columbia Glass Co., Findlay, Ohio	J
Challinor, Taylor & Co., Tarentum, Pa.	C
Doyle & Co., Pittsburgh, Pa.	P
George Duncan & Sons, Pittsburgh, Pa.	D
Gillinder & Sons, Greensburgh, Pa.	G
Hobbs Glass Co., Wheeling, West Va.	H
King Glass Co., Pittsburgh, Pa.	K
Nickel Plate Glass Co., Fostoria, Ohio	N
O'Hara Glass Co., Pittsburgh, Pa.	L
Richards & Hartley, Tarentum, Pa.	E
Ripley & Co., Pittsburgh, Pa.	F

Orders should be sent to the United States Glass Company, but be kind enough in all cases, to name the firm that formerly made the goods. We hope for the continuance of past business, and to be able to merit increased appreciation".

This letter was signed by Mr. A. H. Heisey, Manager, Commercial Department, United States Glass Company. The Commercial Department was what is now known as the Sales Department. This document and hundreds of other papers researched, including the deeds for the glassware companies, gave us definite identification of the original companies that formed the U.S.G.C. Additional companies were added later in the history of the U.S.G.C., and some of the original 10 were lost by fire. Others would be sold outright or consolidated.

The properties of the preceding named firms were appraised by experts and each company received Common Stock of the U.S.G.C., for their factories at the rate of $100.00 per share. To secure a working capital, Preferred Stock was issued in the amount of $640,000, largely purchased by the firms that comprised the organization, at $100.00 per share in cash.

On January 1, 1892, A. J. Beatty & Sons of Tiffin, Ohio was added to the company, which would be known as Factory "R". The old buildings of the A. J. Beatty & Sons Glassworks at Steubenville, Ohio were also taken into the U.S.G.C. at this time, but they were to be used only as a warehouse. The machinery and tooling had been removed in 1888 when the city of Tiffin, Ohio contracted with A. J. Beatty & Sons for the construction of a glassworks there. A simple printing error on one of the first catalogues of the U.S.G.C. listed A. J. Beatty & Sons, Steubenville, Ohio as Factory "S". This error was duplicated many times down through the years by other authors who had not further researched the facts. This property was carried by the U.S.G.C. as Factory "S", as a matter of identification only, having taken it into the organization along with the operating glass works of A. J. Beatty & Sons, Tiffin, Ohio.

On October 6, 1892, the Novelty Glass Co., Fostoria, Ohio sold all of its molds, tooling, chemicals and office furniture to the U.S.G.C. for $1,545.20. There were 183 molds involved in this sale. The land

and buildings were then leased to the U.S.G.C. The factory was operated by U.S.G.C. as Factory "T" until April 1, 1893, when a fire almost completely destroyed the factory. At the time of the fire, this factory was producing tumblers and bottles. The plant remained virtually idle until February, 1896, at which time the stockholders of the Novelty Glass Co. disposed of the property.

Glass factories were considered a bad fire risk, largely because of the flimsey, poorly planned construction. The U.S.G.C. suffered heavy losses, not only from fires, but from the insolvency of many of the fire insurance companies. While collecting extortionate rates for fire insurance coverage, little or nothing was paid on claims as a result of a fire. In researching the many fire claims, especially in the early years of the company, it was necessary to insure their factories with at least forty different fire insurance companies in order to even partially cover their fire losses. This researcher noted that a number of fire insurance claims would be returned by mail to the United States Glass Co. stamped by the Post Office **"Left Town, No Forwarding Address"**.

In the first annual report of the United States Glass Co. dated August 17, 1892, President Daniel C. Ripley advises: "The delay in getting underway, caused partly by unsettled differences between the Conference Committees of the American Flint Glass Union, and the workmen, shortened the production to three and one-half months. The delays and inconveniences inevitable in organizing and conducting so large a business, necessarily limited our product and our profits. These delays were beyond our control and necessitated considerable loss to the company. The natural prejudice which accompanies the organization of any large industry has been met and overcome. The economics which we expected to realize by purchasing in large quantities, and consolidating of offices at home and abroad, has been partly accomplished. It is natural to expect that in the future, with the experience gained, the affairs of the company and the profits can be greatly improved."

In comparing the amount of work done by the individual companies the year previous to formation of the U.S.G.C., we find the old companies worked 22 furnaces, with 360 pots, on an average of 36 weeks; while for the first year the United States Glass Company worked 23 furnaces with 371 pots on an average of 40 weeks, an increase of about 15%.

The first dividend on the preferred stock, was paid on March 31, 1892, in the amount of $21,200.00. Net sales from December 31, 1891 to June 30, 1892 were $2,747,736.93.

Mr. William P. Shinn, a member of the Board of Directors, whose vast business experience and advice was invaluable in originally setting up the record systems of the company, passed away on May 5, 1892. He had accomplished a monumental task.

During the winters of 1892-1893, the shortage of gas in the city gas lines of Findlay, Ohio resulted in numerous complaints from the citizens, contending that the private residences were suffering while the manufacturers were using the gas. As a result of these complaints, the Board of Gas Trustees, on November 25, 1892, sent notices to thirteen of its manufacturing firms who were their largest consumers. Factory "M"

and Factory "J" of the U.S.G.C. were among those notified. Upon receipt of this notice, the management of the U.S.G.C. ordered a plant for the burning of oil for each of its two factories, delivery of which was promised by January 20, 1893. A representative of the U.S.G.C. went before the Board of Gas Trustees and requested allowance of enough gas for the two plants to prevent the pots from breaking until the oil plants would arrive. Upon being refused, it was asked that they be allowed enough gas to work out the glass in the pots, which would have taken about three or four days. The Board again refused, and the gas was shut off on January 12, 1893, causing a loss of glass and pots valued at over $5,000. After the manufacturer's gas supply was shut off, it was found that the gas supply for the citizen's homes was no better than it was when the manufacturers were using gas, thus demonstrating what had always been the opinion and argument of men with experience: "The trouble in the supply of gas in Findlay was caused by the gas mains being too small". Shortly afterwards, the gas was turned on again to the manufacturers, but at a higher rate. As a result of this action of the Findlay Glass Trustees, the U.S.G.C. rebuilt all of its furnaces in all of its plants, whereby they could be changed over to coal or fuel oil at short notice and without further expense.

From the first meeting of the Board of Directors of the U.S.G.C., it was felt that there would be many advantages and increased profits to the company if the various plants were consolidated into one or two locations. This conclusion became more and more apparent, and the Board gave considerable attention to this matter without taking actual steps to accomplish it. They had a number of liberal offers from many places in desirable locations, which were to be strongly considered in months to come.

In the early part of 1893, the company purchased about 500 acres of land on the east bank of the Monongahela River, about one and one half miles above McKeesport, Pennsylvania. This property had been plotted to reserve the land between the Monogahelia River and the railroad for manufacturing sites—the balance being laid out into town lots. Thus, the U.S.G.C. originally founded and built the town of Glassport, Pennsylvania.

The contract had been issued to erect a two furnace, fire-proof plant, which would be ready for operations by January 1, 1894. This property would by that time be connected with McKeesport, Pa. by an electric street car. A single fare of five cents would deliver a passenger to any of the principal streets of McKeesport, Pa. This property, which was to be called Glassport, was so well located that the U.S.G.C. would make a considerable profit on its investment in a very few years. In addition, they would reserve sufficient river frontage for the proposed consolidation of all of its factories in Pennsylvania and West Virginia.

When the U.S.G.C. organized, naturally there was only one President, but each member company had their own set of officers. These men were given executive positions in the parent company, so it started out over-staffed with plenty of brass hats.

Mr. Daniel C. Ripley was President of the U.S.G.C. until August 22, 1893. The management foresaw trouble ahead and felt a number of radical steps had to be taken in the way of retrenchment.

On August 22, 1893 Mr. Ralph Baggaley was elected by the Board of Directors to the position of President with the sole purpose of reorganization. He was an executive of high standard, but not a glass manufacturer. In October of the same year, a large number of the company's officers, men of unquestioned ability, ripe with experience and loyalty, were dispensed of. This resulted in a lot of these men starting independent glass companies which would soon become competitors of the U.S.G.C. The clerical force in the general office at Pittsburgh, Pa. was reduced about one-half, and the office forces employed at the company's various factories were reduced to a minimum. In short, economics were inaugurated whenever and wherever possible. Subsequent events showed that this course was necessary for the company's welfare, if not for its salvation.

The years of 1892 and 1893 were ones of disturbances and loss of revenue; all businesses were in a depressed state. Strikes were almost universal, few undertakings showed profit and many showed losses.

The prospect of a major conflict between the American Flint Glass Workers Union and the new management of the U.S.G.C. had engaged the attention of laboring classes all over the world. This union was second in numbers among labor organizations. There was only one other union that was more powerful, also located on the south side of Pittsburgh known as the Window Glassworkers Association. The combined wealth of these two labor organizations was over a half million dollars in 1893. The "flints" or glassware workers were a little better off financially than the "window workers", but they did not control the trade effectively. If a window glass worker was not a member of the union, he could not work in the business anywhere in North America.

Because of the depression, all of the factories of the U.S.G.C., as well as others, had been idle or had operated in a desultory way, throughout the first six months of 1893. Only four of the factories of the U.S.G.C. were operating at all, and only for very short periods.

The company had besought the officers of the American Flint Glass Workers Union for permission to produce glassware according to the production capacity of its various factories. It did not wish to have its four million dollars of invested capital curtailed to the production power of a two million dollar glassware concern—which was still further curtailed by the arbitrary summer shut down. Many times the company asked permission from the union to make jelly tumblers and packers glassware, so that it might be able to compete with others in the market. It asked that the arbitrary summer shutdown of from six to eight weeks be abolished as this was the only time of the year when fruit and vegetables were ready for processing. Also, during the summer months the supply of natural gas was greatest, and cost much less.

Management had asked the union permission to produce competitive ware, such as beer mugs, tumblers, etc., at equal rates with those paid by its competitors for the same items. All of these were refused by the union and consequently a dispute arose with the skilled glass workers. On Thursday, October 12, 1893, the factories of the United States Glass Co. were closed.

On Friday, October 13th, the company through their attorneys, Knox & Reed, acquired the services of Gilkinson's American Detective Bureau and Camps World Detective Agency for the purpose of ascertaining the intentions and probable course of the American Flint Glass Workers Association members. During the length of the strike the two detective agencies used a number of undercover agents who infiltrated the ranks of the strikers and the union. These daily reports of the two detective agencies were also found in the old records of the United States Glass Co., and provided this researcher information as to the true nature of the strike.

As it was impossible to operate the business successfully on the lines laid down by the labor unions, the company concluded that the only way it could operate at all was on a non-union basis. By its quick action the company caught the strikers "off-guard" by opening Factory "K" the following Monday, October 16, 1893, with green non-union help. It was evident that the strikers had not formulated a plan to circumvent the employment of non-union men, but were content with their self-assurance that the company could not obtain a sufficient number of skilled non-union workmen to make a success of opening any of their factories. The opening of this first non-union factory was nevertheless bloody, necessitating that the men sleep and eat in the factory. Their needs were taken care of at the expense of the company. In the early days of the strike, the T. M. Morley Club on South 19th Street, Pittsburgh, was the location where the non-union men were taken, with food and lodging furnished them in preparation for the employment in one of the factories. On the 30th of October, 1893, Factory "F" was also started with non-union workmen, plus the company had secured nearly 100 applications from flint glass workers and machinists. Six of the mold makers also returned to work at this factory, advising that they could not afford to remain idle. In starting this factory, a number of special policemen were hired so that the workers could come and go to their jobs without being attacked by the strikers.

While on strike, the flint glass workers received from their union $6.00 per week, which was the same for both single and married men. It was not enough, especially if a striker had a large family. The churches on the south side of Pittsburgh were kept busy gathering used clothing, shoes and food donated by local merchants, thinking that the strike would last only a short time. In November, 1893, at one church alone, 300 applicants for charity were received. Women of the Ladies Aid Society and kindred institutions were given the task of investigating these applications. The strike cost the union $1,200.00 per week in member benefits.

The company had no problems from the union workers when they opened Factory "B" on Monday, December, 18, 1893, primarily because of the number of special guards which were hired. It was fast becoming a bitter pill to swallow for the striking flints, as they had been led to believe by their union management that it would be an impossibility to successfully man the factories non-union. All along they had been advised by union leaders that the company had men in all the larger eastern cities soliciting non-union workmen, when in fact the newly hired men had for the most part been located right in the city of Pittsburgh and surrounding counties.

After the successful opening of this third factory, the attitude of the strikers began to change. Many wanted to return to work but were fearful to do so because they did not want the label of "scab" attached to them or their families. As the strike dragged on, the south side merchants became weary of having to carry these men, especially when they would be seen in the taverns spending their strike benefits on drinks, instead of paying their grocery bills.

This was not a strike of wages. It was over the union's demands on the company to limit production to the same level as that of their fathers and grandfathers. It was therefore fair to assume that the company had concluded after mature deliberation to operate the factories on a non-union basis or close them. In two special meetings of the company directors on September 26, 1893, and January 8, 1894, they were unanimous in their decision to operate on a non-union basis. Another meeting was held on July 24, 1894, with the stockholders ratifying the action of the directors. The announcement of the stockholders' endorsement, as well as a 4% dividend on preferred stock of the company, hit the striking flints like a thunderbolt.

When this new policy was announced, a number of efficient factory heads who held positions of importance handed in their resignations, which for a time weakened the non-union working forces. Management then prepared a set of independent, non-union rules and invited men to make application for work under these rules. They were pronounced fair and equitable, both by the company and its former workers, but loyalty to the union and fear that they would lose the power they had so long enjoyed kept many men from accepting work at the different factories.

From the beginning of the strike, the flints had set up committees to patrol each plant and report to their officers the number of employees and their progress in production. It was taking the company a lot of time to select men who were endowed with the patience and intelligence necessary to learn the trade.

In those days it was a well-known fact that glassmakers working under union rules were not allowed to introduce any improvements in machinery which might lessen the labor and thus lower the cost of production, unless the workers derived all the benefits of those improvements. It was during this time of transition in which machinery was being developed that would permanently displace many of the striking glass workers.

After the opening of Factory "P" on February 13, 1894, the condition of the striking workers became exceedingly worse. The following month, the single men had their benefits cut to $5.00 per week, as the drain on the treasury was quite large.

On the other hand, the non-union men were doing so well at learning their trade that on April 30, 1894, two shifts were initiated at Factory "K". The following week all four factories started working double shifts.

On Monday, April 29, 1894, the company opened Factory "A" without incident. The workmen were roomed by the company in the old offices directly across the street from the main gates of the factory. On May 28, 1894, Factory "U" at Gas City, Indiana opened for the first time, also without incident.

In the early months of the strike, the flints were successful in getting a number of the new non-union workmen to quit work and join the union. While these men were working for the U.S.G.C. they were considered "green hired hands", but upon joining the union, they were officially "skilled glass workers". These unsuspecting men were given union cards, which unbeknown to them, were coded. Some went to other cities seeking employment in union factories, but were refused since the union could tell by the coded card that they had "scabbed" for U.S. Glass in Pittsburgh. It wasn't long before the word got back to the other non-union workmen, and from then on the union had a difficult task in wooing any new members.

In June of 1894 the merchants joined together in refusing additional credit to the strikers. A local publication sums up the activities of the striking flints this way:

"For the present we desire to say that many are laboring at Jones & Laughlin's and Oliver's mills, a few are doing police duty, some are wearing the livery of the city ring, doing duty in the fire department, in the parks, in the station houses, at the Court House, and some are wearing the white garments of the angels of the street sweeping department, and handling brush, broom and hoe with a deftness and dexterity which has repeatedly astonished their oldest friends. A few are still loafing, and eating up their own or other people's substance. Many are living off the labor of good strong mothers, daily bending over the washtub in an incessant battle with dirt; while a few others are trying to inveigle unsuspecting men of means to go into the spectacle and optical glass business, so as to enable themselves to see things and their world as magnified by lenses paid for suckers. Others are in jail, more ought to be . . . "

It was announced on Friday, June 29, 1894, that all factories of the U.S.G.C. would close from July 2 through July 8, allowing the workmen a chance to be with their families over the Independence Day holiday and to allow time for some repairs to be made in the factories. The strikers were exuberant when they learned this, mistakenly thinking the company had failed and was calling it quits. The final disappointment came when the non-union workmen returned to all operating factories on July 9. The strike and the union rapidly weakened, for without credit the striking flints were forced into looking for work at other union factories. This was a depressed time and any kind of work was hard to find.

On July 1, 1894, President Ralph Baggaley announced that the following factories were being operated on a non-union basis: A, B, K, P, R, F and U, and that the net cost of running the seven since the beginning of the strike was $55,239.27. He also announced that the new workmen were producing greater amounts of glassware under the unlimited system.

During this transition period, the company was negotiating with various parties for the sale of some

(Continued on page 181) 11

ABBREVIATION KEY
(See also Bibliography, page 187)

APP—Approximately
ATT—Attribution
D & B—Daisy & Button
EPD—Estimated Production Date
FIG—Figure (Illustration) Number
K 1, 32—KAMM Book 1, pg. 32
LVG, 32—LEE "VICTORIAN GLASS", plate 32
LP—Limited Production

MMA—Metropolitan Museum of Art
NBA—Name by Author
OMN—Original name of Manufacturer for pattern
POP NOM—Popular Nomenclature
ORIG—Original
PROD—Production
SPEC—Speculative
U.S.G.C.—United States Glass Company

COLOR KEY

A—AMBER
AM—AMETHYST
AF—AMETHYST FLASHED
AG—APPLE GREEN
AS—AMBER-STAINED
B—BLUE
BF—BLUE FLASHED
C—CRYSTAL (Clear)
CB—COBALT BLUE
CG—CUSTARD GLASS (Opaque Ivory)
DC—DECORATED CRYSTAL
EG—EMERALD GREEN
FC—FROSTED CRYSTAL
FW—FRANCES WARE DECORATED
G—GREEN (Color can vary)

GF—GREEN FLASHED
LABV—LIMITED AMBER, BLUE & VASELINE
LC—LIMITED COLOR PRODUCTION
LRS—LIMITED RUBY-STAIN (Possibly by an
    independent decorator)
MG—MILK GLASS (White Opaque)
OB—OPAQUE BLUE
OG—OPAQUE GREEN
OP—OPAQUE PINK
PS—PURPLE SLAG (Mosaic)
RF—ROSE FLASHED (Maiden's Blush)
RS—RUBY-STAINED
SB—SAPPHIRE BLUE
VC—VASELINE OR CANARY

FACTORY KEY

Factories in boldface were those still in operation after 1900.

A—ADAMS & COMPANY, Pittsburgh, Pa.
B—BRYCE BROTHERS, Pittsburgh, Pa.
C—CHALLINOR, TAYLOR & CO., Tarentum, Pa.
D—GEORGE DUNCAN & SONS, Pittsburgh, Pa.
E—RICHARDS & HARTLEY, Tarentum, Pa.
F—RIPLEY & CO., Pittsburgh, Pa.
G—GILLINDER & SONS, Greensburg, Pa.
H—HOBBS GLASS COMPANY, Wheeling, W. Va.
J—COLUMBIA GLASS COMPANY, Findlay, O.
K—KING GLASS COMPANY, Pittsburgh, Pa.
L—O'HARA GLASS COMPANY, Pittsburgh, Pa.
M—BELLAIRE GLASS COMPANY, Findlay, O.
N—NICKEL PLATE GLASS CO., Fostoria, O.

O—CENTRAL GLASS COMPANY, Wheeling,
    W.Va.
P—DOYLE & COMPANY, Pittsburgh, Pa.
R—A. J. BEATTY & SONS, Tiffin, O.
S—A. J. BEATTY & SONS, Steubenville, O.
    (non-operating)
T—NOVELTY GLASS COMPANY, Fostoria, O.
    (non-operating)

OTHER GLASS FACTORIES BUILT BY U.S.G.C
U—At Gas City, Indiana
GP—At Glassport, Pa. (Factory O)

U.S. GLASS COMPANY PATTERNS NUMERICAL SEQUENCE

Provided here are patterns in the "15,000" series, listed in numerical sequence, produced by the United States Glass Company from 1891 to about 1920. This list is incomplete, with several voids noticeable, and hopefully can be completed in the future through continued research by myself and others. This list is by no means to be construed as the entire output of U.S. Glass, as there was also a "9,000" and a "5,000" series, but the series offered here was their major production of complete table sets.

NUMBER	YEAR	PATTERN NAME	FACTORY
15001	1891	SAWTOOTH & STAR (O'Hara's Diamond)	L
15002	1891	NAIL	F
15003	1891	PLEATING (Flat Panel)	F, B
15004	1891	BARRED OVAL	D
15005	1891	COIN	O, H
15006	1892	POINTED JEWEL (Long Diamond)	N, J
15007	1892	FROSTED CIRCLE (Horn of Plenty)	N, B
15008	1892	RUFFLES	G
15009	1892	FLEUR-DE-LIS & TASSLE	F, A
15010	1891	RIBBON CANDY	B
15011	1891	ALL-OVER-DIAMOND (Westmoreland)	G, D
15012	1892	FLOUR THUMBPRINTS	E
15013	1892	U.S. THUMBPRINT	N
15014	1892	HEAVY GOTHIC	J, K
15015			
15016	1893	MILLARD (Fan & Flute)	H
15017			
15018	1893	DIAMOND & SUNBURST VARIANT	
15019			
15020	1891	BERKELEY (Blocked Arches)	B, U
15021	1891	BROKEN COLUMN	J
15022	1892	FLUTED RIBBON (Panel & Flute)	N
15023	1892	PRISM COLUMN	
15024	1892	DOUBLE ARCH (Interlocking Crescents)	L
15025	1892	U.S. DIAMOND BLOCK (Diamond Waffle)	G, B
15026	1892	SCALLOPED SWIRL (York Herringbone)	F
15027			
15028	1892	LOOP WITH DEWDROP	
15029	1897	INDIANA	U
15030		ROMAN ROSETTE	B
15031	1896	SUPERIOR	F
15032		TEARDROP & THUMBPRINT	F
15033			
15034	1896	LEAFY SCROLL	G
15035			
15036	1895	ACANTHUS SCROLL	F
15037			
15038	1891	ELECTRIC	
15039			
15040		DIAMOND BRIDGES	
15041		PINEAPPLE & FAN (Cube with Fan)	G, A
15042	1895	ZIPPERED SWIRL & DIAMOND	
15043		FEATHER DUSTER	
15044	1895	STIPPLED BAR	
15045		BLOSSOM (A decorated opal glass)	
15046	1896	VICTOR or SHOSHONE	K, GP
15047	1896	PLAIN SCALLOPED PANEL (Colonial)	GP
15048	1897	PENNSYLVANIA (Balder)	O, G
15049	1897	MARYLAND (Inverted Loop & Fan)	B
15050	1897	OHIO (plain pattern used for etching)	F
15051	1897	KENTUCKY	K
15052	1897	ILLINOIS	GP
15053	1898	LOUISIANA	B
15054	1898	MASSACHUSETTS	K
15055	1898	MINNESOTA	F, GP
15056	1898	EMERALD GREEN HERRINGBONE or FLORIDA	B
15057	1898	COLORADO	K, E
15058	1899	MISSOURI	
15059	1899	CALIFORNIA or BEADED GRAPE	B, F
15060	1899	VERMONT	
15061	1899	U.S. RIB	GP
15062	1899	ALABAMA	GP
15063	1899	BOHEMIAN (Floradora)	
15064	1899	TENNESSEE (Jewel & Crescent)	K
15065	1899	DELAWARE	B, K
15066	1899	MAINE	
15067	1900	TEXAS (Loop with Stippled Panels)	F, B
15068	1900	CONNECTICUT	K
15069	1900	IOWA	GP
15070	1900	NEW JERSEY	GP
15071	1901	VIRGINIA (Banded Portland)	G, U, E
15072	1901	KANSAS (Jewel & Dewdrop)	K
15073	1901	OREGON (Beaded Loop)	
15074	1901	WASHINGTON	F, K
15075	1902	NEVADA	
15076	1902	GEORGIA (Peacock Feather)	E
15077	1902	MICHIGAN (Loop with Pillar)	GP
15078	1902	MANHATTAN	GP
15079	1903	WISCONSIN (Beaded Dewdrop)	U
15080	1903	UTAH	U
15081	1903	WYOMING	U, E
15082	1903	CHURCH WINDOWS (OMN, Columbia)	K, E
15083	1903	CAROLINA (Iverness)	B
15084	1903	NEW HAMPSHIRE (Bent Buckle)	

NUMBER	YEAR	PATTERN NAME	FACTORY
15085	1904	BEADED SWIRL WITH LENS	B
15086	1904	GALLOWAY (OMN, Mirror)	GP, U
15087	1904	FRAZIER	K
15088	1904	PANAMA	
15089	1904	SERRATED PANELS	U
15090	1905	BULLSEYE & FAN (Daisy in Oval Panels)	
15091	1905	ARCHED OVALS (Concaved Almond)	F
15092	1905	STAR-IN-BULLSEYE	GP
15093	1905	THE STATES	
15094	1906	CANNON-BALL PINWHEEL (OMN, Caledonia)	
15095	1906	PANELLED PALM (OMN, "Brilliant")	F
15096	1906	WREATHED SUNBURST (OMN, Radiant)	
15097	1906	WESTERN STAR (Georgia Belle)	
15098	1906	U.S. REGAL	GP
15099	1907	SPINNING STAR (OMN, Royal)	
15100	1907	GLOVED HAND (OMN, Banner)	U
15101	1907	BUZZ-STAR (OMN, Comet)	B
15102	1907	TENNIS RACKET (OMN, Windsor)	F
15103	1907	STELLAR	GP, U
15104	1907	U.S. VICTORIA	GP
15105	1907	MARLBORO	B
15106	1907	BUCKINGHAM	GP
15107	1907	BEVELLED WINDOWS (OMN, St. Regis)	GP
15108	1908	STAR AND CRESCENT	K, F
15109	1908	DIAMOND WHIRL	GP, U
15110	1908	RISING SUN (OMN, Sunshine)	GP, F
15111	1908	U.S. PEACOCK	GP
15112	1909	PATTEE CROSS	E, B
15113			
15114			
15115	1909	U.S. PURITAN	K
15116	1908	SOLAR	U, B
15117	1909	BULLSEYE & DAISY (OMN, Newport)	GP, F, B
15118	1909	CANE HORSESHOE	F
15119	1909	PALM BEACH	GP
15120	1910	STARGLOW	U
15121	1910	PORTLAND	GP, F, O
15122	1910	FEATHER BAND (OMN, Wreath)	B
15123	1910	FORT PITT	GP, F
15124	1910	OMNIBUS	GP, O
15125	1911	INTAGLIO SUNFLOWER	GP
15126			
15127			
15128			
15129			
15130			
15131	1912	EVANGELINE	U
15132			
15133	1912	INTAGLIO DAISY	GP
15134			
15135	1912	SNOWFLOWER	B
15136	1912	RAMBLER	U
15137			
15138	1912	TWO FLOWERS	
15139	1912	TWIN SNOWSHOES (OMN, Sunbeam)	U
15140	1912	PANELLED 44 (OMN, Athenia)	GP
15141	1912	FLOWER WITH CANE	GP
15142	1912	FIELD THISTLE	U
15143			
15144	1912	U.S. SHERATON	
15145	1913	COLONIS	GP
15146	1913	PANELLED SUNBURSTS & DAISY	
15147	1913	FLOWER & DIAMOND	
15148			
15149			
15150			
15151	1915	POMPEIAN	GP
15152	1915	U.S. GEORGIAN	GP, K
15153			
15154			
15155	1915	KNOBBY BULLSEYE (OMN, "Cromwell")	GP
15156	1915	ALPHA	K, GP
15157	1915	BETA	U
15158	1915	U.S. OPTIC	GP
15159			
15160			
15161	1915	PANELLED DOGWOOD	B
15162	1915	U.S. NIAGARA	GP
15163			
15164			
15165			
15166			
15167	1915	FLORICUT	GP

13

THE UNITED STATES GLASS COMPANY
PATTERN GUIDE

Listed here are more than 300 different glass patterns known to have been made by the U.S. Glass Company, or it's member factories at the time of the 1891 merger. Also included are a number of "possible" U.S. Glass patterns about which I am reasonably certain. This list consists primarily of those glass items which are collectible in "sets", and does not include information on the thousands of pieces of plain and etched bar ware known to have been produced by U.S. Glass. Nor does it include novelty items, or single items for which no other matching pieces were made.

The data is broken down into eight major factors. The **Pattern Name** is the one most often used today by collectors. The **Source** is usually the glass historian who named the pattern. The **Other Names** used on the same pattern are then listed. If the **Factory** where the glass was primarily produced is known, it is listed according to code. An estimate of the earliest production date (**EPD**) by U.S. Glass is offered, but this is not meant to be interpreted as the single year of production, as many patterns were produced for several years. Then **Colors** are listed according to code. A reference to an **Illustration** of the pattern in this book is listed—in the case of patterns not shown in this book, the best known illustration of the pattern in other references is offered. Finally, I present any important **Notes** concerning the pattern.

I have not listed patterns made only in goblets or wines, since they are found in no other form, and thus not collectible in sets.

Pattern Name	Source	Other Name	Factory	U.S.G.C. EPD	Colors	Illustration	Notes
ACANTHUS SCROLL	K5, 105		F	1896	C	Revi, 313	U.S. #15036
ADAMS' #52	OMN		A	1891	C	Page 72	
ADAMS' #329	K4, 28	PLAIN, TWO MOLD	A	1891	C	Page 71	Also U.S. #329
ADAMS' SAXON	OMN	SAXON	A	1891	C, RS	Page 60	
ALABAMA	OMN	BEADED BULL'S EYE AND DRAPE	GP	1899	C, RS, G	K1, 81 H1, 13	U.S. #15062
ALL-OVER-DIAMOND	K3, 134		D	1891	C	Page 103	U.S. #15011
AMAZON	OMN	SAWTOOTH BAND	B	1891	C, LABV	Page 78	See Figure 231
ALPHA	NBA		GPK	1919	C	Page 160	U.S. #15156
APOLLO	OMN		A	1891	C, RS	Page 65	
AQUARIUM	K4, 119			1908	C, A, EG	Page 169	Pitcher only
ARGENT	OMN		B	1891	C	Page 85	
ARCHED OVALS	Md 2, 80	CONCAVED ALMOND	F	1908	C, RF, LRS, LG	Page 154	U.S. #15091
ART	OMN		A	1891	C, LRS	Page 66	K3, 77
ATLAS	OMN		A, B	1891	C, RS	Page 75	Do not confuse with "Cannon Ball"
BALTIMORE PEAR	LPG, 66	FIG (OMN)	A	1891	C	Page 69	Reproduced
BAMBOO BEAUTY	NBA		J	1891	C	Page 128	Prev. Unlisted
BANQUET	OMN		J	1891	C	Page 130	See also "Thumbprint Block"
BAR AND BEAD	K4, 65	RIBBED WARE (LVG)	G	1891	C	K8, 169	
BAR AND BLOCK	K4, 128	AKRON BLOCK	N	1891	C	Page 136	Part of Richmond pattern set
BAR AND DIAMOND	LVG, 62	R & H SWIRL BAND	E	1891	C, RS	Page 116	Also etched
BAR AND FLUTE	K2, 106	CORSET & THUMBPRINT		1893	C, RS	Page 30	Speculative Att.
BARRED OVAL	K6, 25		D	1891	C, RS	Page 97	See Fig. 146

Pattern Name	Source	Other Name	Factory	U.S.G.C. EPD	Colors	Illustration	Notes
BARRED STAR	LVG, 49		G	1891	C	LVG, 49	Gillinder #414
BEAD AND SCROLL	K2, 112			1901	C, FC, RS, CB, G	Figs. 53-55, 244	Att. based on color and pattern design
BEADED BLOCKS	NBA		M	1891	C, B, A	Fig. 254	Similar to Pillow Bands pattern
BEADED GRAPE	K4, 94	CALIFORNIA	B, F	1899	C, EG	Figs. 82-87	Some repro's U.S. #15059
BEADED SWIRL	LVG, 41	SWIRLED COLUMN	D	1891	C, EG	Pgs. 96, 103	With or without feet
BEADED SWIRL & DISC	K8, 36		B	1904	C, B, G, YS	Page 164, 177	
BELLAIRE	K5, 114		M	1891	C	K5, 114	MMA catalogue
BERKELEY	LVG, 45	BLOCKED ARCHES	B, U	1891	C, FC, RS	Fig. 241	U.S. #15020
BERLIN	K1, 98		A	1891	C	Page 72	Orig. produced in 1874
BETA	NBA		U	1919	C		U.S. #15157
BEVELLED BUTTONS	NBA		D	1891	C	Page 99	Duncan's #320
BEVELLED DIAGONAL BLOCK	K2, 19	Challinor #311 CROSSBAR (LVG)	C	1891	C, LRS	Page 93	Also by Bryce, 1888
BEVELLED DIAMOND AND STAR	K2, 74	DIAMOND PRISMS		1895	C, RS	Fig. 207	Att. speculative
BEVELLED WINDOWS	NBA	ST. REGIS (OMN)	GP	1907	C	Page 146	U.S. #15107
BIG TOP	NBA	Challinor #316-318	C	1891	C	Page 92	compotes only
BIG LEAF & BUTTON	NBA	Duncan's #1002	D	1891	C, AS	Page 97	bowls only
BLEEDING HEART	K1, 8			1898	C	Kamm 1, 8	Also made earlier
BLOCK AND FAN	LVG, 41		E	1891	C, MG, RS	Page 108	R & H #554
BLOCKADE	LVG, 65	Challinor #309	C	1891	C	Page 93	
BOHEMIAN	K6, pl. 59	FLORADORA		1899	C, FC, RF, EG	Figs. 14-18, 166, 255	U.S. #15063
BOHEMIAN GRAPE	NBA			1899	C, EG, RF	Figs. 97-98	Att. Spec.—LP
BRACELET BAND	NBA		D	1891	C	Page 101	
BROKEN BANDS	K3, 48	Doyle's #65	P	1892	C, B, A	K3, 48	MMA Catalogue
BROKEN COLUMN	K6, pl. 30		J, E	1891	C, RS, LCB	Fig. 179-184	U.S. 15021
BRYCE PANEL	NBA		B	1891	C, B, V	Fig. 127	Syrup only See H3, 77
BUCKINGHAM	OMN		GP	1907	C, DC	Page 146	U.S. #15106
BUCKLE AND STAR	K1, 20	ORIENT (OMN)	B	1891	C	Page 85	
BULBOUS BASE	NBA	HOBB's #331	H	1891	C, Cr, AS, FW	Page 30	Also made with an "Optic" effect
BULLET	POP NOM	BULLET-EMBLEM		1898	C, DC	Page 1	See Quote on page 31
BULLSEYE & FAN	K1, 58	DAISY IN OVAL PANELS		1905	C, SB, G	Page 150	U.S. #15090
BULLSEYE & DAISY	Mz1, 215	NEWPORT (OMN)	GP	1909	C, RS, EG, DC	Page 151	U.S. 15117
BUTTERFLY	K2, 123	U.S. 6406		1908	C	Page 169	Pitcher only

Pattern Name	Source	Other Name	Factory	U.S.G.C. EPD	Colors	Illustration	Notes
BUZZ-STAR	K4, 140	WHIRLIGIG (toy set)	B	1907	C	Page 150, 174	U.S. 15101
CAFE SET	OMN			1908	C	Page 146	
CANE HORSESHOE	K1, 100	PARAGON (OMN)	F	1909	C	Page 151, 168	
CANNON-BALL PINWHEEL	K4, 140	CALEDONIA (OMN)		1906	C	K4, 140	MMA Catalogue #15094
CAROLINA	K2, 28	IVERNESS	B	1903	C, LRS	Page 167	"States" pattern #15083
CATHEDRAL	K1, 19	ORION (OMN)	B	1891	All	Page 83; Fig. 243	Limited but extensive color prod.
CELESTIAL GLOBE	K1, 119			1893	C	K1, 119	Reissued 1898
CHALLINOR FORGET-ME-NOT	PET SAL	Challinor #20	C	1891	MG, OPBG	Page 56	Limited items
CHALLINOR #313	OMN	TREE OF LIFE	C	1891	MG, OBGP	H3, 64	
CHALLINOR #314	OMN		C	1891	MG	K4, 84	Table set only
CHALLINOR THUMBPRINT	LVG, 58	Challinor #312	C	1891	C	Page 94	
CHANDELIER		CROWN JEWELS (OMN)	L	1891	C	K2, 114 LVG, pl. 68	MMA Catalogue
CHURCH WINDOWS	K4, 115	COLUMBIA (OMN)	K, E	1903	C, DC	Page 145	U.S. 15082
CLIMAX	LVG, 70		J	1891	C, B	Page 130	Kamm calls it SMOCKING BANDS
CLIO	OMN	D & B WITH ALMOND BAND	C	1891	C, B, G, V	Page 89	
CLOVER	OMN		E	1891	C, EG	Page 117	Often confused for Panelled D & B
COIN	K3, 80	U.S. COIN SILVER AGE (OMN)	H, O	1891	C, FC, LRS	K7, 103-106	
COLONIS	OMN	COLONIS #45	GP	1913	C	Page 157	U.S. #15145
COLORADO	OMN		K, E	1898	C, G, B, RS, AF	Page 166	See Figs. 38-46, 48-51, 56-60
COLUMN BLOCK	K3, 75	PANEL & STAR	L	1891	C, V	K3, 75	O'Hara #500 MMA Catalogue
CONNECTICUT	OMN		K	1900	C	Page 180	"State" pattern U.S. #15068
CORDOVA	OMN		L	1891	C, RS, G	Page 162	Lengthy production
COTTAGE	OMN		A	1891	C, A, G, LRS, LB	Page 63; Fig. 253	
CRUSADER CROSS	Md 2, 44	STAR (LVG) CROSS-IN-DIAMOND (K5)	C	1891	C	Page 90	Challinor #9
CRYSTAL ROCK	OMN			1905	C	Page 175	
CRYSTAL WEDDING	OMN		A	1891	C, RS, LCB	Page 64	
CRYSTALINA	OMN		H	1891	C, RS, EG	Page 126	
CUBE AND BLOCK	NBA	R & H #401	E	1891	C, LRS	Page 107	Similar to "Plume and Block"
CUT SUNBURST	OMN			1908	C	Page 175	
DAISY & BUTTON	POP NOM		D, G, H R. O	1891	All	See Revi	Many variations by several factories
D & B WITH CROSSBARS	K3, 53		E	1891	C, B, V, A	Page 112	
D & B WITH RED DOTS	POP NOM		D	1891	RS	Page 102	See Fig. 185-189

Pattern Name	Source	Other Name	Factory	U.S.G.C. EPD	Colors	Illustration	Notes
D & B WITH THIN BARS	NBA		G	1891	C, V	Page 124	Tumblers do not have the bars
D & B WITH THUMBPRINT	K3, 73		A	1891	All	Page 33, 70; Fig. 257	Also with blue-stained panels
DAISY IN DIAMOND	K3, 77		L	1891	C, A	K3, 77	O'Hara #725 MMA Catalogue
DAKOTA	OMN		F	1891	C, LRS	Page 119-120	"State" pattern
DELAWARE	OMN	FOUR PETAL FLOWER	B, K	1899	C, RF, EG, CG, LMG	Page 148	Lengthy Production U.S. #15065
DERBY	OMN	PLEAT & PANEL	B	1891	C	Page 81	First made in 1882
DEWDROP & ZIG-ZAG	NBA	Challinor #418	C	1891	C, PS	Page 94	Limited items
DIAGONAL BAND WITH FAN	LPG, 156	GREEK (OMN)	F	1891	C	LPG, 156	Not Prev. Attributed MMA Catalogue
DIAMOND BRIDGES	NBA			1896	C, EG	Figure 240	U.S. #15040
DIAMOND & SUNBURST, VARIANT	K6, pl. 30			1893	C, LRS	K6, pl. 30 Page 164	U.S. #15018—remake of early pattern
DIAMOND WAFFLE	K3, 60	U.S. DIAMOND BLOCK		1892	C	Revi, 307	U.S. #15025 Lee calls it "Patricia"
DIAMOND WHIRL	NBA			1915	C	Page 162, 177	U.S. #15109
DOUBLE ARCH	K5, 73	INTERLOCKING CRESCENTS	L, K	1892	C, RS	K6, pl. 30	U.S. #15024
DOUBLE DAHLIA AND LENS	K8, 23			1900	C, EG, RF, DC	Figure 101	Att. based on color & pattern design
DOUBLE EYE HOBNAIL	K1, 57	DEWDROP (OMN)	J	1891	C, B, A	Figs. 173-176 Pg. 130	See H3, pg. 68 for ad reprint
DOUBLE FAN	LVG, 57	Challinor #305	C	1891	C	Page 90	
DOYLE'S COMET	K7, 9	COMET	P	1891	C, A, V	K7, 113	See also U.S. Comet
DOYLE'S DOT	K8, pl. 1		P	1891	C	K8, pl. 1	
DOYLE'S SHELL	K8, pl. 4	CUBE WITH FAN	P	1891	C, RS	Fig. 271	
DOYLE'S #65	OMN		P	1891	C	K3, 48	See "Broken Bands"
DUNCAN BLOCK	LVG, 41	BLOCK	D	1891	C, RS	Page 101	Also made by Doyle
DUNCAN DOT	NBA		D	1891	C, B, A	Page 106	
DUNCAN'S #88	OMN		D	1891	C, AS	Page 104	"Amberette" decorated
DUNCAN'S #320	OMN		D	1891	C, RS		Same as Red Block
EARLY OREGON	NBA	OREGON (OMN)	E	1891	C, RS	Page 115	Not part of state series
ELECTRIC	K3, 78			1891	C	K3, 78	U.S. #15038
ELEPHANT TOES	NBA			1905	C, CSC	Page 28	Spec. Attribution
ETCHED GRAPE	K2, 122			1904	C, EG	K2, 122	Kamm attribution
EVANGELINE	OMN		U	1918	C	Page 168	U.S. #15131
EYEBROWS	K5, 11	Doyle's #11	P	1891	C	K5, 11	
FAN & STAR	LVG, 66	CHALLINOR #304	C	1891	C, PS, MG	Page 91	
FAN-TOP HOBNAIL	LPG, 71		P	1891	C, B, RS	K7, pl. 9	Doyle's #150

Pattern Name	Source	Other Name	Factory	U.S.G.C. EPD	Colors	Illustration	Notes
FEATHER BAND	K4, 134	WREATH (OMN)	B	1910	C	Page 156	
FEATHER DUSTER	K2, 42			1895	C, EG	REVI, 309	U.S. #15043
FIELD THISTLE	Hartung	JUNGLE (OMN)	U	1912	C, Carnival	Page 157	U.S. #15142
FILE	K2, 30		J	1891	C	K2, 30	Lengthy production
FINECUT	K8, 21			1891	C, A, B, V	Figs. 116-119	Spec. Att.
FINE CUT & BLOCK	LPG, 161		K	1891	C, AS, DC	Figure 267	Stained amber, blue or pink
FINE CUT & PANEL	LPG, 61	RUSSIAN (OMN)	B	1891	C, A, B, V	Page 80	See Figure 213
FISHSCALE	K1, 58	CORAL (OMN)	B	1891	C	Page 79	
FLORICUT	OMN		GP	1916	C	Page 161	U.S. #15167
FLORIDA	K1, pl. 93	EMERALD GREEN HERRINGBONE	B	1898	C, EG	Fig. 68-74	U.S. #15056 See page 173
FLEUR-DE-LIS AND DRAPE	LVG, 59	FLEUR-DE-LIS AND TASSLE (K3)	A	1891	C, EG, MG	Page 61	U.S. #15009
FLOWER & DIAMOND	NBA			1913	C	Page 170	U.S. #15147
FLOWER WITH CANE	K7, 29		GP	1912	C, DC	Page 164	U.S. #15141
FLUTED RIBBON	K3, 95	PANEL & FLUTE	N	1891	C	REVI, 264	U.S. #15022
FOOTED PANELLED RIB	LVG, 59	Challinor #308	C	1891	C	Page 90	
FORT PITT	OMN		GP, F	1910	C	Page 156	U.S. #15123
FOSTORIA	K6, 76	Nickel's #27	N	1891	C	Page 136	
FOUR THUMBPRINTS	K5, 57		E	1892	C	K5, 57	U.S. #15012
FRAZIER	Bt, pl. 14		K	1904	C, AF, RS	Page 166	U.S. #15087
FROSTED CIRCLE	K4, 19	HORN OF PLENTY	N	1891	C, FC	REVI, 264	U.S. #15007
GALLOWAY	M1, 218	Virginia (misnomer) MIRROR (OMN)	GP, U	1904	C, RF, LRS	Page 145, 154	Toothpick repro's U.S. #15071
GEORGIA	OMN	PEACOCK FEATHER	E	1902	C	U2, 231	U.S. #15076
GEORGIAN	OMN		GP, K	1915	C	Page 159, 160	U.S. #15152
GIANT BULLS EYE	K2, 101	U.S. #157		1898	C	K2, 101	
GLOVED HAND	K6, 59	COAT OF ARMS	U	1907	C	Page 164	OMN—"BANNER" U.S. #15100
HAND AND BAR	M2, 82	HAND	B	1891	C	Page 84	
HANOVER	K1, 113	BLOCK WITH STARS	E	1891	C, A, B	Page 108	
HARTLEY	OMN		E	1891	C	Page 110	
HEAVY FINECUT	H3, 55	BAG WARE (OMN)	D	1891	C, A, B, V	Page 104	Often confused for Finecut pattern
HEAVY GOTHIC	K2, 109	WHITTON	J, K	1891	C, RS	Page 131	U.S. #15014
HEAVY PANELLED FINECUT	K2, 24	PANELLED DIAMOND CROSS	D	1891	C, B, A, V	Page 105	
HENRIETTA	K1, 110		J	1891	C, LRS	Page 128	

Pattern Name	Source	Other Name	Factory	U.S.G.C. EPD	Colors	Illustration	Notes
HEXAGON BLOCK	PET SAL, 30-T		H	1891	C, AS, RS	Page 126	Often confused for Henrietta
HIDALGO	K3, 56		A	1891	C, FC, LRS	Page 68	
HOBBS' BLOCK	K3, 95	DIVIDED SQUARES	H	1891	FDC	H3, 67	
HOBBS' HOBNAIL	POP NOM		H	1891	All	Page 125,	See toy set, Figure 263-264
HOBNAIL WITH BARS	LVG, 66	HOBNAIL IN BIG DIAMOND	C	1891	C	Page 91	Challinor #307
HOBNAIL WITH CURVED BARS	M2, 100		P	1891	C	K7, 110	Doyle's #240
HOBNAIL WITH THUMBPRINT BASE	K1, 70		P	1891	C, A, B, LRS	Fig. 259	
IDAHO	OMN		F	1891	C	Page 117	
ILLINOIS	OMN		GP	1897	C, LEG	Page 143	U.S. #15052 See Fig. 102
INDIANA	OMN		U	1897	C	LVG, pl. 39	U.S. #15029
INTAGLIO DAISY	NBA		GP	1911	C, DC	Page 170	U.S. #15133
INTAGLIO SUNFLOWER	K7, 53		GP	1911	C, DC	Page 178	U.S. #15125
IOWA	OMN	PANELLED ZIPPER	GP	1900	C, RF	Page 173	U.S. #15069
JACOB'S LADDER	K1, 20	MALTESE (OMN)	B	1891	C, LABV	Page 85	See Page 33 for a rare colored item
JACOB'S LADDER LATE	K1, 98		B	1898	C	K1, 98	Similar to Jacob's Ladder
JASPER	K2, 13	LATE BUCKLE	B	1891	C	Page 84	
KANSAS	OMN	JEWEL & DEWDROP	K	1901	C	U2, 235	U.S. #15072
KENTUCKY	OMN		K	1897	C, EG, LCB	Fig. 143	U.S. #15051
KING'S BLOCK	NBA	KING'S #312	K	1891	C, LV	Page 132	Late production on wine glass
KING'S CROWN	LPG, 162	RUBY THUMBPRINT	A	1891	C, RS, AS	Pages 58-59	
KING'S #500	OMN	PARROT	K	1891	C, CB	Figure 52	MMA Catalogue
KNOBBY BULLS EYE	M1, 214	CROMWELL (OMN)	GP	1919	C, DC	Page 159	
LACY DAISY (LATE)	K2, 73	DAISY		1918	C, LC	Page 162	
LACY MEDALLION	K1, 106	JEWEL (OMN)		1905	C, G, LCB, RS	Page 149	See Figures 64-66
LATE BLOCK	K1, 118	WAFFLE BLOCK	D	1891	C, RS	Page 100	
LATTICE	K4, 40	DIAMOND BAR	K	1891	C	LPG, pl. 78	
LEAF AND FLOWER	LVG, PL. 50		H	1891	FC, AS	Page 126	See Figure 125
LEAFY SCROLL	K4, 91		GP	1896	C	Page 172	U.S. #15034
LENS AND STAR	K2, 36	STAR AND OVAL	L	1891	C, FC	K2, 36	MMA Catalogue
LIGHTNING	K3, 100		U	1893	C	K3, 100	
LITTLE BALLS	K3, 44	Bryce #88	B	1891	C	K3, 44	
LOG & STAR	K5, 140	CUBE & DIAMOND	M	1891	C, A, B	Fig. 269	Limited service

Pattern Name	Source	Other Name	Factory	U.S.G.C. EPD	Colors	Illustration	Notes
LONG DIAMOND	K8, 54		J	1891	C	K8, 54	Part of Pointed Jewel line
LOOP WITH DEWDROP	K1, 72			1892	C	REVI, 309	U.S. #15028
LOOP HERRINGBONE	NBA			1901	C	Page 173	Syrup only to date
LOUISIANA	OMN		B	1898	C	Page 164	U.S. #15053
MAINE	OMN	STIPPLED PANELLED FLOWER		1899	C, EG, DC	Figure 169	See rare syrup in color, Fig. 126
MAJESTIC CROWN	NBA	FLUTED	C	1891	C, PS	Page 88 Fig. 258	
MALTESE CROSS	MD 1, 35		D	1891	C	Page 104	DUNCAN'S #1003
MANHATTAN	OMN		GP	1902	C, RF, GF	Pg. 144, 166; Fig. 260-262	U.S. #15078
MARIO	OMN		H	1891	C, AS, RS	H3, 69	
MARLBORO	OMN	U.S. #15105	B	1907	C, RF	Page 150	Similar to Cambridge "Sweetheart" pattern
MARYLAND	OMN		B	1897	C, RS	K1, 60	U.S. #15049
MASCOTTE	OMN		F	1891	C	Page 123	
MASSACHUSETTS	OMN		K	1898	C, LG, LRS	Page 144	U.S. #15054
MEDALLION	LPG, pl. 102		?	1891	C, B, A, V	Fig. 112-115	Spec. Attribution
MICHIGAN	OMN	LOOP & PILLAR	GP	1902	C, LRS, RF, GF, DC	Fig. 19-24 Page 144	U.S. #15077
MIKADO FAN	M2, 149	Bryce #128	B	1891	C	Page 86	Limited items
MILLARD	LVG, pl. 42	FAN & FLUTE	H	1893	C, AS, RS	Fig. 221	U.S. #15016
MINNESOTA	OMN		F, GP	1898	C, LRS, LG	Page 144	U.S. #15055
MIRROR & FAN	NBA		B	1891	C, EG, RS	Page 73	Long production
MISSOURI	OMN	U.S. #15058		1899	C, EG	U2, 239	See H3, Fig. 441 for rare cruet
MITRED BARS	K2, 33	MITRED DIAMOND	B	1891	C, A	Page 80	
MOON AND STAR	K1, 80	PALACE (OMN)	A	1891	C, LRS	Page 67	See Fig. 245-246
MONTANA	OMN		F	1891	C	Page 123	Little-known "State" pattern
NAIL	K2, 87		F	1891	C, RS	Page 121 Fig. 242	U.S. #15002
NEVADA	OMN			1902	C, DC	Page 28	U.S. #15075
NEW JERSEY	OMN	LOOPS & DROPS	D	1900	C, RS	Page 144, 148	U.S. #15070
NEW YORK	OMN	NEW YORK HONEYCOMB	P	1891	C, LRS	Fig. 268	
NEW HAMPSHIRE	OMN	BENT BUCKLE		1903	C, RF, LRS	Fig. 25-36	U.S. #15084
NEWPORT	OMN		E	1891	C	Page 118	Pitchers only
NIAGARA	OMN		GP	1919	C	Page 161	U.S. #15162
NICKEL PLATE'S #26	OMN		N	1891	C	K5, 102	
NICKEL'S ROYAL	OMN		N	1891	C	Page 136	Nickel's #77 pattern

Pattern Name	Source	Other Name	Factory	U.S.G.C. EPD	Colors	Illustration	Notes
NICKEL'S RICHMOND	OMN	BAR & BLOCK	N	1891	C	Page 136	
NOTCHED OVALS	NBA		N	1891	C	Page 136	Nickel's #82
O'HARA DIAMOND	K5, pl. 32	SAWTOOTH & STAR	L	1891	C, RS	Figure 251	U.S. #15001
OHIO	OMN		F	1897	C	Page 147	U.S. #15050 State pattern
OLD COLUMBIA	NBA		J	1891	C	Page 131	
OMNIBUS	NBA		GP, O	1911	C	Page 168	U.S. #15124
OPALESCENT SWIRL	POP NOM		N	1891	See H3	Page 135	Also made by other companies
OREGON	OMN	BEADED LOOP		1901	C	Page 164	U.S. #15073
OVAL LOOP	K4, 135		E	1891	C	Page 114	
OVAL PANEL	K2, 120		C	1891	PS	K2, 120	
OWL PITCHER	K1, 56		C	1891	C, B, MG, A, AM	Page 176	
PALM BEACH	LVG, pl. 58	U.S. #15119	GP	1909	C, DC	Page 151	Also opalescent & carnival colors
PANAMA	OMN	FINE CUT BAR		1904	C	Page 178	U.S. #15088
PANELLED CABLE	K6, 14	ACME (OMN)	B	1891	C	Page 84	Previously unattributed
PANELLED DAISY	K6, 35	BRAZIL (OMN)	B	1891	C, B, MG	Page 74	
PANELLED 44	MD 1	ATHENIA (OMN)	GP	1912	C, DC	Page 156	U.S. #15140
PANELLED DAISY & BUTTON	K1, 80	ELLROSE (OMN)	D	1891	C, AS, BS LABV	Page 104	"Amberette" decorated
PANELLED DOGWOOD	NBA		B	1919	RF, EG	Page 161	U.S. #15161
PANELLED FORGET-ME-NOT	K3, 43		B	1891	C, A, B	LPG. 79	Reportedly also made by Doyle
PANELLED PALM	MD2, 37	BRILLIANT (OMN)	F	1906	C, RF	Page 43	U.S. #15095
PANELLED SUNBURSTS & DAISY	NBA			1915	C	Page 170	U.S. #15146
PATTEE CROSS	K2, 121		E, B	1909	C, RF, EG	Page 151, 167	U.S. #15112
PAVONIA	OMN		F	1891	C, LRS	Page 122	
PEAS AND PODS	NBA		B	1891	C, LRS	Page 73	Wine set only
PENDANT	NBA			1919	C, RF	Page 163	Liquer set only
PENNSYLVANIA	OMN	BALDER	O, GP	1897	C, RS, EG	Page 143, 166	2 different butters U.S. #15048
PINEAPPLE & FAN	K3, 79	CUBE WITH FAN	A, GP	1895	C, RS, LEG	Page 143	Similar to Czarina
PITTSBURGH	OMN		B	1891	C	Page 77	
PLAIN SCALLOPED PANEL	K1, 81	U.S. COLONIAL	GP	1896	C, EG, LCB	Page 143	U.S. #15047
PLEATED RIBBON	NBA	Challinor #82	C	1891	C	Page 92	
PLEAT & PANEL	LPG, 157	DERBY (OMN)	B	1891	C, A, B, V	LPG, 157	See Page 81
PLEATING	K3, 53	FLAT PANEL	B, F	1891	C, RS	Page 81	See Figures 248-249

Pattern Name	Source	Other Name	Factory	U.S.G.C. EPD	Colors	Illustration	Notes
PLUME	K2, 64		A	1891	C, RS	Page 62	
PLUME & BLOCK	K3, 74	FEATHER & BLOCK	E	1891	C, RS	K3, 74	
POINTED JEWEL	K6, pl. 1		J	1891	C	Page 131	U.S. #15006
POMPEIAN	NBA		GP	1918	C	Page 157	U.S. #15151
PORTLAND	K1, 107		GP, F, O	1918	C	Page 155	U.S. #15121
PRESSED DIAMOND	LV, pl. 70		O	1891	C, B, V, A	H3, 36	Cruet shown in MMA catalogue
PRESSED SWIRL	NBA		O	1891	C, A, B	Page 33	Cruet only known MMA catalogue
PRISM COLUMN	K6, 15			1892	C, LG	K6, pl. 31	
QUEEN'S NECKLACE	K3, 78		M	1891	C	K3, 78	MMA catalogue
RADIANT	LVG, pl. 70		J	1891	C	Page 129	Also MMA catalogue
RAMBLER	NBA		U	1912	C	Page 169	U.S. #15136
RED BLOCK	K1, 105	BARELLED BLOCK (in C or AS)	P	1891	RS	K7, pl. 11	Also made by D, E and others
RETICULATED CORD	M1, 130		L	1891	C, LAB	M1, 130	MMA Catalogue
RIBBED FORGET-ME-NOT	LPG, Pl. 137		B	1891	C, LAB	Page 84	
RIBBON CANDY	K1, 32	BRYCE (Lee)	B	1891	C, LG	Page 76	U.S. #15010
RICHMOND	OMN		E	1891	C	Page 116	Do not confuse for Nickel's Richmond
RING & BLOCK	K4, 128		K	1891	C	K4, 128	
RISING SUN	K2, 61	SUNSHINE (OMN)	GP, F	1908	C, CSC	Page 142	Rare in carnival colors; U.S. #15110
ROANOKE	OMN		F	1891	C, G, LRS	Page 122	See Fig. 219, 250
ROMAN ROSETTE	LPG, pl. 157		B	1891	C, RS	Page 33	U.S. #15030
ROSETTE	K4, 46	MAGIC (OMN)	B	1891	C	Page 79	
RUBY THUMBPRINT	K1, 104	KING'S CROWN (In C or AS)	A	1891	RS	Pages 58-59	See page 48
RUFFLES	K6, pl. 36		G	1891	C	REVI, 167	U.S. #15008
SANBORN	LVG, 62	IRON KETTLE	C	1891	C	Page 91	Challinor #83
SAWTOOTH	K4, 15	DIAMOND	B, G	1891	C	Page 83	Made by several companies
SCALLOPED DAISY & FANS	MD2, 35			1905	C, EG	Page 33	MMA Catalogue Goblet & 2 tumblers
SCALLOPED SWIRL	K6, pl. 32	YORK HERRINGBONE	F	1892	C, RS, LG	K6, pl. 32	See Figure 252
SCROLL & FLOWER	LVG, 48		C	1891	MG	Page 55	Table set only Challinor #314
SCROLL WITH STAR	LVG, 28		C	1891	C	Page 94	Limited service
SEAWEED OPALESCENT	NBA	BEAUMONT BEAUTY	H	1891	OP Color	H2, 50	MMA Catalogue
SERRATED PANELS	NBA		U	1904	C	Page 164	MMA Catalogue U.S. #15089
SHELL ON RIBS	NBA	SHELL (OMN)	J	1891	C	Page 129	Not prev. listed

Pattern Name	Source	Other Name	Factory	U.S.G.C. EPD	Colors	Illustration	Notes
SHOSHONE	MD2, 88	VICTOR (OMN)	K, GP	1896	C, RS, EG	Fig. 227	Misspelled in H1 & 3 U.S. #15046
SILVER QUEEN	OMN		F	1891	C, LRS	Page 121	See Figure 265
SNAIL	K2, 69	DOUBLE SNAIL (a variant)	D	1891	C, RS	Figure 204	See Page 33. Lee calls it "Compact"
SNOWFLOWER	NBA		B	1912	C	Page 169	U.S. #15135
SOLAR	OMN	FEATHER SWIRL	U, B	1908	C	Page 155	U.S. #15116
SPINNING STAR	NBA	ROYAL (OMN)		1907	C	Page 146	U.S. #15099
SPIREA BAND	LVG, 29			1891	C, A, B	Figures 110-111	Speculative Attribution
STAR & CRESCENT	MD1, 50		K, F	1908	C	Page 151	U.S. #15108
STARGLOW	NBA		U	1910	C	Page 155	U.S. #15120
STAR-IN-BULLSEYE	K1, 100		GP	1905	C, RF	Page 43	U.S. #15092
STAR-IN-DIAMOND	K1, 62	U.S. #414		1891	C	K1, 62	
STARS AND BARS	K1, 64	DAISY AND CUBE	M	1891	C, A, B	H3, 58	MMA Catalogue
STELLAR	OMN		GP, U	1907	C	Page 162, 177	U.S. #15103
STIPPLED BAR	LVG, 63			1895	C	REVI, 311	U.S. #15044
STYLIZED FLOWER	K2, 127	FLOWER & PANEL	C	1891	PS, MG	Page 94	
SUPERIOR	OMN		F	1896	C	Page 172	U.S. #15031
SWAG BLOCK	K3, 130		D	1891	C, RS	Page 101	Duncan's #326
TARGET	NBA		E	1891	C, LRS	Page 117	Wine set only
TEARDROP & THUMBPRINT	K3, 32		F	1896	C, LRS, LCB	REVI, 291	U.S. #15032
TENNESSEE	OMN	JEWEL & CRESCENT	K	1899	C	Page 147	U.S. #15064
TENNIS RACKET	M2, 176	WINDSOR (OMN)	F	1907	C	Page 174	U.S. #15102
TEXAS	OMN		F, B	1900	C, RF, LRS	Page 173	U.S. #15067 See H1, Fig. 359
THE STATES	OMN	CANE & STAR MEDALLION		1908	C, EG	Page 145	U.S. #15093
THOUSAND EYE	LPG, 137		A, E	1891	C, A, B, V, OP	Pages 71, 111	Two variants
THREE FACE	LPG, 89		D	1891	C, FC	Page 106	Orig. prod. before 1891 merger
THREE PANEL	K3, 115		E	1891	C, A, B, V	Page 113	R & H #25
THUMBPRINT BLOCK	K7, 19		J	1891	C	Page 129	Not Prev. attributed
TINY FINECUT	M2, 134			1900	C, RS, EG	Figure 157	
TREE OF LIFE	POP NOM		H	1891	C, A, B	Not Illus.	MMA Catalogue
TREMONT	OMN		E	1891	C	Page 113	
TRILBY	LVG, 54	VALENTINE	GP	1895	C	LVG, 54	
TRIPLE BAR	LVG, 59	U.S. #84	P	1891	C	K8, 103	Doyle's #84

Pattern Name	Source	Other Name	Factory	U.S.G.C. EPD	Colors	Illustration	Notes
TRIPLE TRIANGLE	LVG, 56	DOYLE'S #76	P	1891	C, RS	Figure 266	See K8, 104
TWIN SNOWSHOES	K8, 54	SUNBEAM (OMN)	U	1918	C	Page 156	U.S. #15139
TWO FLOWER	NBA			1918	C	Page 170	U.S. #15138
TWO PANEL	K3, 45		E	1891	C, A, B, V, LAG	Fig. 212	Primarily produced before merger
TYCOON	OMN		J	1891	C	Page 129	
U.S. BLOSSOM (OMN)	LVG, 40	U.S. #15045		1895	MG	LVG, 40	
U.S. COMET	OMN			1895	C	K3, 82	Similar to Doyle's COMET
U.S. OPTIC	OMN		GP	1919	C	Page 160	U.S. #15158
U.S. PEACOCK	OMN		GP	1908	C	Page 155	U.S. #15111
U.S. PURITAN	OMN		K	1909	C	Page 149	U.S. #15115
U.S. RIB	K7, 42		GP	1899	C, EG	Figs. 75-81	U.S. #15061 May be a state???
U.S. REGAL	OMN		GP	1906	C	Page 145	U.S. #15098
U.S. SHELL	K3, 76			1892	C	K3, 76	Similar to Doyle's SHELL pattern
U.S. SHERATON	K5, 100			1912	C, LG	Page 158	U.S. #15144
U.S. THUMBPRINT	K5, 5	GILLINDER #421	N	1891	C	REVI, 264	U.S. #15013
U.S. VICTORIA	OMN		GP	1907	C	Page 146	U.S. #15104
UNITED STATES	K5, 68			1903	C, DC	K5, 68	Similar to NEVADA
UTAH	OMN	FROST FLOWER	U	1903	FC	Page 167	U.S. #15080
VALENCIA WAFFLE	MD1, 71	BLOCK & STAR HEXAGONAL BLOCK	A	1891	C, A, B, AG	Page 71	
VENICE	OMN		A	1891	C	K4, 105	
VERMONT	OMN	HONEYCOMB WITH FLOWER RIM		1899	C, EG, LB	Page 53	U.S. #15060 Also in Custard
VIRGINIA	OMN	BANDED PORTLAND	G, U, E	1901	C, RF, GF LRS	Page 44	U.S. #15071
WAFFLE & FINE CUT	K2, 98	Variant of CATHEDRAL	B	1891	C, B, A, V	Page 83	Note the odd butter in Cathedral
WAVERLY	K4, 107		B	1891	C	Page 80	
WASHINGTON	OMN	BEADED BASE	K, F	1901	C, RS	Page 166	U.S. #15074 Limited custard
WESTERN STAR	OMN	GEORGIA BELLE		1906	C	M1, 228	U.S. #15097 MMA Catalogue
WESTMORELAND	LVG, 49		G	1891	C	LVG, 49	MMA Catalogue
WHEAT & BARLEY	K1, 41	DUQUESNE (OMN)	B	1891	C, A, B	Page 81	
WHIRLIGIG	K2, 103	BUZZ-STAR	B	1907	C	Page 150	U.S. #15101
WIDE STRIPE	H2, 46		N	1891	Op. colors	H3, Figs. 295-296	MMA Catalogue
WILDFLOWER	K1, 36		A	1891	C, A, B, V, AG,	Page 70	Produced many years
WILLOW OAK	K1, 36	WREATH (OMN)	B	1891	C, A, B, V	Page 83	See Fig. 122

Pattern Name	Source	Other Name	Factory	U.S.G.C. EPD	Colors	Illustration	Notes
WISCONSIN	OMN	BEADED DEWDROP	U	1903	C	Page 167	U.S. #15079
WOODEN PAIL	K1, 55	BUCKET (OMN) OAKEN BUCKET	B	1891	C, A, B, V AM	Page 81	
WREATHED SUNBURST	K8, 23	RADIANT (OMN)		1906	C	Page	
WYANDOTTE	OMN	UMBILICATED HOBNAIL	F	1891	C	Page 120	
WYOMING (STATE)	OMN		U	1903	C	U2, 251	U.S. #15081
WYOMING, RIPLEY'S	OMN		F	1891	C	Page 121	Not state pattern
ZIPPERED BLOCK	K3, 131		D	1891	C, LRS	Page 102	
ZIPPERED SWIRL & DIAMOND	K6, 33			1895	C, LRS	Figure 247	U.S. #15042

THE RIPLEY.

Illustrated here are rare examples of cut glass made by U.S.G.C. in the *Malta* and *Ripley* patterns, circa 1906.

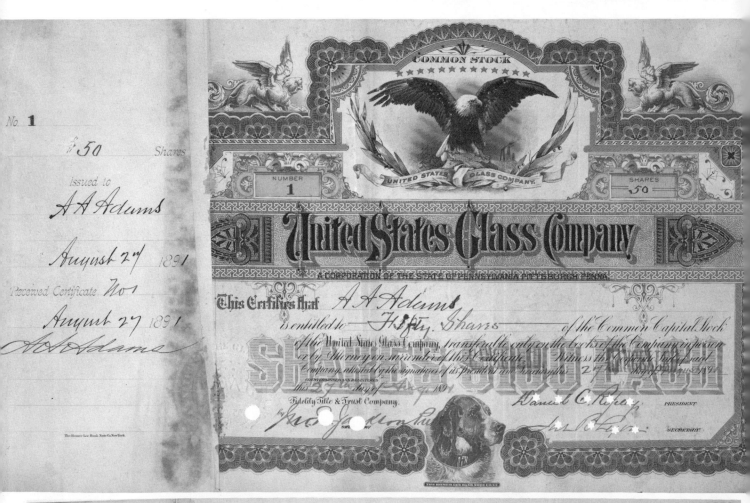

The properties of the firms incorporated into the United States Glass Co. were appraised by experts and each Company received Common Stock of the Company at the rate of $100.00 per share for his plant (no cash). Then to secure a working capital Preferred Stock was issued to the amount of $640,000, which was largely purchased by the firms that comprised the Organization, paying $100.00 per share in cash.

Pictured are the # 1 Common Stock issued to A. A. Adams for 50 shares, and # A-1 Preferred Stock issued to Mr. John D. McCord for 100 shares. These were the first shares of Common and Preferred Stock issued by the United States Glass Co. A total Capital Stock of the company was issued for $4,148,100.00.

SALES REPORT
UNITED STATES GLASS COMPANY
(Fiscal Year—July-July)

1891-92	$2,887,609.13
1892-93	2,969,423.14
1893-94	1,039,855.43
1894-95	974,256.30
1895-96	1,103,951.52
1896-97	1,052,394.11
1897-98	1,242,362.07
1898-99	1,297,651.96
1899-1900	1,568,117.68
1900-01	1,777,081.32
1901-02	1,995,501.24
1902-03	2,196,037.70
1903-04	2,238,808.25
1904-05	2,322,029.60
1905-06	2,420,087.84
1906-07	2,737,738.26
1907-08	1,967,524.41
1908-09	2,184,139.98
1909-10	2,633,453.72

Original U.S.G.C. invoice for March 14, 1893.

Nevada pattern table set, frosted background with enamel decoration; U.S. Glass #15075 pattern, circa 1902.

Table set in crystal with gold *Elephant Toes* pattern, previously unlisted. This pattern can also be found with the base thumbprints stained amethyst or green.

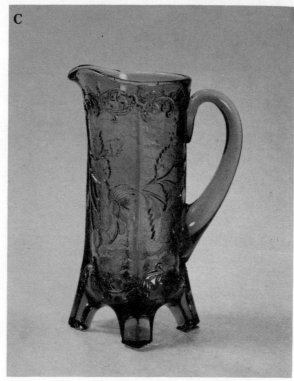

(**Figure A**) Rare butter dish in custrard (ivory) colored *Delaware*, part of the state series; (**Figure B**) Tiny cruet (stopper missing) in amber *Hobnail with Bars* pattern, made by Challinor; (**Figure C**) Unusual syrup pitcher in green with gold *Bohemian* pattern, circa 1899.

Water pitcher in ruby-stained *Bar with Flute* pattern (I mistakenly called this "Corset & Thumbprint" in my Book 3), and milk pitcher in *Washington* (state) pattern.

Water pitcher in rare Frances-Ware decorated *Bulbous Base* pattern, and cranberry cruet in same (Factory H, circa 1891).

GLIMPSES AT U.S. GLASS

The following quotes were lifted from various issues of the "Crockery and Glass Journal", some of which prove important in providing documentation concerning patterns produced by the United States Glass Company. I wish to credit here Mr. J. Chris Ramsey for his unselfish help by sending this data to me, which he recorded at the Library of Congress, Washington, D.C. I cannot thank him enough for his continued support of this series.

January 13, 1898

(Reviewing the USGC exhibit at the Monongahela House) . . . "then a table of odd pieces in their old Colonial pattern, and their new Florida in exquisite shade of green with gold decoration. Another table of green and gold of odd pieces, and a new design, very unique, adorns it. The design shows twisted beaded columns, which, decorated in gold, give the green pieces the appearance of an adornment of gold chains."

In this season of cut glass patterns the "Colorado" stands alone in the simplicity and beauty of an entirely plain pattern of a delicate exquisite mold. It is simple beauty unadorned. The sugars and butters have covers with beaded edges and when decorated in gold present the appearance of a string of gold beads. This line also has feet with a large bead in the center, and some have sand-blast decoration. One of the sugars, with sand-blast decorations on the cover, gold decorations on the beaded edges, and solid gold decorations on the foot, except for the bead, reminds one very much of a delicate, chaste Puritan maiden, with face kerchief, gold beads, and golden slippers with diamond buckles."

April 21, 1898

The U.S.G.C. have just gotten out some pretty vases in strikingly original shapes. There are six new original designs. They are both crystal and emerald. The colored have an exquisite shade of green. The shapes are dainty and unique. One is an inverted truncated, triangular pyramid, so to speak, with beaded corners and sides neatly figured. Another represents a kind of twisted horn of plenty . . . (they) are making one line of their lamps—9851—in emerald this year as an experiment.

July 7, 1898

"The U.S.G.C. have just got from one of their factories a newly-designed short table-ware line of a number of pieces that are patriotically unique. The set is footed and the feet are United States shields (decorated in white and blue) and standing on these shields is the eagle in a kind of bas-relief in the ware. On the cover of the sugar, butter, etc., is a shield, on top of which is a loaded cartridge or shell."

"They have just put on their table a series of cute little globe colognes—one, two, four and six ounce. These have gold decors on the feet and on the edge of the rim at the top, on the crystal sets, while in the green or emerald sets the stoppers and feet are decorated with gold."

July 14, 1898

"The U.S.G.C. report a gratifying continuence in orders for their invaluable clinch-collar lamps—stem, body and collar all in a single piece, requiring no repair during the lamp's existence. This is a boon to every household in the world using lamps. They have just brought out . . . a new pattern of fruit dish for lemons, limes, etc. It is an open globe, sitting on a ring for a foot and is unique in design."

August 11, 1898

"The U.S.G.C. are now showing two lines of tableware—Nos. 30 and 500—in Dewey blue, both with and without gold decors. This is an exquisite shade of rich blue — the exact thing to meet the demands of cultivated taste. It is very difficult to get a shade of this color that does not look cheap. This Dewey line is simply superb. The gold decors are not heavy and are in excellent taste."

September, 1, 1898

"The U.S.G.C. have an enviable reputation for their decorations. This is the largest department of its kind among glassware manufacturers and is the one branch that runs full the year round."

September 15, 1898

"Movement in tableware has improved a little, though it is still very quiet. There is a tendency among manufacturers to test the market with a blue glass this fall. Blue is a patriotic color now—popular in dress and various articles. Most shades of blue look cheap in glass, hence there is a hesitancy on the part of the manufacturers in testing the public taste on this color. There is a shade of blue now shown by the U.S.G.C., however, that is a striking success, nearly perfect, and it is reported to be winning its way on the market."

December 1, 1898

"Colored ware, decorated, and novelties have a better movement than anything else these days, according to the manager of the U.S.G.C. He also said blue is making some impression on the trade, but the fine shades of emerald, gold decorated, hold the palm. The United States are preparing four or five new lines for next year . . . "

December 15, 1898

"The U.S.G.C. are receiving a good many econiums on their No. 30 line in an elegant shade of blue, enamelled in white and yellow with cupids, scrolls, etc. These may be somewhat conventional, but they are entirely in line with the best decorations of the day. The delicate shade of the yellow cannot fail to be most pleasing to people of taste. This line embraces a great variety of pieces of graceful shapes in tankards, salad bowls, celery dishes, etc."

December 22, 1898

" . . . new California pattern is square shaped and has figured designs of sections of grape vines. It is shown in crystal and green—also in both, gold decorated. The Missouri is plain with the exception that four ferns are apparently attached to the bowls, nappies, etc., about halfway up the side, and extend down and are curved out below into feet upon which the piece stands giving it a graceful, unique appearance."

December 29, 1898

"The U.S.G.C. show a large line of novelties and specialties for '99 in colored, gold decorated and crystal.

"... A swan bowl in jet black glass gives a striking effect from the unusual polish and sheen of the black bowl in contrast with the head and neck of the swan in solid gold color."

January 1, 1903

"H. H. McBride, who is making an extended tour of Europe on behalf of the U.S.G.C., is expected to reach New York either the latter part of February or early in March. When last heard from Mr. McBride was in South Africa."

February 19, 1903

"At the U.S.G.C. salesroom there is no feature more deserving of observation than the No. 15,082 line of pressed tableware. There are fully one hundred distinct pieces on show, including rose bowls, cracker jars, water jugs, tankards, syrups, peppers, salts, nappies, stemware and a complete assortment of vases. The metal is excellent, and every piece has been well finished. The line is both crystal and decorated."

March 12, 1903

"An enormous sale is being made of the U.S.G.C.'s No. 15,082 tulip pattern in tableware. The various prismatic colors of the flowers are pleasingly blended in the glass, producing an effect that is both delicate and harmonious. The crystal decoration, a genuine colonial flute design, shows a high polish and a galaxy of desirable shapes. Then there is No. 15,084 assortment of half-cut and half-plain, the last mentioned portion being colored in claret with gold mounting. This claret, it may be stated incidently, differs materially from the old style ruby-stain."

April 2, 1903

"(The U.S.G.C.'s) 1903 glass lamps, both plain and decorated are out. There is a gorgeous decoration on the 9873 lamp, being a color combination of ruby and gold."

June 11, 1903

"The U.S.G.C., which is non-union, will shut down at the close of the month, take stock, make repairs and probably take the same vacation as the union plants."

July 30, 1903

"A delicate shade of green, bearing a close resemblance to the color of creme de menthe, is the most recent finish shown on the U.S.G.C. line of table glassware. The tint covers the upper half of each piece, merging at the centre into the plain crystal very nicely. This combination of green and crystal enlivened in some instances by the application of gold on the edge and around the body, is decidedly pretty."

September 3, 1903

"The U.S.G.C. sent this week ... thirty samples of long-stem flower vases ... ranging from six to thirty inches in height, they are graceful, artistic, and admirably adapted for the use for which they were designed. They are shown in crystal, amber, blue and emerald."

November 12, 1903

"The U.S.G.C. were disappointed at first with the movement of their "Cafe" ware. It's popularity is, however, now largely increasing, and demands for it have been coming in of late more satisfactorily, especially for the cups and saucers."

December 3, 1903

"The U.S.G.C. will have five new patterns, with twelve new effects. The Rosebud pattern is a beauty, and the Magenta no one will overlook. The Sea Foam is another pretty effect, while their white and gold is one of the daintiest creations ever shown by them. The pattern is largely plain, of excellent proportions, with figured edges, delicately illuminated with gold petals, the outline of which are enamelled. Their mirrored plate pattern is rich and striking, and the finest crystal design probably they ever put out ..."

Glass figurals made by U.S.G.C., circa 1935 (from advertising cuts found at Tiffin, Ohio)

Bullseye & Fan

1   2   3   4

U.S. Glass In Color

(Includes patterns made by member factories)

4A   4B   4C   4D   4E   4F   4G

(Fig. 4A) Scarce blue AMAZON cruet with one of two possible stoppers—see also Figure 231; **(Fig. 4B)** Emerald green SCAL-LOPED DAISY & FAN goblet, previously unattributed; **(Fig. 4C)** Very rare blue JACOB'S LADDER cruet with original stopper; **(Fig. 4D)** Ruby-stained SNAIL pattern syrup pitcher; **(Fig. 4E)** Ruby-stained ROMAN ROSETTE salt shaker; **(Fig. 4F)** Amber-stained DAISY & BUTTON WITH THUMBPRINT goblet; **(Fig. 4G)** Amber PRESSED SWIRL cruet, made by Factory O, and known only in this cruet.

5	6	5	7	8
TUMBLER	TANKARD	TUMBLER	PITCHER	PIN TRAY

Delaware

9	10	11	12	13
TOOTHPICK	SUGAR	CREAMER	SPOONER	BUTTER

Bohemian

14	15	16	17	18
TOOTHPICK	SUGAR	CREAMER	SPOONER	BUTTER

DELAWARE (Figs. 5-13) One of the most popular of the "states" patterns, with a long production life, 1898-1910, it remains equally sought after by collectors today. It was made in a wide variety of items, including a dresser set, in several colors. See also the cruet (Fig. 229), and the catalogue reprint, as well as the scarce custard glass pieces shown in Book 4, page 54.

BOHEMIAN (Figs. 14-18) Also known as "Floradora", this pattern is sometimes confused for "Delaware". It is illustrated here to show the similar, but obviously different, pattern characteristics. The easiest way to differentiate between the two is that all pieces of "Bohemian" are footed, except for the tumbler and covered butter. No cruet has been seen in this pattern to date. See also Figures 159 and 166.

Michigan

19 SPOONER   **20 BUTTER**   **21 SUGAR**   **22 CREAMER**   **23 PITCHER**   **24 TUMBLER**

25 BUTTER   **26 SUGAR**   **27 CREAMER**   **28 SPOONER**   **29 CRUET**

New Hampshire

30 GOBLET   **31 WINE**   **32 CUSTARD**   **33 TOOTHPICK**   **34 SALT**   **35 BREAKFAST SUGAR**   **36 BREAKFAST CREAMER**

MICHIGAN (Figures 19-24) Produced primarily in crystal, the only colored version of this pattern would be of the color-stained variety. The "Maiden's Blush" decoration seems to be the most commonly found today, but occasional items are found in crystal with yellow, blue or green staining— sometimes with tiny enamel decorated flowers. "Michigan" is rare in ruby-stained, and is made in a complete table service. The toothpick has been reproduced in all colors, including carnival glass.

NEW HAMPSHIRE (Figures 25-36) Another pattern known only in crystal and color-stained crystal, this popular state series pattern is also known as "Bent Buckle". Ruby-stained is rare, usually found only in souvenir items. "New Hampshire" was made in a complete table service, and has never been reproduced. The stopper in the Figure 29 cruet is original.

37
Wooden Pail
WATER PITCHER

38
COMPOTE

39
TUMBLER

40
PITCHER

41
VASE

Colorado

42
CELERY

43
TUMBLER

44
WINE

45
IND. SUGAR

46
IND. CREAMER

47
Maine

48
SPOONER

49
SUGAR

50
BUTTER

51
CREAMER

Colorado

WOODEN PAIL (Figure 37) Originally called the "Bucket Set" by Bryce Brothers, this popular figural pattern was revived by U.S. Glass after 1891. Made in several colors, the amethyst is quite scarce. See the table set on page 44.

MAINE (Figure 47) This little-known pattern in the state's series was made in crystal and emerald green. Lee called it "Stippled Panelled Flower". The colored production was limited, but the value of this pattern today is relatively low due to minimal collectability. See also Figures 126 and 169.

COLORADO (Figures 38-46, 48-51) Perhaps the most popular state's pattern among collectors today, "Colorado" had a long production life when introduced in 1898. This lengthy production explains the considerable variations in the emerald green color most often found today. The cobalt blue color shown on the next page is the most sought after, and is quite scarce because of this demand. See the catalogue reprint in this book, and the very rare perfume bottle on page 43.

Bead & Scroll

52
Kings 500
PITCHER

53
SUGAR

54
BUTTER

55
CREAMER

56
ANDLED TUMBLER

57
IND. SUGAR
(with handles)

58
SHERBERT

59
VIOLET BOWL

60
TOOTHPICK

Colorado & Lacy Medallion

61
SOUVENIR CREAMER

62
HANDLED TUMBLER

63
CUSTARD

64
SALT

65
TOY OPEN SUGAR

66
TOY CREAM

67
VIOLET BOWL

KING'S 500 (Figure 52) This exciting piece of glass is in the rich "Dewey Blue" introduced by USGC in 1899. Originally produced by the King Glass Co., production was continued for some time after the 1891 merger. This pattern was made in an incredible number of items, too numerous to list here. Primarily found in crystal, scarce in cobalt.

BEAD & SCROLL (Figures 53-55) I may be climbing out on a limb, but I am basing attribution of this pattern on color and pattern characteristics. It was also made in an odd color of green (Fig. 244) ruby-stained crystal, as well as plain crystal. The toy table set in "Bead & Scroll" is charming, and can also be found in a frosted crystal.

COLORADO (Figures 56-60, 63, 67) Shown here and on page 44 in the rich "Dewey Blue". Rare in a salt shaker. Except for the tumbler, all pieces of "Colorado" are footed.

LACY MEDALLION (Figures 61-66) Originally the "Jewel" line of USGC, dating around 1908, this line was almost exclusively marketed as souvenir ware. See the catalogue reprint section.

68
GOBLET

69
PITCHER

70
SALT

71
SYRUP

70
PEPPER

72
Long Loops
VASE

Florida

73
MASTER BERRY

74
IND. BERRY

75
CRUET

76 77
BREAKFAST SUGAR & CREAMER

U.S. Rib

78
SUGAR

79
BUTTER

80
SPOONER

81
CREAMER

FLORIDA (Figures 68-71, 73-74) This is the original name for this state series pattern, popularly known today as "Emerald Green Herringbone". However, since the pattern was also made to a considerable degree in crystal, this name often proves inappropriate. Care should be taken not to confuse this with the "Florida" pattern made by Greensburgh Glass ("Sunken Primrose"). The syrup illustrated is quite rare in color.

LONG LOOPS (Figure 72) One of a variety of vases released by U.S. Glass in 1899—see catalogue reprint.

U.S. RIB (Figures 75-81) Kamm based her attribution and naming of this pattern on color and characteristics, and she was correct in her guess. Appeared in their catalogue as #15061. Seen to date only in crystal and emerald green, usually with gold decoration. Not a very rare or collectible pattern on today's market, but the wide variety of available shapes makes it's future promising.

California
(Beaded Grape)

| 82 CREAMER | 83 SUGAR | 84 BUTTER | 85 SPOONER | 86 WINE | 87 PITCHER |

| 88 SUGAR | 89 CREAMER | 90 BUTTER | 91 SPOONER |

Daisy & Button with Crossbars

| 92 SYRUP | 93 GOBLET | 94 CRUET | 95 KETCHUP |

96
Thousand Eye
(cruet set)

CALIFORNIA (Figures 82-87) Better known as "Beaded Grape", this popular state series pattern is only rarely called by it's original name. Introduced in 1899, it was made only in crystal and emerald green in a wide variety of shapes.

DAISY & BUTTON WITH CROSSBARS (Figures 88-95) Originally the "Mikado" pattern of Richards & Hartley (Factory F), this line can be found in crystal and amber, with minimal items in blue and vaseline. See my Book 3, page 72, for more items in this pattern.

THOUSAND EYE (Figure 96) This amber cruet set was made by Factory A (Adams & Co.), which also produced colors of crystal, blue, vaseline, apple green and a few items in opalescent white. See the catalogue reprint for Factory A for other items in this pattern. See also Figure 130.

97
98
Bohemian Grape
JUICE TUMBLER & TANKARD

99
U.S. Colonial
WINE

100
California
CAKE STAND

101
Dbl. Dahlia W. Lens
WINE

102
Illinois
PITCHER

103
Wildflower
PITCHER

104
Hanover
BUTTER

105
LEMONADE PITCHER

106
TUMBLER

107
WATER PITCHER

Bullseye & Fan

BOHEMIAN GRAPE (Figures 97-98) Previously unlisted, this lovely breakfast juice set has a scroll design and wave-like stippling identical to the Bohemian pattern. No other items known. See pattern listing.

U.S. COLONIAL (Figure 99) Also known as "Plain Scalloped Panel", this line was made primarily in crystal and emerald green, with limited production in cobalt blue.

CALIFORNIA (Figure 100) See notes page 39.

DOUBLE DAHLIA WITH LENS (Figure 101) I am basing attribution of this pattern on the luscious "Rose" stained crystal (identical to the color on page 34) in which the pattern has been found. Also made in color-decorated crystal and emerald green in a limited table service.

ILLINOIS (Figure 102) This state series pattern was made primarily in crystal with limited production in emerald green. Never listed by Kamm, Metz or Lee.

WILDFLOWER (Figure 103) See Factory A catalogue reprint. A very popular pattern shown here in scarce apple green color. Beware or repro's!!

HANOVER (Figure 104) Made primarily in crystal, this pattern is scarce in amber and rare in blue. See Factory A catalogue reprint.

BULLSEYE & FAN (Figures 1-4, 105-107, 167) Also known as "Daisy in Oval Panels", this popular pattern is shown here in the rich sapphire blue. Also made in crystal and two shades of green. See catalogue reprint, page 150.

40

108	**109**	**110**	**111**	**110**
D & B With Thumbprint CELERY	*Wheat & Barley* SYRUP	GOBLET	PITCHER	GOBLET

Spirea Band

112	**113**	**114**	**115**
BUTTER	SPOONER	SUGAR	CREAMER

Medallion

116	**117**	**118**	**119**
CREAMER	SUGAR	BUTTER	SPOONER

Finecut

*Possible U.S. Glass Patterns

DAISY & BUTTON WITH THUMBPRINT (Fig. 108) This pattern is very similar to and often confused for the highly collectible "Amberette" (Fig. 233), which does not have thumbprints in the panels. Made in crystal, color & color-stained crystal. See also Figure 257. Factory A.

WHEAT & BARLEY (Fig. 109) Made in crystal and color by Factory B.

SPIREA BAND (Figs. 110-111) I am including this and the next two patterns as "possible U.S. Glass" since no maker has been listed to date.

MEDALLION (Figs. 112-115) Again, I am only speculating that this pattern was made by one of the member factories of USGC. No maker has been determined to date and pattern & color characteristics date the glass about 1890-1895.

FINECUT (Figs. 116-119) Another pattern of the early USGC variety, no maker has been discovered on this pattern either. It was made in all the usual colors, and should not be confused for the similar "Heavy Finecut" (Fig. 132)

41

120 *Palm Beach* **PITCHER**

121 *Finecut* **GOBLET**

122 *Willow Oak* **GOBLET**

123 *Spirea Band* **GOBLET**

124 *Medallion* **PITCHER**

125 *Leaf & Flower* **CELERY**

126 *Maine* **SYRUP**

127 *Bryce Panel* **SYRUP**

128 *Kings 500* **SYRUP**

129 *Kings 500* **CRUET**

130 *Thousand Eye* **THREE-KNOB**

131 *Wooden Pail* **SPOONER**

132 *Heavy Finecut* **SPOONER**

133 *Three Panel* **SUGAR**

134 *Three Panel* **CREAMER**

PALM BEACH (Fig. 120) See catalogue reprint and Book 2 for more information.

WILLOW OAK (Fig. 122) Factory B in crystal and color.

LEAF & FLOWER (Fig. 125) Factory H—see catalogue reprint.

BRYCE PANEL (Fig. 127) This syrup is shown in the catalogue reprint, Book 3, page 77.

HEAVY FINECUT (Fig. 132) This was originally called Duncan & Sons "Bag Ware", with continued production by USGC. Made in crystal, amber, blue and canary. See catalogue reprint—also Book 3, pg. 71.

THREE PANEL (Figures 133-134) Made by Factory E, this popular colored glass pattern was made in crystal, amber, blue, canary and apple green.

(Figures 121, 123, 124 are discussed on page 41, Figures 126, 128-131 are covered on earlier pages.)

Pattee Cross
PITCHER & TUMBLERS

135

136

Ruby Thumbprint

137
Panelled Palm
BUTTER

138
SUGAR

139
CREAMER

140
Colorado
PERFUME

141
Star-in-Bullseye

142
Mirror & Fan

143
Kentucky

144
Pavonia

145
Thousand Eye

PATTEE CROSS (Figures 135-136) Not previously attributed, this is U.S.G. #15112, made in crystal, color-flashed crystal and emerald green. See catalogue reprint.

PANELLED PALM (Fig. 137) Made in crystal and rose-flashed crystal, after 1906.

RUBY THUMBPRINT (Figs. 138-139) See page 49

COLORADO (Fig. 140) See notes page 36 on this very rare perfume bottle.

STAR-IN-BULLSEYE (Fig. 141) Made only in crystal and rose-flashed crystal, after 1908.

MIRROR & FAN (Fig. 142) Part of a wine set made by Factory B from 1891 to as late as 1910. See catalogue reprint.

KENTUCKY (Fig. 143) Part of the state series, this pattern was made in crystal, emerald green and is rare in cobalt.

PAVONIA (Fig. 144) Made by Factory F (Ripley) in crystal and rare in ruby-stain.

146
Barred Oval
PITCHER

147
Bullseye & Daisy
SPOONER

148
BUTTER

149
VASE

Virginia

150
SUGAR

151
BUTTER

152
CREAMER

Colorado

153
SPOONER

154
BUTTER

155
SUGAR

156
CREAMER

Wooden Pail

BARRED OVAL (Fig. 146) U.S.G. #15004 pattern made in crystal and scarce in ruby-stain. See catalogue reprint for Factory D.

BULLSEYE & DAISY (Fig. 147) This pattern is rather late, dating after 1909, made in crystal, color-stained crystal, ruby-stain and emerald green.

VIRGINIA (Figs. 148-149) I personally believe an end should be put to calling this "Banded Portland", to prevent further confusion concerning it's origins. This is part of the state series, dating after 1901. It was made in crystal, rose-flashed crystal (Lee calls this pattern "Maiden's Blush"), and variations of color-staining in yellows, blues and greens.

COLORADO (Figures 150-152) See notes on page 34 and 35.

WOODEN PAIL (Figures 153-156) See notes on page 34 concerning this pattern.

157
Tiny Finecut
WINE DECANTER

158
Panelled Dogwood

159
Bohemian
COLOGNE

160
Delaware
CELERY

161

162
Beaded Swirl
PITCHER & TUMBLERS

161

163
*U. S.
Sheraton*
NIGHT LAMP

164

165
Panelled Dogwood
BERRY BOWL & SAUCES

164

TINY FINECUT (Figure 157) Made only in a wine set in crystal, emerald green and scarce in ruby-stain (see Fig. 215)

PANELLED DOGWOOD (Fig. 158, 164-165) Made only in assorted bowls after 1908, in crystal, emerald green, rose-flashed and amethyst flashed. See catalogue reprint.

BOHEMIAN & DELAWARE (Figs. 159-160) See notes on page 34.

BEADED SWIRL (Figures 161-162) A pattern made by Factory D, it was made in both a plain and footed variation. See catalogue reprint for more information. Made in crystal and emerald green.

U.S. SHERATON (Figure 163) Made primarily in crystal, illustrated here is the tiny night lamp in emerald green. See catalogue reprint for more items in this late pattern.

166
Bohemian
STRAW JAR

167
Bullseye & Fan
LEMONADE

168
Bearded Man

NOT U.S. GLASS

169
Maine
MILK PITCHER

170
Pavonia
CELERY

171

172
Late Block
WATER SET

173
SUGAR

174
CREAMER

175
SPOONER

176
BUTTER

177
Two Panel
MASTER & INDIV. SA

178

Double-Eye Hobnail

BEARDED MAN (Fig. 168) This is not U.S. Glass—it was made by LaBelle Glass Co., Bridgeport, O., and was originally called "Queen Anne" in 1879 when it was introduced.

PAVONIA (Fig. 170) This scarce ruby-stained celery vase is inscribed in German.

LATE BLOCK (Figures 171-172) A poor name for such an early pattern, this was made by Factory D in crystal and ruby-stain. See catalogue reprint.

DOUBLE-EYE HOBNAIL (Figures 173-176) Made by Factory J (Columbia) in crystal and color—see ad reprint Book 3, pg. 68

TWO PANEL (Figs. 177-178) Factory E pattern, made in crystal and several colors.

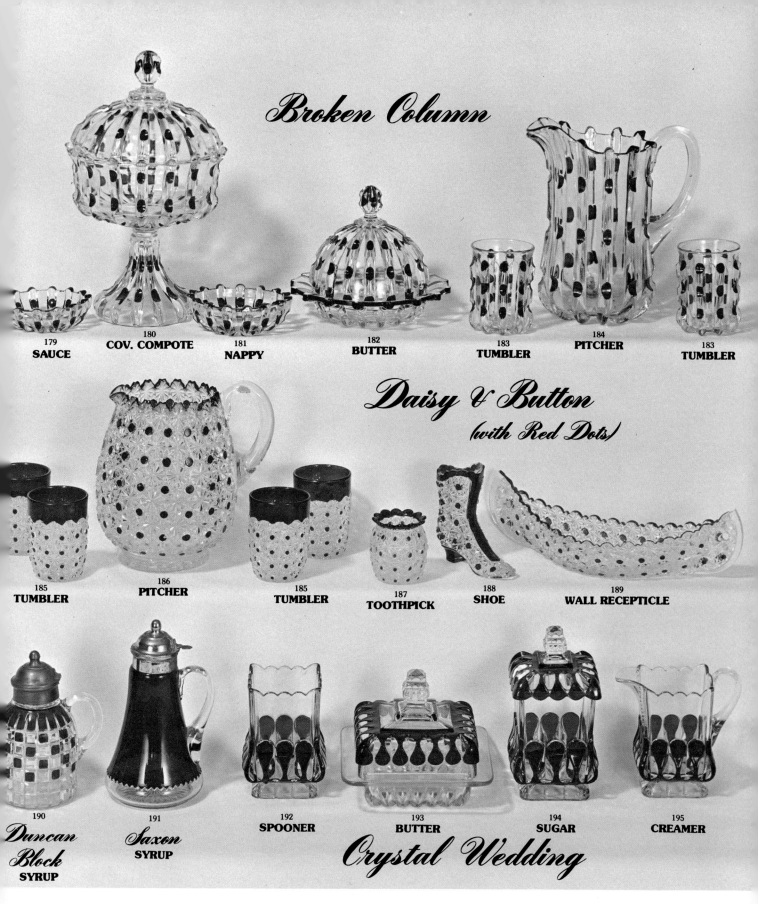

Broken Column

179 SAUCE · **180 COV. COMPOTE** · **181 NAPPY** · **182 BUTTER** · **183 TUMBLER** · **184 PITCHER** · **183 TUMBLER**

Daisy & Button
(with Red Dots)

185 TUMBLER · **186 PITCHER** · **185 TUMBLER** · **187 TOOTHPICK** · **188 SHOE** · **189 WALL RECEPTICLE**

190 Duncan Block SYRUP · **191 Saxon SYRUP** · **192 SPOONER** · **193 BUTTER** · **194 SUGAR** · **195 CREAMER**

Crystal Wedding

BROKEN COLUMN (Figures 179-183) A highly collectable pattern in ruby-stain, this was made originally at Factory J and later at Factory E. The covered compote shown is quite rare.

DAISY & BUTTON WITH RED DOTS (Figs. 185-189) Made by Factory D, this line was also produced in crystal, amber, blue and amethyst. These other colors should be referred to as "Duncan's Daisy & Button". See catalogue reprint.

DUNCAN BLOCK (Fig. 190) See catalogue reprint, page 101.

SAXON (Fig. 191) Made in crystal and ruby-stain by Factory A. See catalogue reprint, page 60.

CRYSTAL WEDDING (Figs. 192-195) Made primarily in crystal and ruby-stain, a few items have been seen in color. See Factory A catalogue reprint. This pattern has been reproduced in a cheap-looking ruby-stain.

196
TUMBLER

197
BULBOUS PITCHER

196
TUMBLER

198
TUMBLER

199

198
TUMBLER

Ruby Thumbprint

(Figures 196-197, 200-203)

Washington

200
BUTTER

201
CUP & SAUCER

202
MILK PITCHER

203
GOBLET

204
Snail
CRUET

205
Dakota
WINE

206
Peas & Pods
WINE

207
Bevelled Diamond & Star
WINE

208
Washington
CORDIAL

RUBY THUMBPRINT (Figs. 196-197, 200-203) See Factory A catalogue reprint for this very popular ruby-stained pattern which is known as "King's Crown" when in crystal or color (a few items in green and cobalt). A massively reproduced pattern—be especially careful of wine glasses.

WASHINGTON (Figs. 198-199, 208) Part of the state series, dating after 1901, in crystal, ruby-stain and rare in custard glass (limited). See catalogue reprint.

SNAIL (Figure 204) Produced by Factory D in crystal and rare in ruby-stain. The stopper is original in the rare cruet shown here.

DAKOTA (Fig. 206) Another state series pattern, made in crystal and ruby-stain.

PEAS & PODS (Fig. 206) Part of a wine set made by Factory B in crystal & ruby-stain—see catalogue reprint.

BEVELLED DIAMOND & STAR (Figure 207) A possible U.S.G. pattern dating around 1895—no previous attributions on this line, made in crystal and ruby-stain.

209 Bullseye & Daisy	210 Arched Ovals	211 Pennsylvania	212 Two Panel	213 Finecut & Panel	214 Cathedral
215 ny Finecut	216 Ruby Thumbprint	217 Kings Crown	218 Washington	219 Roanoke	220 New Jersey
221 Millard	222 Star-in-Bullseye	223 Minnesota	224 Pennsylvania	225 Bullseye & Fan

Illustrated here are a number of wines, cordials and toothpick holders in patterns made by the United States Glass Company. Several of the patterns have been discussed previously in this color section. Figure 210 is a rather late pattern (circa 1908) in which only a few items are found in emerald green and ruby-stain. Fig. 211 is part of the states series, made primarily in crystal. Figures 220 and 223 are also part of the state series, both quite scarce in color or color-stained crystal. The Figure 224 example was advertised in 1910 by Butler Brothers as a "tumbler-toothpick", although most collectors call it a shot glass today. See the Pattern Guide for further information concerning the patterns illustrated here.

49

U.S. Glass Cruets

226	227	228	229	230
U.S. Colonial	*Shoshone*	*U.S. Rib*	*Delaware*	*Beaded Sw...*

231	232	233	234	235
Amazon	*D & B With Crossbar*	*Panelled D & B (Amberette)*	*Millard* N.O.S.	*Millard* N.O.S.

236	237	238	239
Virginia	*Saxon*	*Pennsylvania*	*Nail*

Illustrated on this page are a wide variety of colored and color-stained cruets in U.S.G.C. patterns. Figure 226 is also known as "Plain Scalloped Panel" but I prefer to use the original name in this book. I have been misspelling the Figure 227 pattern for years (due to a typographical error in Barret's book on ruby-stain), so please note the correct spelling. It was originally called the "Victor" pattern by it's makers when it was introduced in 1896. Figure 231 is an unusual example of Amazon in color, as it was made almost exclusively in crystal. See the catalogue reprint section of Book 3 for other items relative to Figures 230, 232, 233, 237 and 239.

240 Diamond Bridges
241 Berkeley
242 Nail
243 Cathedral
244 Bead & Scroll
245 Moon & Star
246
247 Zippered Swirl & Diamond
248 Pleating
249
250 Roanoke
251 O'Hara Diamond
252 Scalloped Swirl
253 Cottage

DIAMOND BRIDGES (Fig. 240) U.S. #15040 water pitcher, scarce in emerald green.

BERKELEY (Fig. 241) U.S. #15020 water pitcher, in crystal and ruby-stained.

NAIL (Fig. 242) Factory F, very popular pattern, rare in ruby-stained.

CATHEDRAL (Fig. 243) See page 83 for more items in this popular Bryce pattern made in several colors.

MOON AND STAR (Fig. 245-246) Made by Factory A, this pattern was decorated with ruby-staining by Pioneer Glass Company (not part of U.S. Glass)—see Kamm 8, page 171 for others; rare in color-stained crystal. Massively reproduced in crystal and color today.

ZIPPERED SWIRL & DIAMOND (Fig. 247) U.S. #15042 in crystal and color-stained crystal.

PLEATING (Figs. 248-249) U.S. #15003 in crystal and ruby-stained.

ROANOKE (Fig. 250) A rare piece in emerald green shown here; primarily made in crystal and also scarce in ruby-stained.

O'HARA DIAMOND (Fig. 251) Made by Factory L in crystal and ruby-stained crystal only—also called "Sawtooth & Star".

SCALLOPED SWIRL (Fig. 252) Only limited pieces found in emerald green—primarily made in crystal and ruby-stained.

COTTAGE (Fig. 253) Made by Factory A primarily in crystal and rare in color.

51

254
Beaded Block
(cruet)

255
Bohemian
(celery)

256
Michigan
(celery)

257
D & B With Thumbprint
(butter)

258
Majestic Cr
(sugar)

259 (toy set)
Hobnail w. Thumbprint

260 (cruet)

261

262 (syrup)

(salt)

263

264
Manhattan

Hobb's Hobnail
(toy water set)

265
Silver Queen

266
Triple Triangle

267
Finecut & Block

268
New York

269
Log & Star

270
Prism & Daisy Bar

271
Doyle Shell

(wines and cordials)

BEADED BLOCKS (Fig. 254) Made only in the cruet by Factory M (Bellaire) in crystal, rare in color.

MAJESTIC CROWN (Fig. 258) Made by Challinor in crystal and purple slag (see page 88).

HOBNAIL WITH THUMBPRINT (Fig. 259) Made by Factory P (Doyle) in complete table set—shown here in the toy-size child's set (on original tray); made in crystal, amber, blue and limited ruby-stain.

MANHATTAN (Figs. 260-262) U.S. #15078, circa 1902, in crystal and color-flashed crystal; there are two size cruets and the syrup shown here is quite rare in color.

HOBB'S HOBNAIL (Figs. 263-264) This is the rare toy water set in Frances Ware decoration (see page 125).

WINES AND CORDIALS (Figs. 265-271) See pattern listing for more information. Figure 270 was made only in a wine glass and goblet. Figure 268 is a natural favorite of mine, since it has my given name on it.

Vermont

272
VASE

273
PICKLE
TRAY

274
TUMBLER

275
PITCHER

276
WASTE
BOWL

277
SPOONER

278
BUTTER

279
SUGAR

280
CREAMER

281
TOOTHPICK

282
SALT

283
SMALL
CARD
TRAY

284
MEDIUM
CARD
TRAY

285
LARGE
CARD
TRAY

286
SAUCE

287
MASTER
BERRY

VERMONT—Introduced in 1899 by the U.S. Glass Company, this ivory colored glass was their first attempt to compete in the new market for "custard" colored glass. Obviously they did not quite get the color right, as this glass is sometimes ignored by "true" custard glass collectors. However, it most decidedly is not milk glass, and it **was** called "ivory" in the original advertisèments (see Book 4, page 66), which is what Northwood called his version. Every shape known is included here in this book, although there is a candle holder (Book 4, Fig. 408) designed and decorated similarly, which I have named "Jewelled Vermont". **Vermont** is also known as "Honeycomb with Flower Rim", with some sources pointing out that the difference between the two is that one has the honeycombs, while the other does not.

The pieces shown here have the honeycomb inside, but since I have never seen a piece without it, and since the ad for **Vermont** specifically said it was made in ivory, I am going to stick to my conclusions presented in Book 1 of this series. I've been told (but it has not been proven to me) that shards of this pattern have been turned up at Greentown's Indiana factory dump. I am hesitant to mention this rumor here, but I suppose it is better to just tell my readers that it is highly unlikely that this pattern was ever made there. U.S. Glass had a factory at nearby Gas City, Indiana, and it is possible that they used the same dump. Decoration on the pattern can be blue or green, although undecorated pieces are known.

Opal Rooster Eyed.
Decoration C.

Opal Rooster Eyed.
Decoration A.

Black Swan Eyed.

Scale ½

Opal Duck Eyed.
Decoration A.

Opal Hen Eyed.
Decoration A.

U.S Glass Factory "C" (Challinor) featuring a number of decorated fowl-covered dishes in milk glass. The page from which this ad was lifted was hand-decorated for color.

This is the first major offering of a reprint of catalogues released by the United States Glass Company. This reprint is by no means complete. Considerable editing was undertaken in order to include only those patterns of major importance to collectors. Literally hundreds of pages of plain tumblers, stemware, bar ware, bottles, bowls, and vases were passed over for reprint. The sets which are included do not necessarily represent complete sets. Space limitations required that I often eliminate including many bowls and compotes which were shown in several sizes.

This reprint offers varying degrees of quality reproduction. The major reprint from Factory A through E was photographed at great expense for detail. Other reprints of less clarity were from Xeroxes available at the various museums where the catalogues were found.

The catalogues for the first year of U.S. Glass production (1891) were made up of separate catalogues from the member factories, bound together in a leather binding. However, as the years went by and most of the factories were closed, the company catalogue was produced by the parent firm and the location of the manufacturer was not offerred.

Represented here are reprints from five major catalogues available for copying. A sixth is included for data only. The pages included in this book are only a portion of these catalogues. Perhaps the balance of the catalogues can be included in a future volume.

1891 Catalogue (photos)	— Factories A through E
1891 Catalogue (Xeroxes)	— Factories F, H, N, J
1891 Catalogues (data only)	— Factories J, M, N, R and F, G, H, K, L, P
1909 Catalogue (Xeroxes)	— Domestic market
1919 Catalogue (photos)	— Export market
1915 Catalogue (photos)	— Mexican/South American market

"Fan & Star" table set and assorted items in decorated opaque white glass, from 1891 U.S.G.C. catalogue, Factory "C".

"SCROLL AND FLOWER" table set, and assorted decorated pitchers, one of which Lee (LVG, pl. 48) incorrectly connects with this pattern; U.S.G.C., Factory "C".

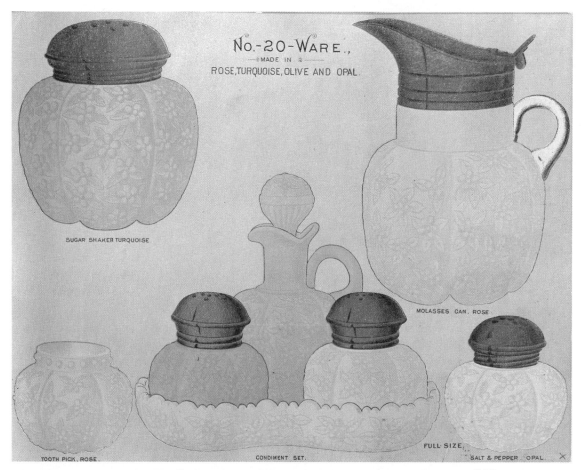

"Challinor Forget-Me-Not" shown in 1891 U.S.G.C. catalogue, Factory "C".

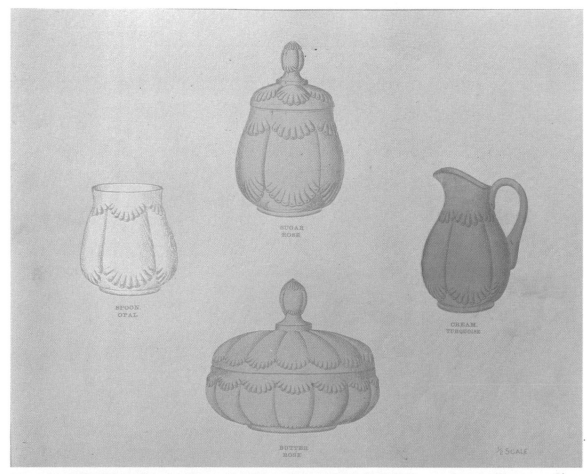

"Banded Shells" table set, illustrated in color in 1891 U.S.G.C. catalogue (Factory C) See also Book 3, pg. 64.

Original letterhead from Adams & Company's stationery, August, 1891.

Factory A

Adams & Company

Pittsburgh, Pa.

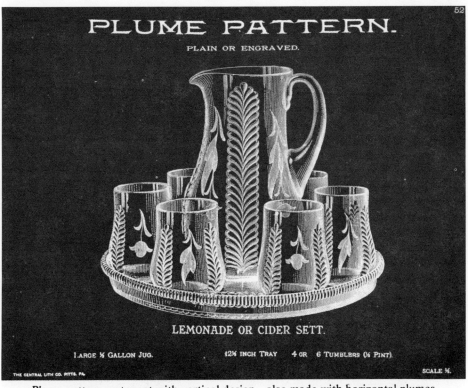

Plume pattern water set with vertical design—also made with horizontal plumes.

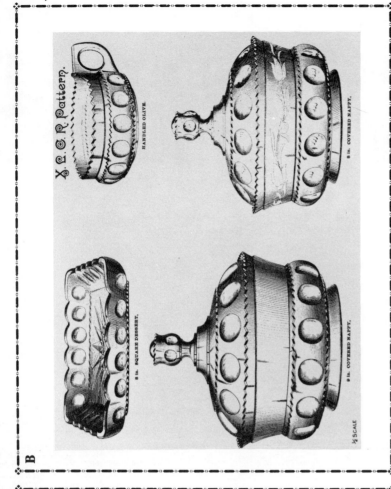

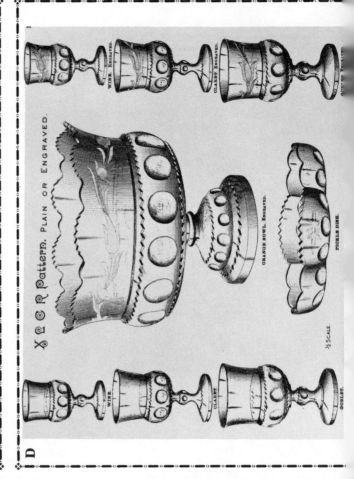

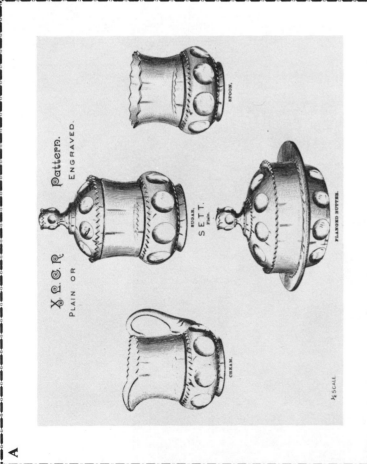

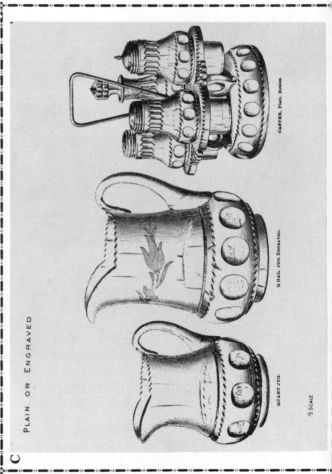

(Plates A—D) Wide assortment of *Ruby Thumbprint* pattern, originally called "X.L.C.R."

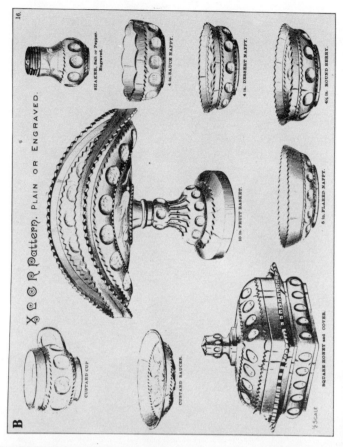

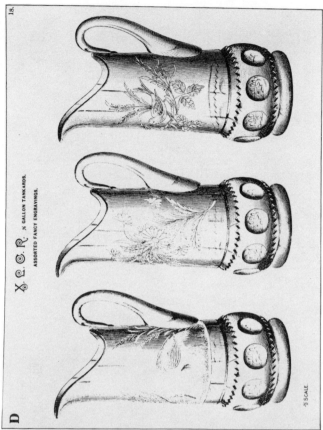

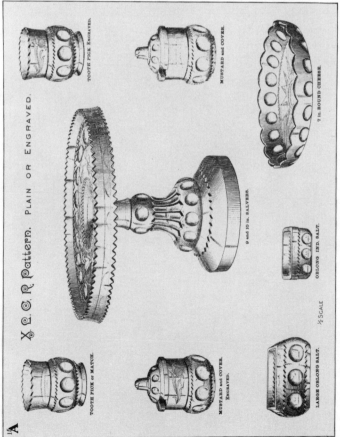

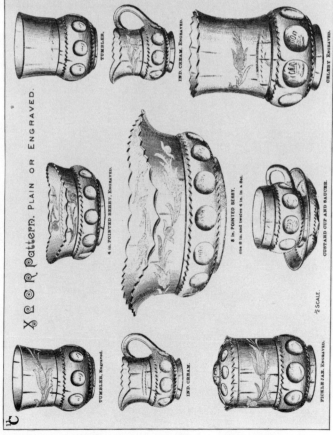

(Plates A—D) More items in *Ruby Thumbprint* (King's Crown), some very rare.

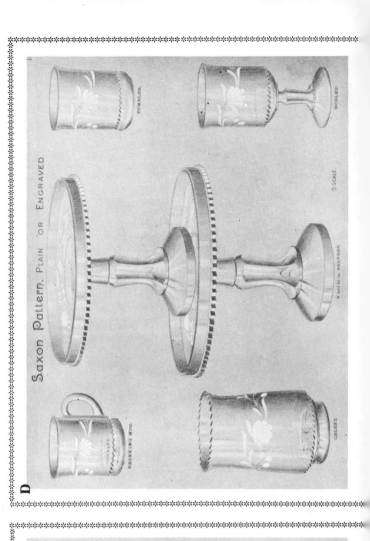

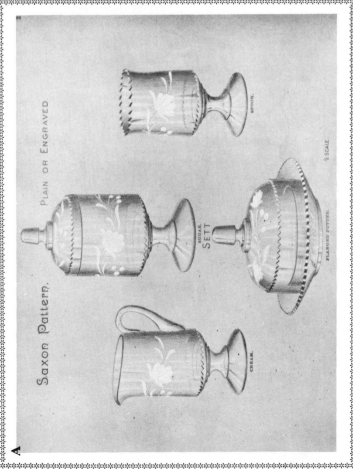

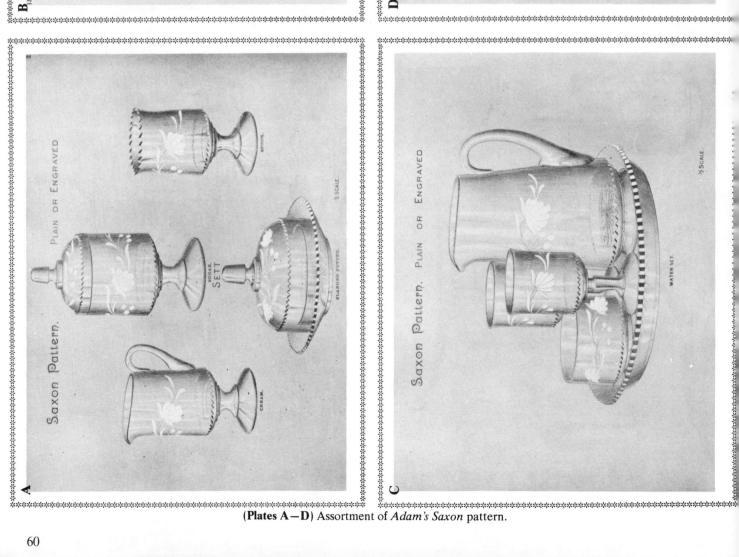

(Plates A – D) Assortment of *Adam's Saxon* pattern.

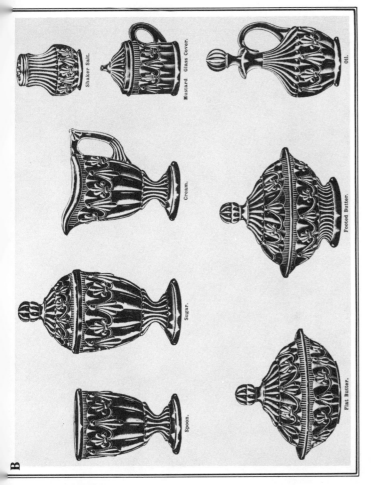

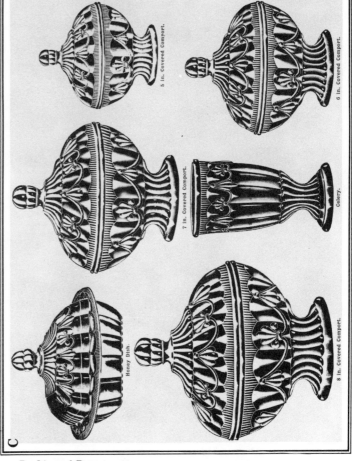

(Plates A—D) Assortment of *Fleur-De-Lis and Drape* pattern.

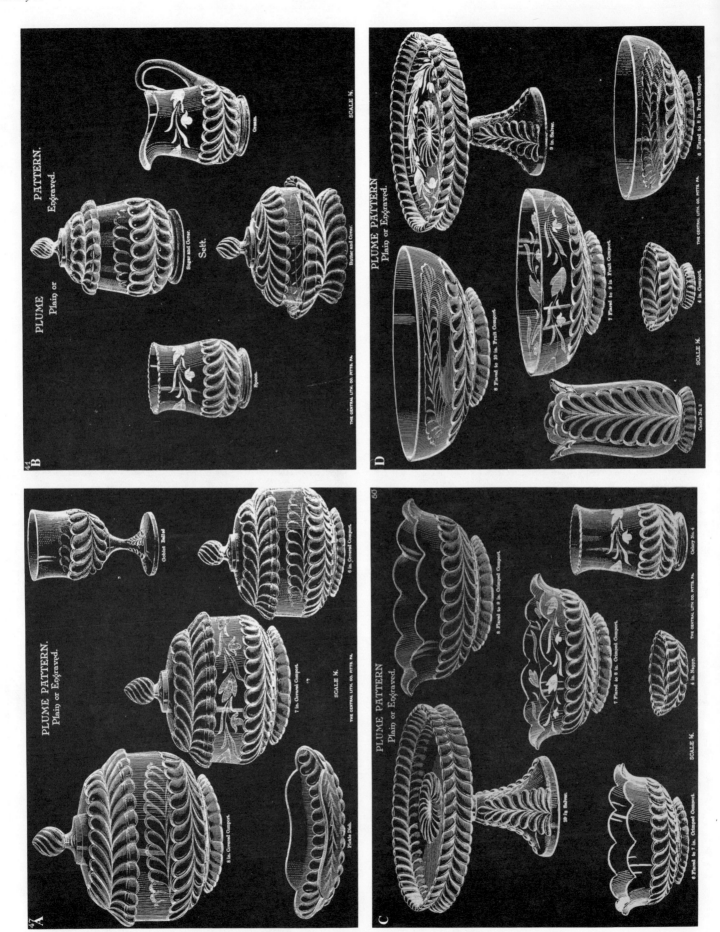

(**Plates A—D**) Wide assortment of the *Plume* pattern; the plumes can be either horizontal or vertical on the pitchers and tumblers (not illustrated).

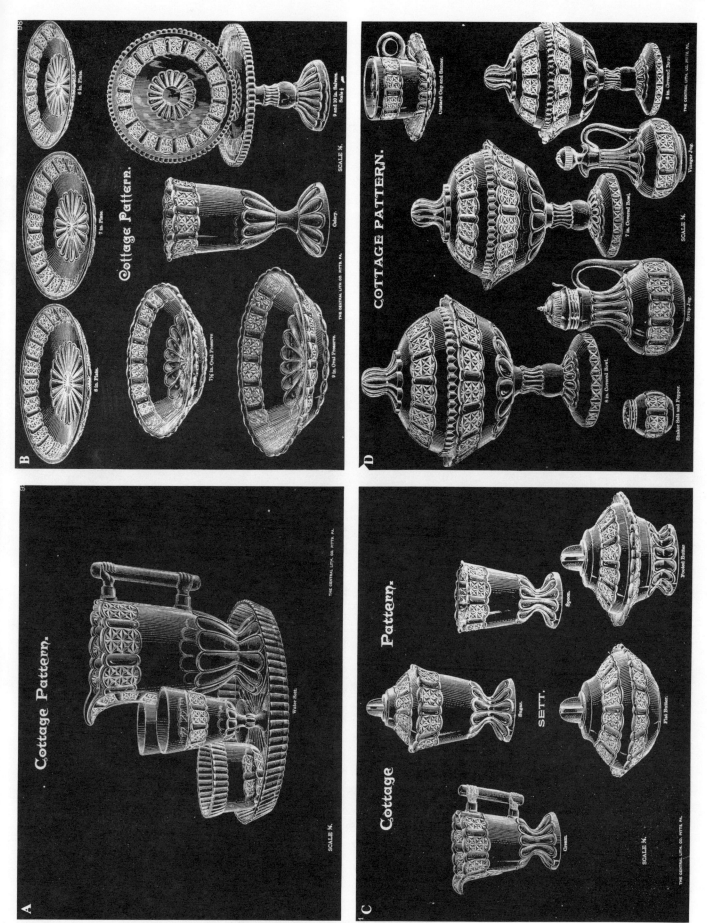

(Plates A – D) Assortment of *Cottage* pattern.

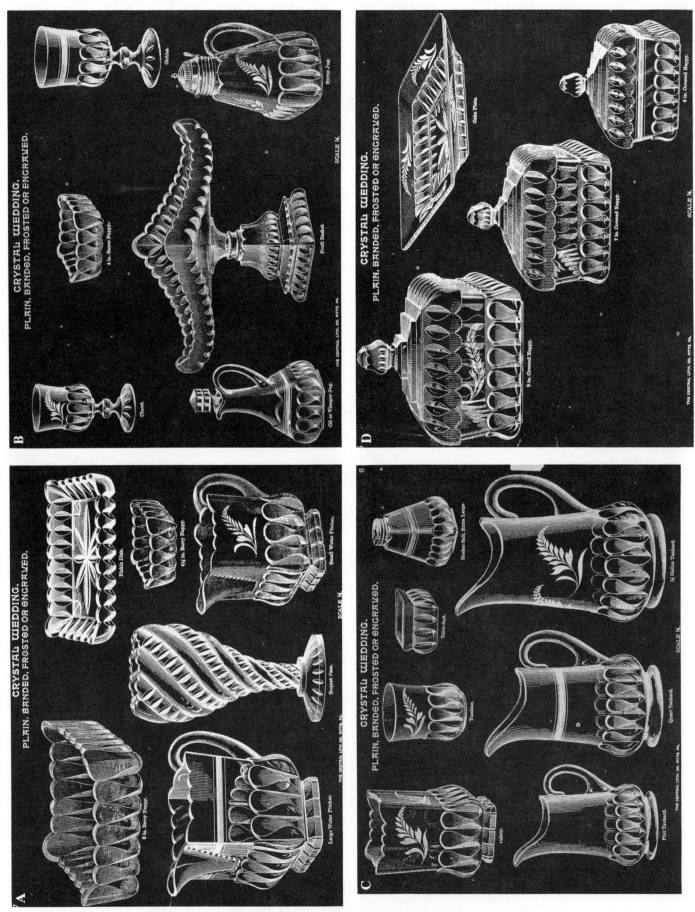

(**Plates A—D**) Assortment of *Crystal Wedding* pattern.

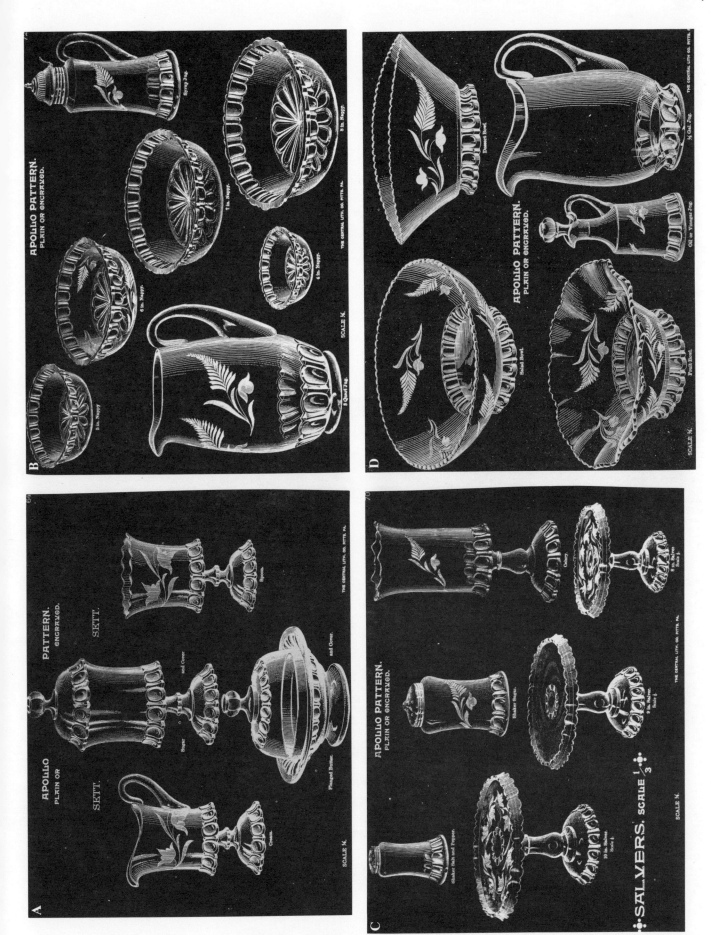

(**Plates A—D**) Assortment of *Apollo* pattern.

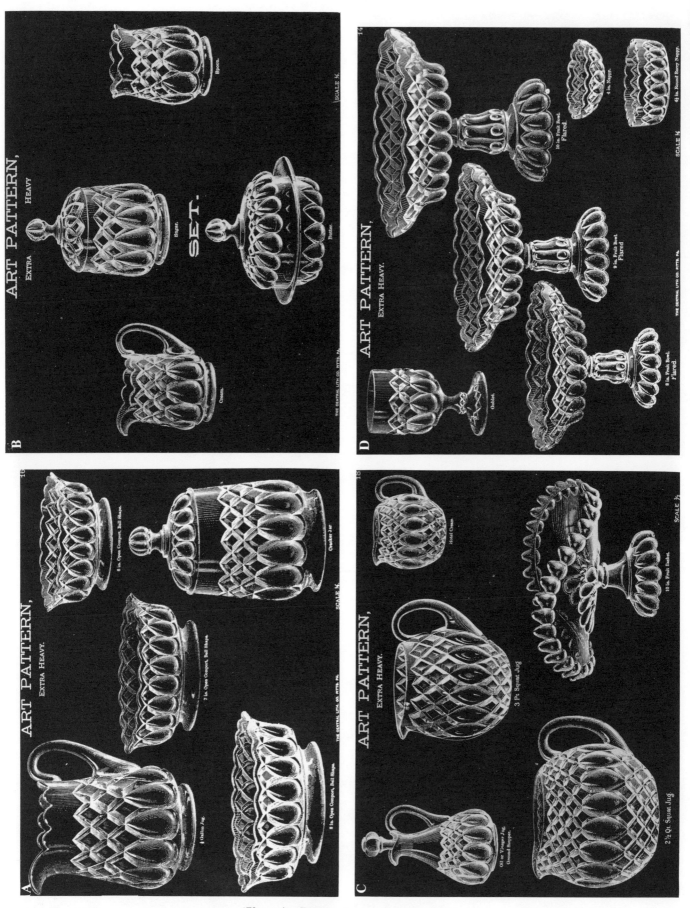

(Plates A—D) Assortment of *Art* pattern.

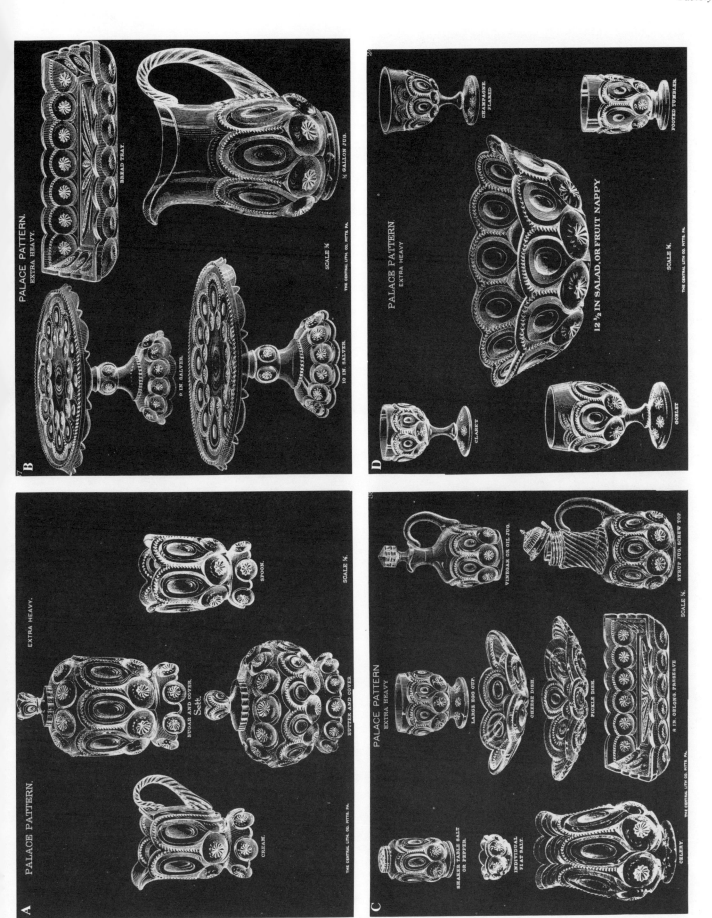

PALACE PATTERN.
EXTRA HEAVY.

BREAD TRAY.

½ GALLON JUG.

SCALE ¼.

THE CENTRAL LITH. CO. PITTS. PA.

9 IN. SALVER.

10 IN. SALVER.

B

PALACE PATTERN
EXTRA HEAVY

CHAMPAGNE, FLARED.

FOOTED TUMBLER.

12 ½ IN. SALAD, OR FRUIT NAPPY

SCALE ¼.

THE CENTRAL LITH. CO. PITTS. PA.

CLARET

GOBLET

D

PALACE PATTERN.

EXTRA HEAVY.

SPOON.

SUGAR AND COVER.

Sett.

BUTTER AND COVER.

SCALE ¼.

THE CENTRAL LITH. CO. PITTS. PA.

CREAM.

A

VINEGAR OR OIL JUG.

SYRUP JUG, SCREW TOP.

PALACE PATTERN
EXTRA HEAVY

LARGE EGG CUP.

CHEESE DISH.

PICKLE DISH.

8 IN. OBLONG, PRESERVE

SCALE ¼.

THE CENTRAL LITH. CO. PITTS. PA.

SHAKER TABLE SALT OR PEPPER.

INDIVIDUAL FLAT SALT.

CELERY.

C

(**Plates A—D**) Assortment of *Moon & Star* pattern, reproduced today in color.

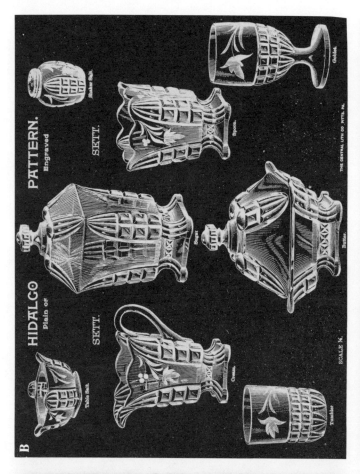

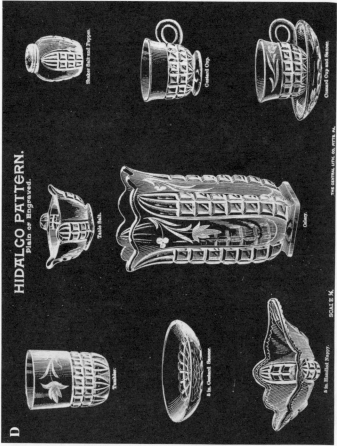

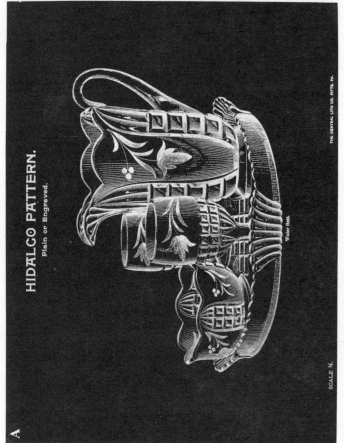

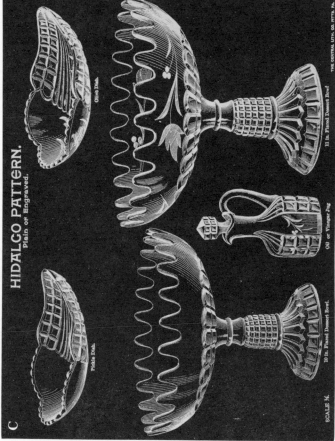

(**Plates A—D**) Wide assortment of *Hidalgo* pattern.

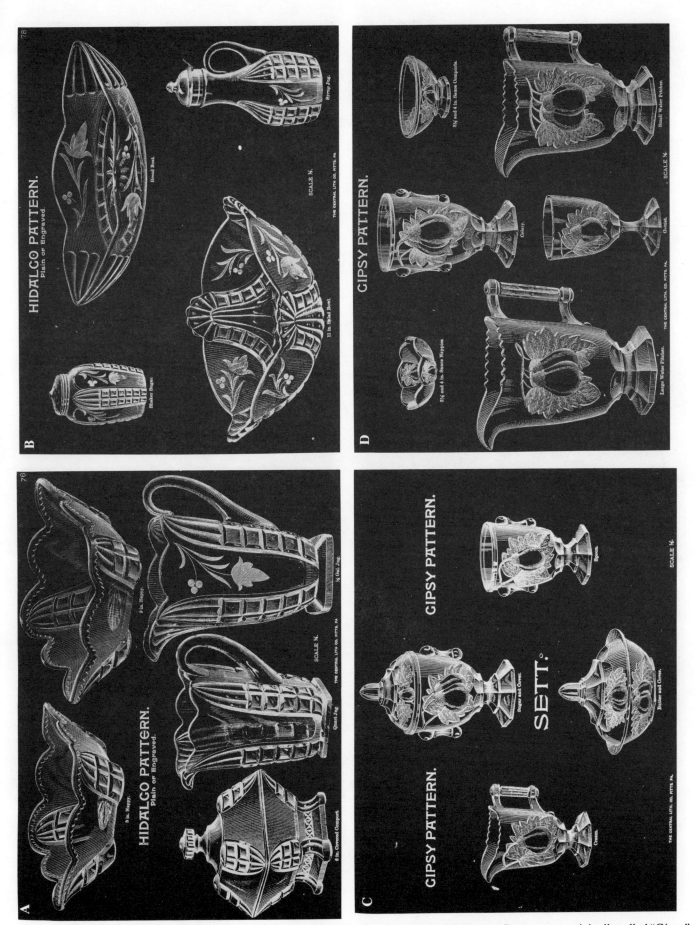

(**Plates A – B**) More items in the *Hidalgo* pattern; (**Plates C – D**) Assortment of *Baltimore Pear* pattern, originally called "Gipsy".

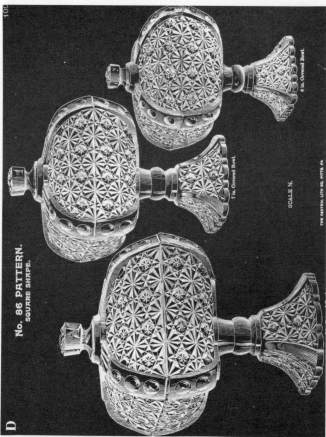

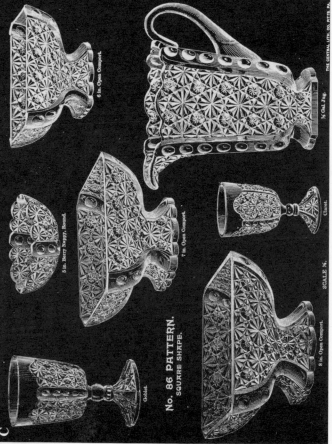

(Plates A — B) Assortment of popular *Wildflower* pattern; **(Plates C — D)** Assortment of *Daisy & Button with Thumbprint* pattern.

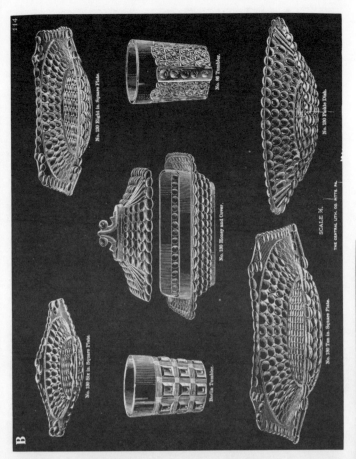

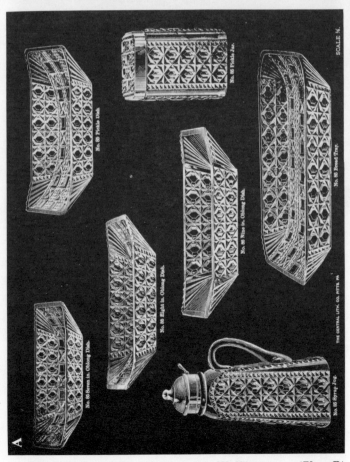

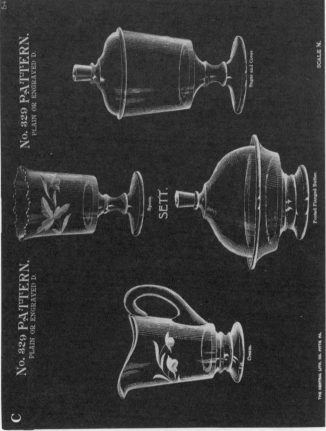

(Plate A) Several items in *Valencia Waffle* pattern; **(Plate B)** Assortment of Adam's "Three-Knob" variant of *Thousand Eye;*
(Plate C) The simple *Adam's #329* pattern, plain or engraved.

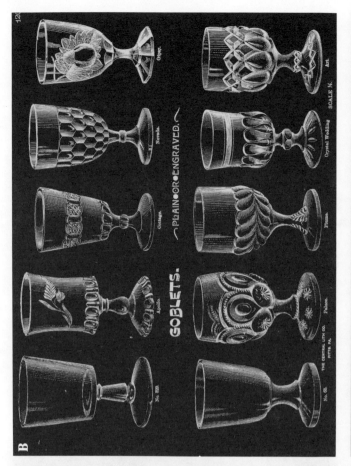

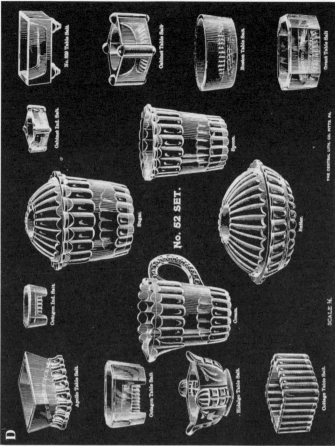

(Plate A) Assortment of Adams tumblers; **(Plate B)** Assorted goblets in Adams patterns; **(Plate C)** Caster sets in "Derby" and "Paragon", the latter similar to "Heavy Panelled Finecut"; **(Plate D)** Table set in *Adam's #52,* and assorted salt dips.

OFFICE AND WORKS, TWENTY-FIRST AND WHARTON STREETS, SOUTH SIDE.

BRYCE BROTHERS,

Crystal Colored and Decorated Table, Lamp and Perfumery Glass Ware.

GLASS WARE.

Original letterhead for Bryce Brothers stationery.

Factory B

Bryce Brothers

Pittsburgh, Pa.

UNITED STATES GLASS COMPANY, FACTORY B.
5602. Wine Set.
5601. Wine Set.

Wine sets in *Peas and Pods* and *Mirror and Fan* patterns, made in crystal and scarce in ruby-stained.

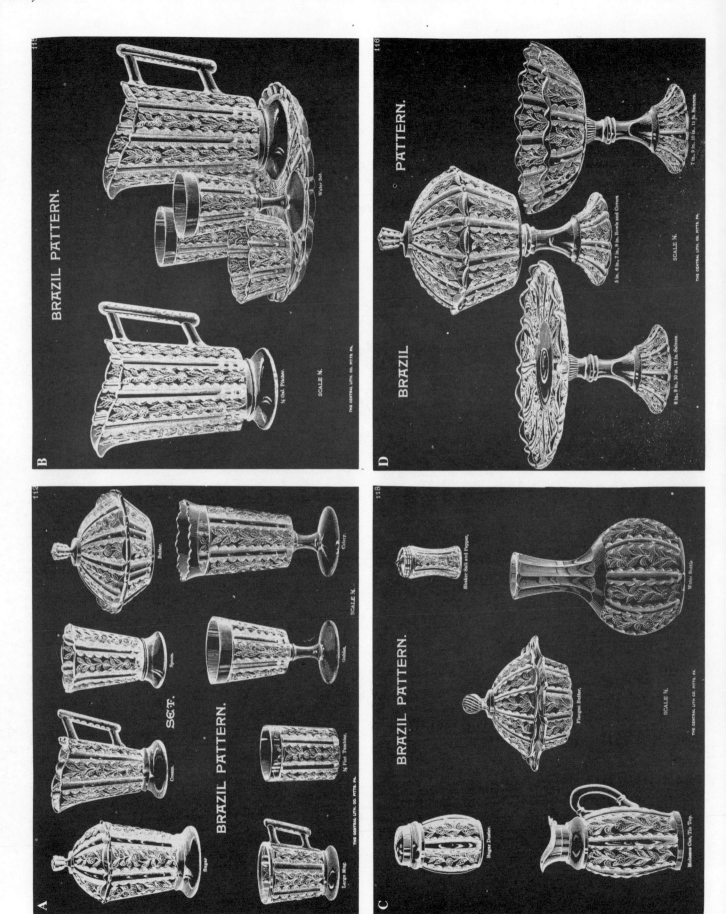

(Plates A—D) Assortment of *Panelled Daisy* pattern, originally called "Brazil";.

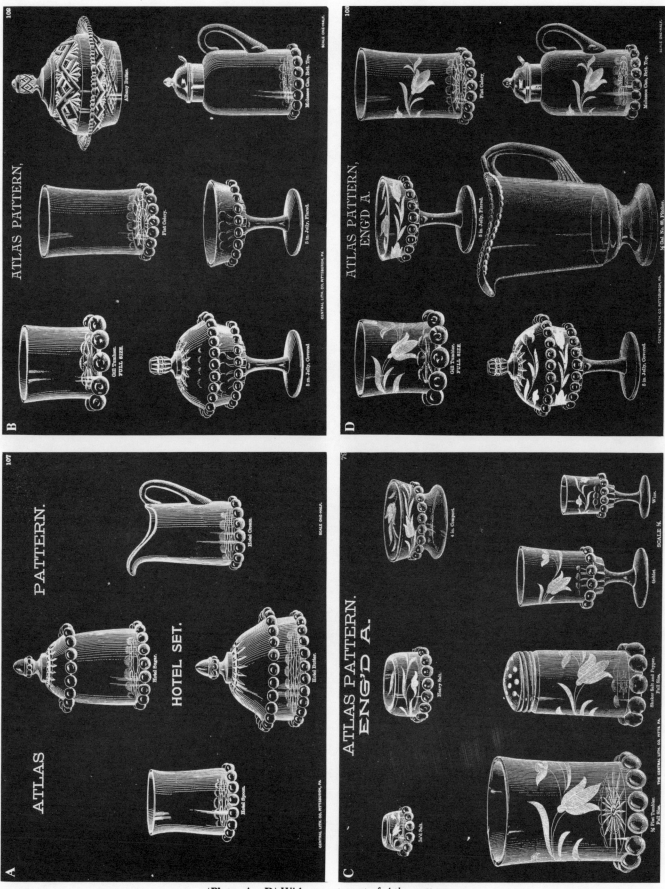

(Plates A—D) Wide assortment of *Atlas* pattern.

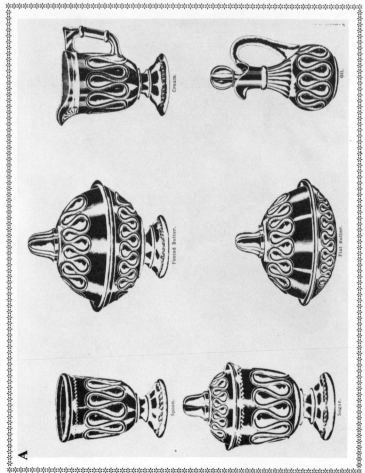

(Plates A—D) Assortment of *Ribbon Candy* pattern.

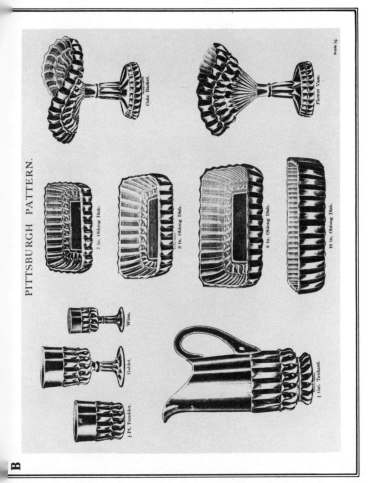

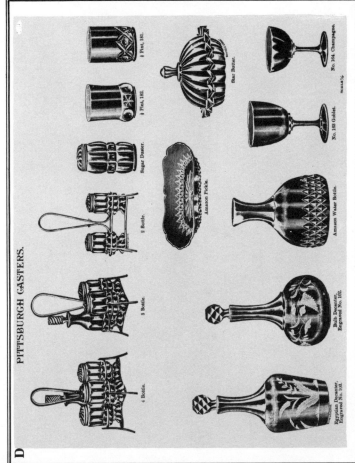

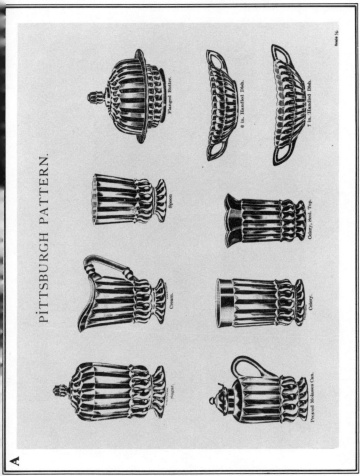

(Plates A–D) Assortment of *Pittsburgh* pattern.

BRYCE BROS., PITTSBURGH, PA.

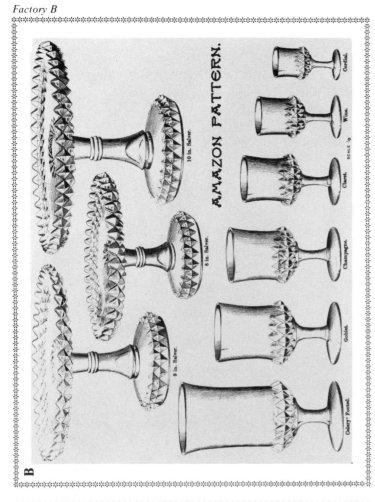

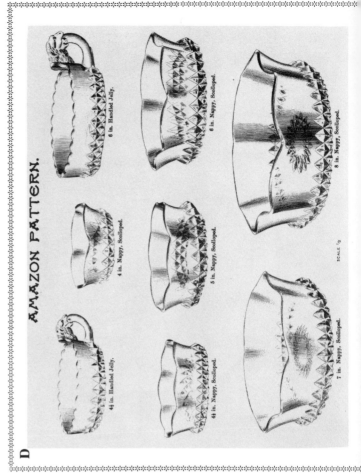

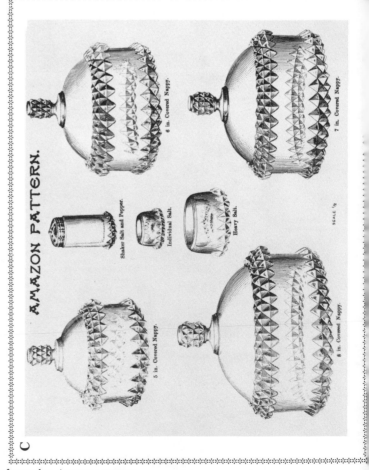

(Plates A—D) Assortment of popular *Amazon* pattern.

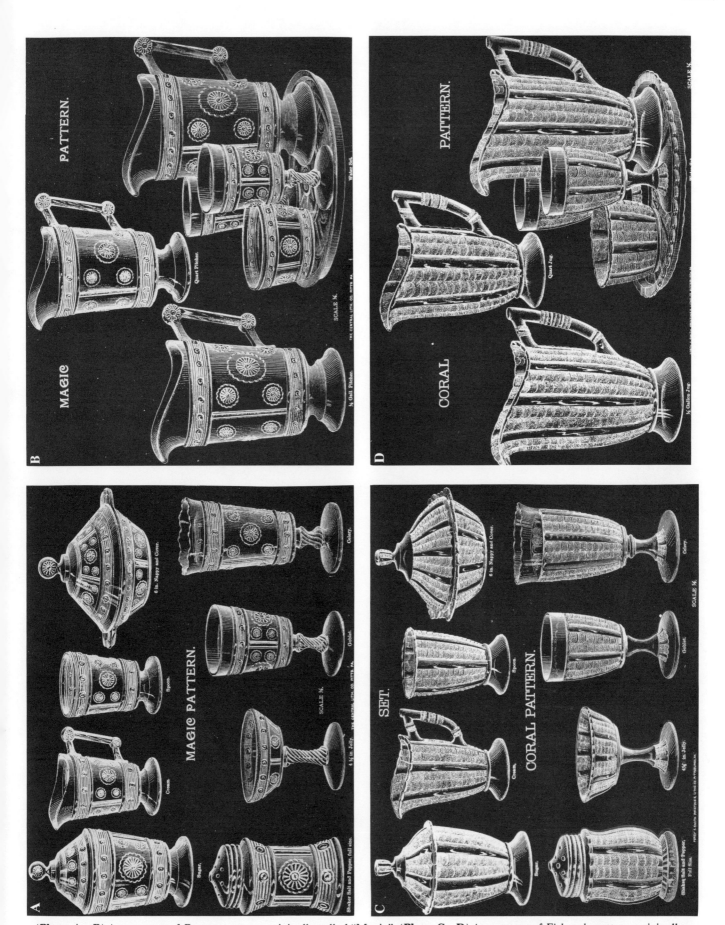

(**Plates A—B**) Assortment of *Rosette* pattern, originally called "Magic"; (**Plates C—D**) Assortment of *Fishscale* pattern, originally called "Coral".

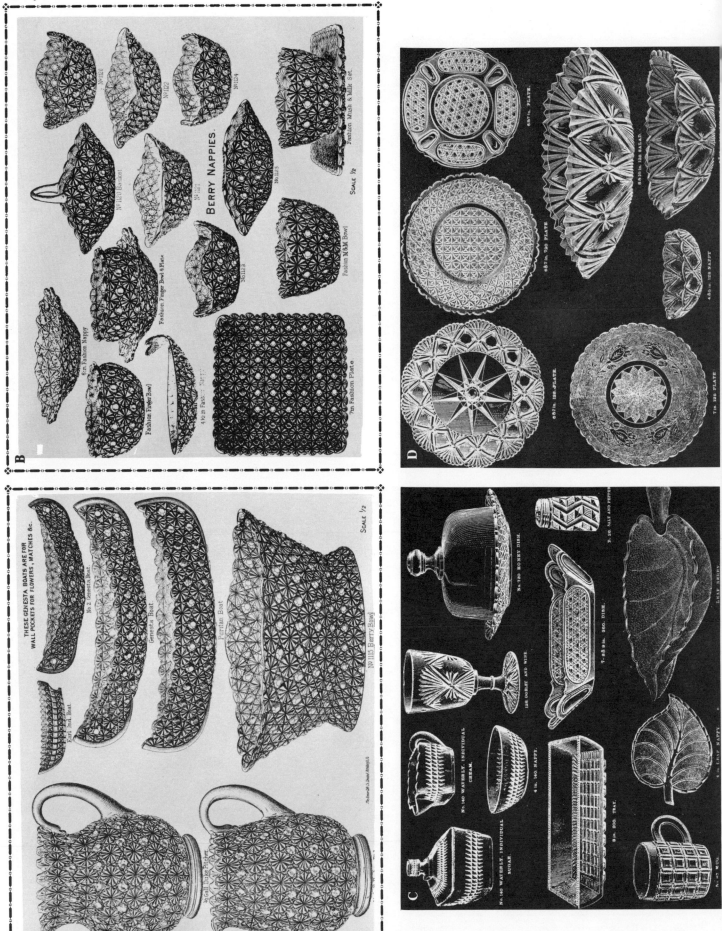

(Plate A & B) *Daisy & Button*, as produced by Bryce, originally called "Fashion"; **(Plate C)** Assortment of items, including *Waverly*, *Mitred Diamond*, and *Fine Cut & Panel*; **(Plate D)** Assortment of plates and bowls.

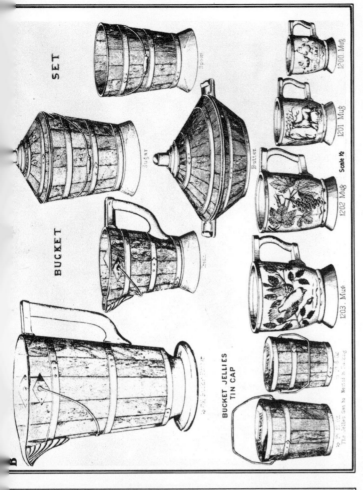

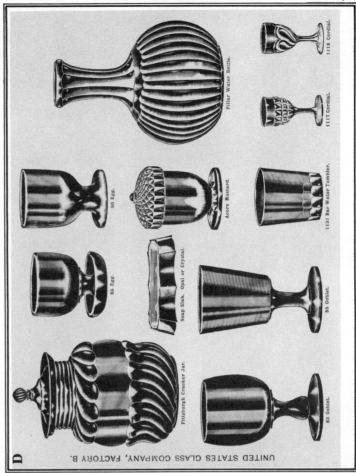

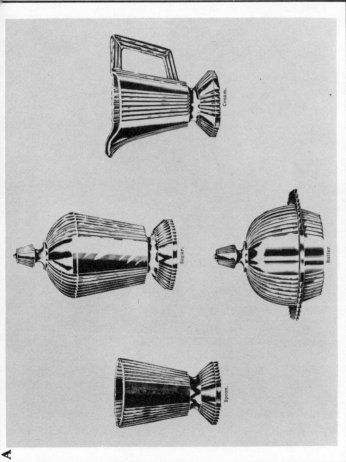

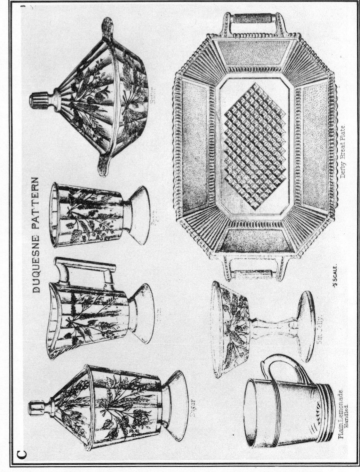

(**Plate A**) *Pleating* pattern table set; (**Plate B**) *Oaken Bucket* table set and a variety of bird and animal mugs; (**Plate C**) *Wheat & Barley* table set and jelly compote, and *Derby* pattern bread plate; (**Plate D**) Bryce assortment, including *Pittsburgh* cracker jar, an unusual "Acorn" covered mustard, and a soap dish.

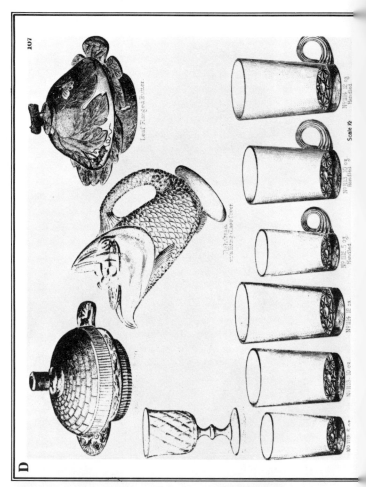

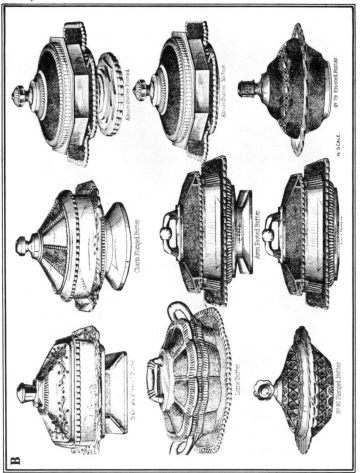

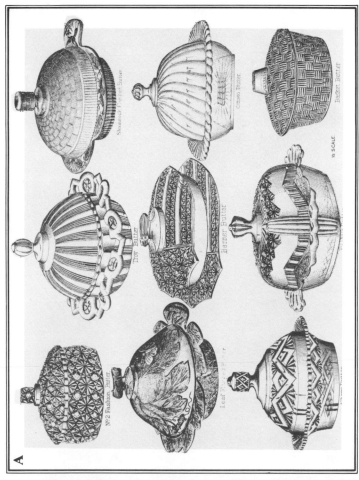

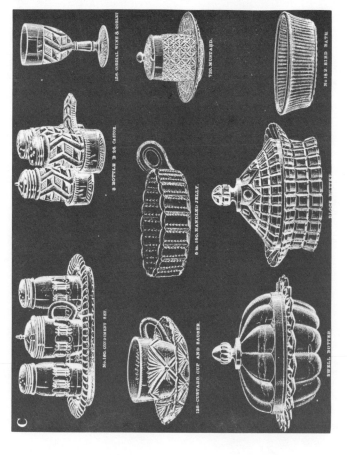

82 (**Plate A & B**) A wide variety of covered butter dishes, most of which are not part of a larger matching table service —made in crystal and color; (**Plate C**) Assortment of caster sets, covered butters, etc.—note even a bird bath; (**Plate D**) Note the unusual fish creamer with a tilting glass cover.

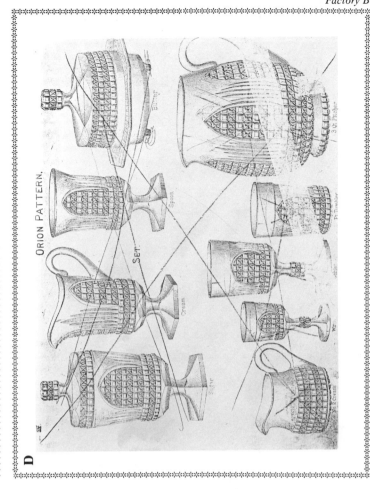

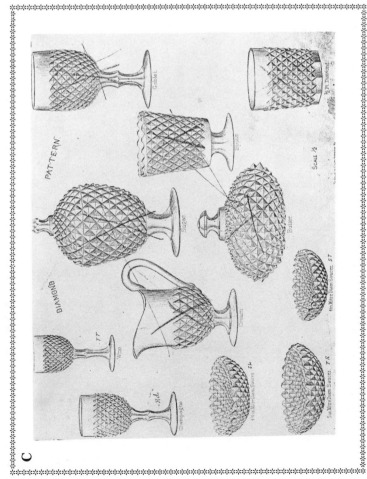

(**Plate A & B**) *Willow Oak* pattern, originally called "Wreath"; (**Plate C**) *Sawtooth* pattern by Bryce—this pattern also made at Sandwich in flint glass; (**Plate D**) *Cathedral* pattern, originally called "Orion".

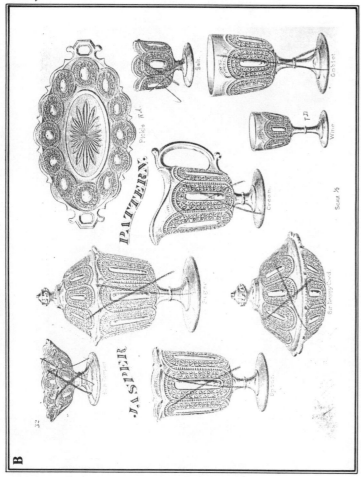

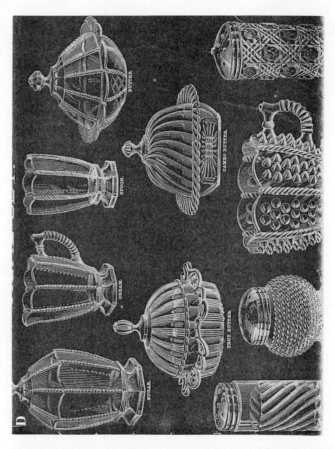

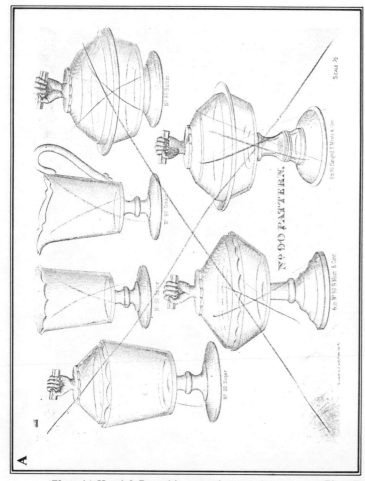

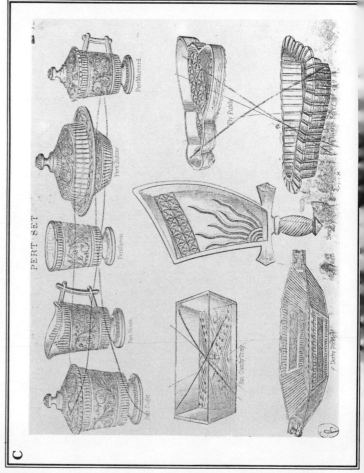

(Plate A) *Hand & Bar* table set and covered compotes; **(Plate B)** *Late Buckle* table set, originally called "Jasper"; **(Plate C)** *Ribbed Forget-Me-Not* breakfast set, and assorted items including a "Sword" and "Fly" shaped pickle dish; **(Plate D)** *Panelled Cable* table set, assorted sugar shakers, etc.

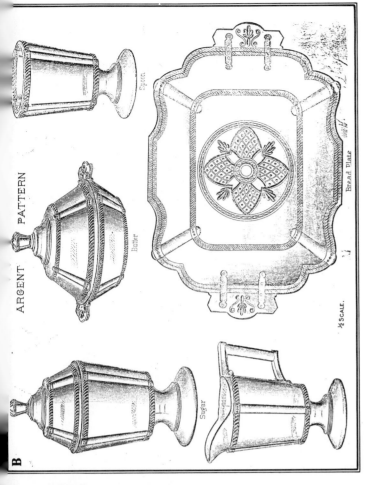

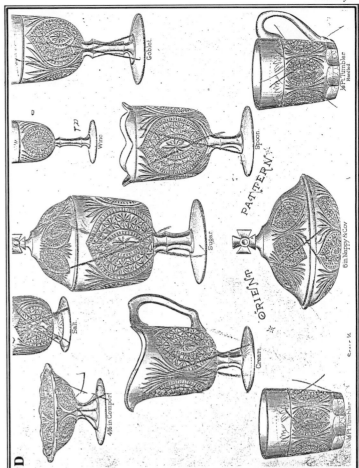

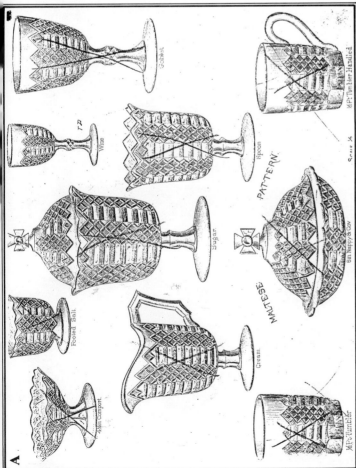

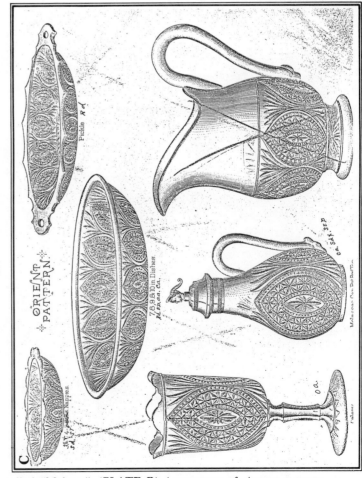

(PLATE A) Assortment of *Jacobs Ladder* pattern, originally called "Maltese"; **(PLATE B)** Assortment of *Argent* pattern; **(PLATES C-D)** Assortment of *Buckle and Star* pattern, originally called "Orient."

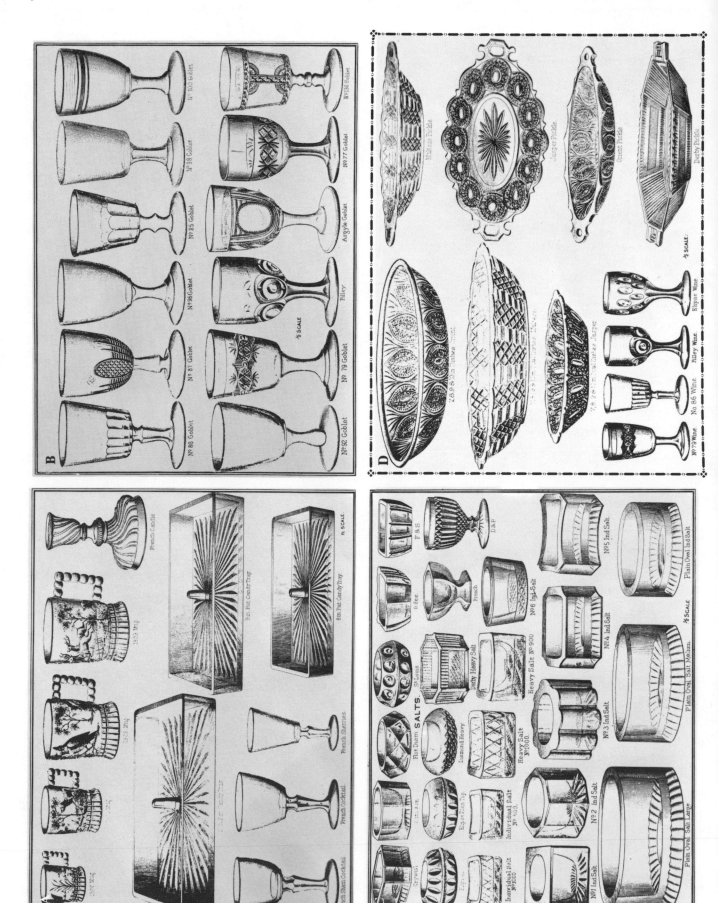

(**Plate A**) Note the variety of bird and animal mugs offered; (**Plate B**) A variety of goblets, including the "Filley" and "Argyle" patterns; (**Plate C**) A wide assortment of salt dips; (**Plate D**) Bowls, pickles and wines in a variety of Bryce patterns.

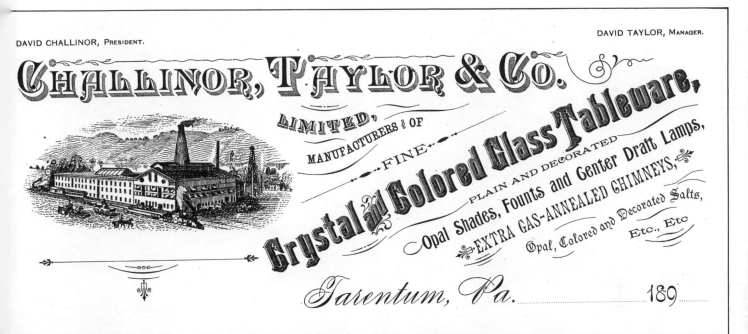

DAVID CHALLINOR, President.

DAVID TAYLOR, Manager.

CHALLINOR, TAYLOR & Co.

LIMITED,

MANUFACTURERS OF

FINE

Crystal and Colored Glass Tableware,

PLAIN AND DECORATED

Opal Shades, Founts and Center Draft Lamps,

EXTRA GAS-ANNEALED CHIMNEYS,

Opal, Colored and Decorated Salts,

Etc., Etc

Tarentum, Pa. _____ 189_

Original undated letterhead from Challinor, Taylor & Co. stationery, circa 1890.

Factory C

Challinor, Taylor & Co.

Tarentum, Pa.

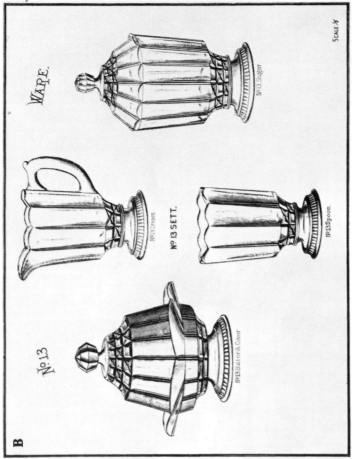

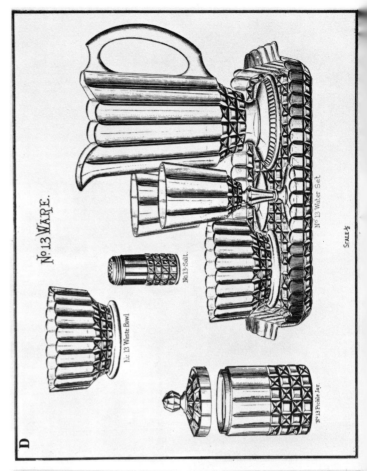

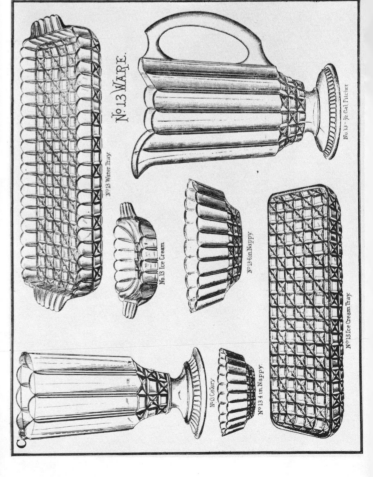

(Plate A) Original title page for Factory C: (Plate B-D) *Majestic Crown* pattern.

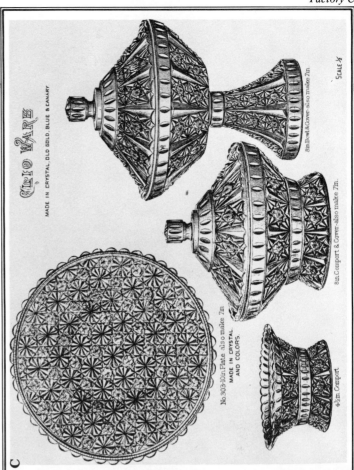

CLIO WARE

MADE IN CRYSTAL, OLD GOLD, BLUE & CANARY.

Scale ⅓

8in Bowl & Cover-also make 7in.

8in Comport & Cover-also make 7in.

No 303-10in Plate also make 7in.
MADE IN CRYSTAL
AND COLORS.

4½in Comport.

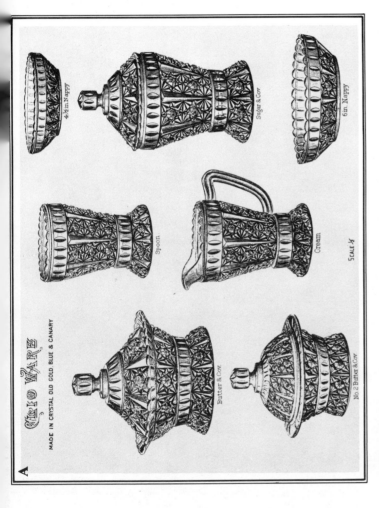

CLIO WARE

MADE IN CRYSTAL OLD GOLD, BLUE & CANARY

4½ in Nappy

Sugar & Cover

6 in Nappy

Spoon

Cream

Scale ½

Butter & Cover

No 2 Butter & Cover

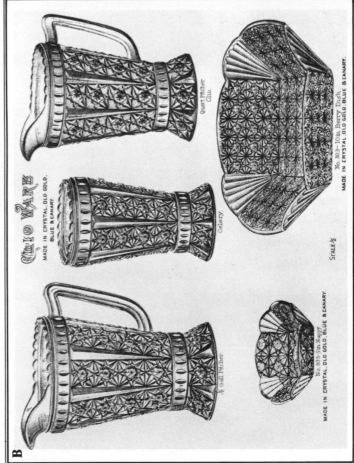

CLIO WARE

MADE IN CRYSTAL, OLD GOLD, BLUE & CANARY.

Quart Pitcher Clio.

No. 303-10in, Berry Dish.
MADE IN CRYSTAL, OLD GOLD, BLUE & CANARY.

Celery

No 303-5in Nappy
MADE IN CRYSTAL, OLD GOLD, BLUE & CANARY.

½ Gal Pitcher

Scale ½

(**Plate A—C**) *Clio* pattern—note the plate lacks pattern characteristics.

89

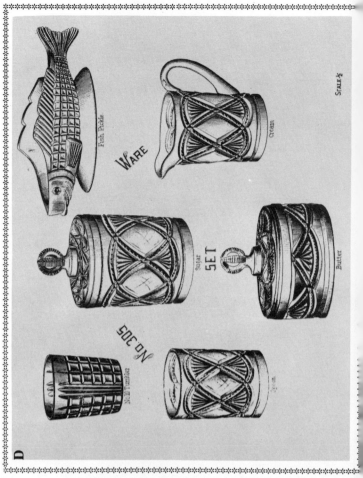

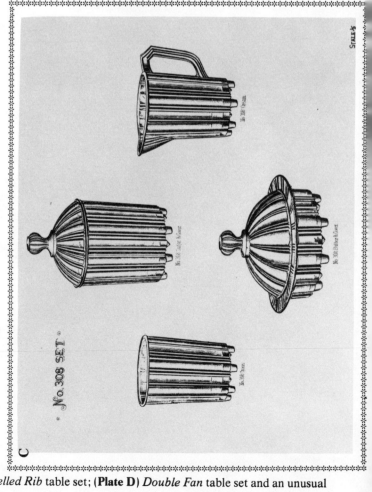

(**Plate A & B**) *Crusader Cross* assortment; (**Plate C**) *Footed Panelled Rib* table set; (**Plate D**) *Double Fan* table set and an unusual figural fish pickle tray.

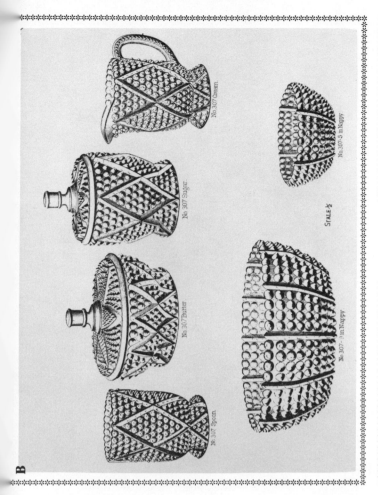

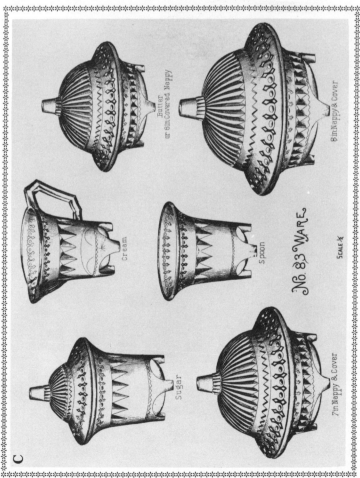

(**Plate A**) *Fan & Star* table set; (**Plate B**) *Hobnail with Bars* table set—note the berry set has different characteristics; (**Plate C**) *Sanborn* table set and two covered nappies in same; (**Plate D**) Assortment of naturalistic mugs and patterned goblets.

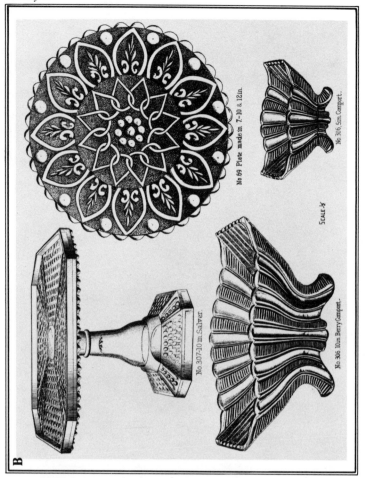

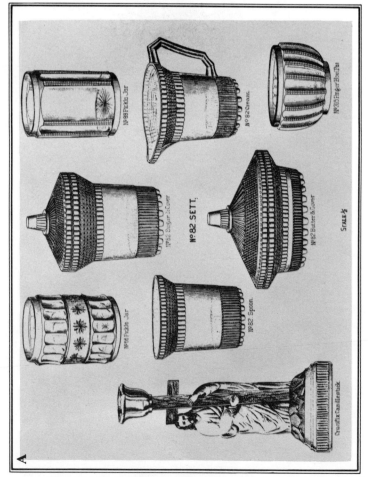

(Plate A) *Pleated Ribbon* (No. 82) table set, also a rare crucifix candlestick; **(Plate B)** *Hobnail with Bars* cakestand and other miscellaneous items; **(Plate C)** *Fan & Star* items; **(Plate D)** *Big Top* compotes.

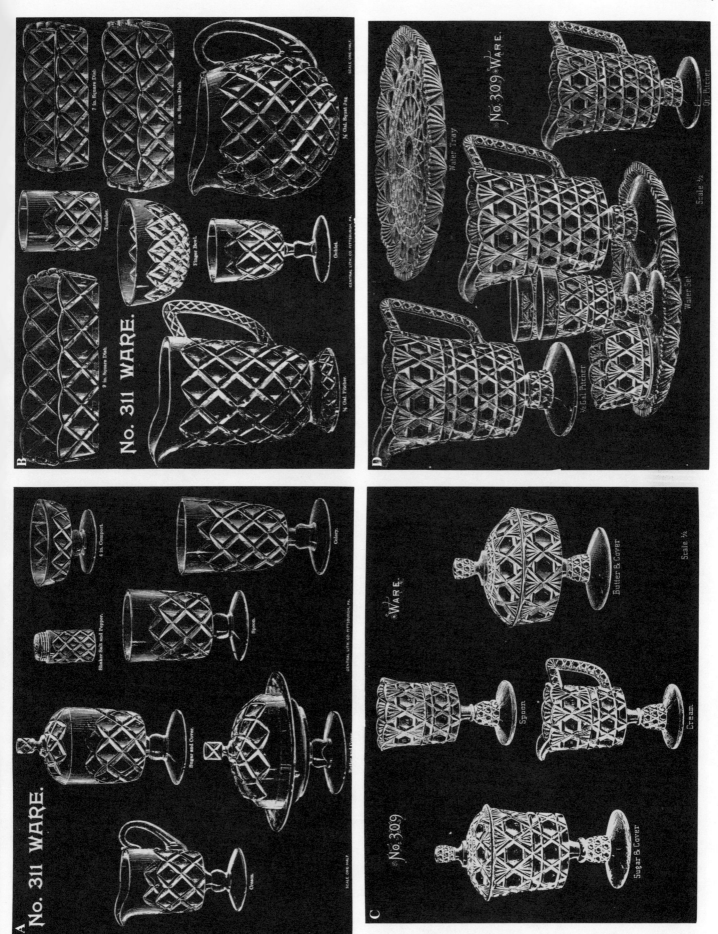

(**Plate A & B**) *Bevelled Diagonal Block* pattern; (**Plate C & D**) *Blockade* pattern.

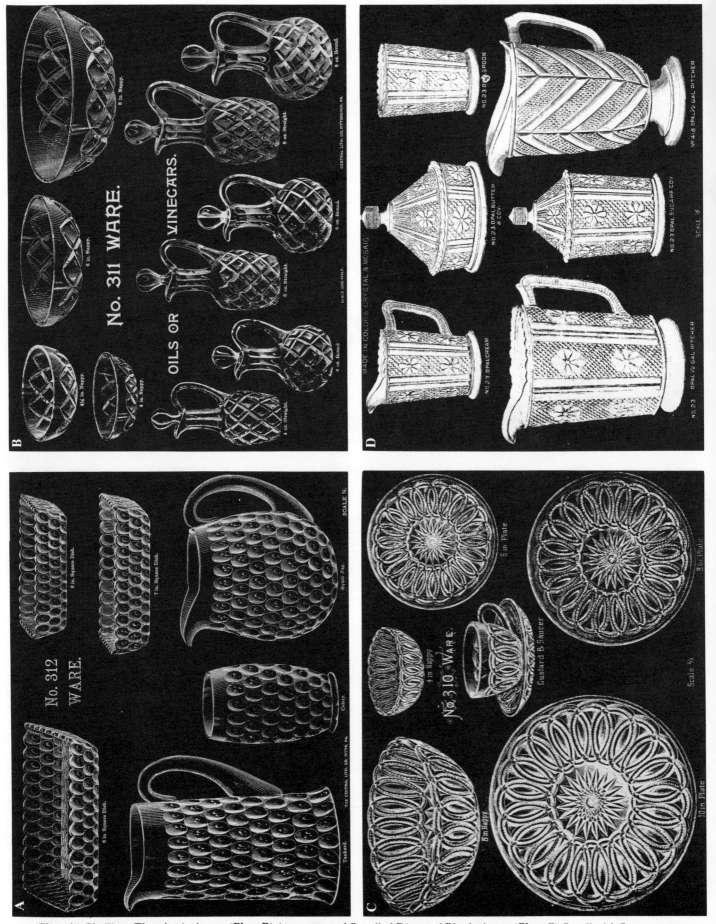

(**Plate A**) *Challinor Thumbprint* items; (**Plate B**) Assortment of *Bevelled Diagonal Block* pieces; (**Plate C**) *Scroll with Star* pattern; (**Plate D**) *Stylized Flower* table set—also *Dewdrop & Zig-Zag* water pitcher.

Jas. E. Duncan,   A. H. Heisey,

Geo. Duncan and Sons,

Manufacturers of

Fine Flint Glassware,

40th Street South Side,   *Pittsburgh, Pa.*   Aug. 6/91

Wm. P. Shinn Esq.

Original stationery letterhead dated August 6, 1891.

Factory D

George Duncan & Sons

Pittsburgh, Pa.

Manufactured by Geo. Duncan & Sons, Pittsburgh, Pa.

B

No. 335 SET. LOW SHAPE.

No. 335 Spooner.—Low.

No. 335 Sugar and Cover.—Low.

No. 335 Butter and Cover.—Low.

No. 335 Cream.—Low.

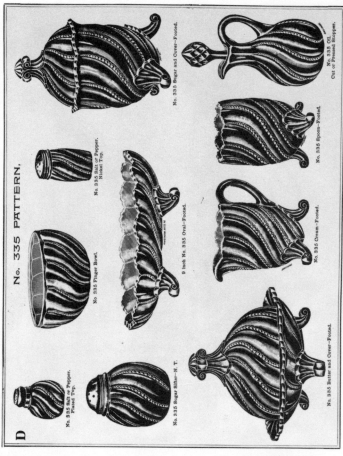

D

No. 335 PATTERN.

No. 335 Sugar and Cover.—Footed.

No. 535 Oil. Cut or Pressed Stopper.

No. 335 Salt or Pepper. Nickel Top.

No. 335 Spoon—Footed.

No. 335 Finger Bowl.

9 inch No. 335 Oval—Footed.

No. 335 Cream—Footed.

No. 335 Salt or Pepper. Plated Top.

No. 335 Sugar Sifter—N. T.

No. 335 Butter and Cover—Footed.

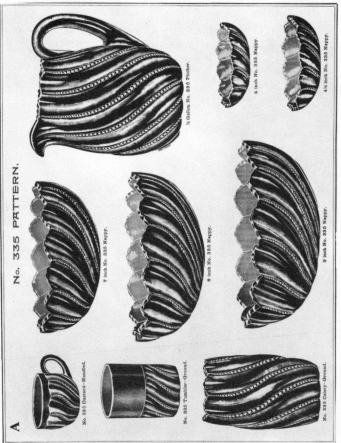

A

No. 335 PATTERN.

½ Gallon No. 335 Pitcher.

4 inch No. 335 Nappy.

4½ inch No. 335 Nappy.

7 inch No. 335 Nappy.

8 inch No. 335 Nappy.

9 inch No. 335 Nappy.

No. 335 Custard—Handled.

No. 335 Tumbler—Ground.

No. 335 Celery—Ground.

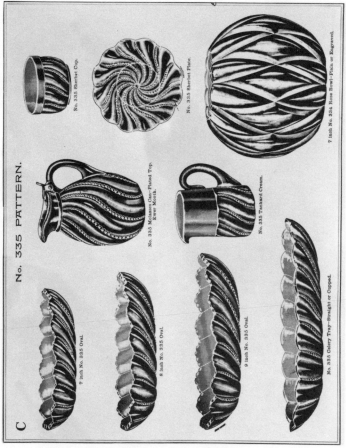

C

No. 335 PATTERN.

No. 335 Sherbet Cup.

No. 335 Sherbet Plate.

7 inch No. 334 Rose Bowl—Plain or Engraved.

No. 335 Molasses Can—Plated Top. Ever Mouth.

No. 335 Tankard Cream.

7 inch No. 335 Oval.

8 inch No. 335 Oval.

9 inch No. 335 Oval.

No. 335 Celery Tray—Straight or Cupped.

(Plate A—D) Assortment of Beaded Swirl pattern.

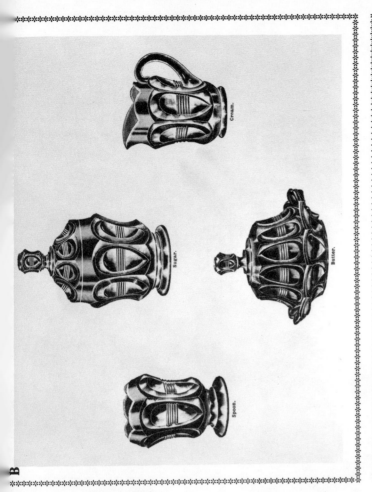

B

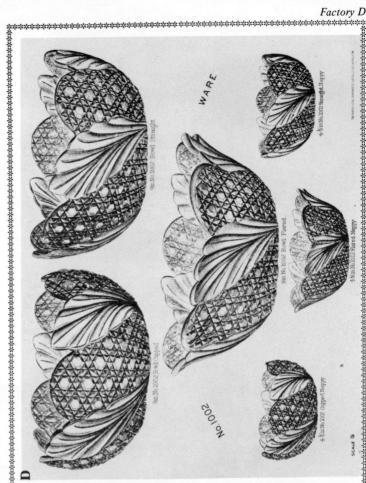

D

WARE

9 in No.1002 Bowl Straight

9 in No.1002 Bowl Flared

9 in No.1002 Bowl Cupped

4½ in No.1002 Straight Nappy

4½ in No.1002 Flared Nappy

4½ in No.1002 Cupped Nappy

No.1002

SCALE ½

A

Oil or Vinegar Jug.

Water Bottle.

½ Gallon Jug.

Tumbler.

Celery.

Quart Jug.

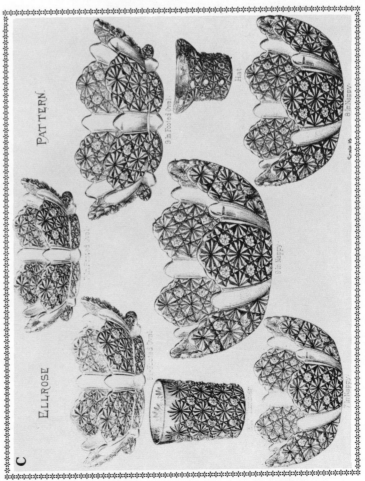

C

PATTERN

ELLROSE

9 in Footed Bowl

Hat

8 in Nappy

Scale ½

7 in Nappy

(**Plates A & B**) Variety of *Barred Ovals* pieces; (**Plate C**) *Panelled Daisy & Button* bowls, plain tumbler & novelty hat; (**Plate D**) *Big Leaf and Button* assortment.

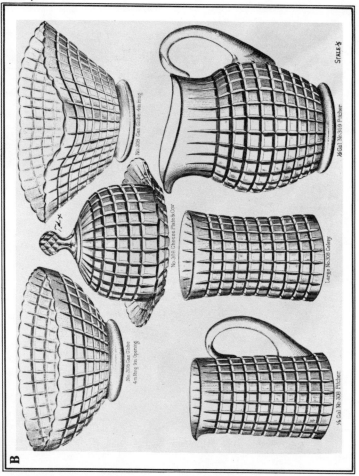

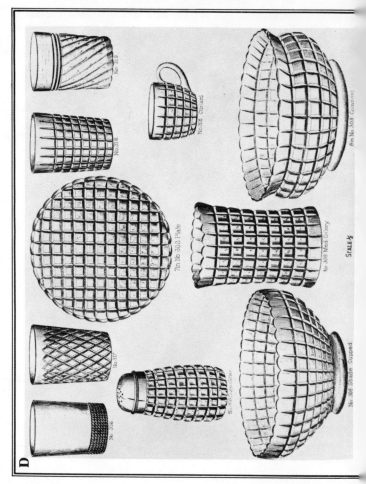

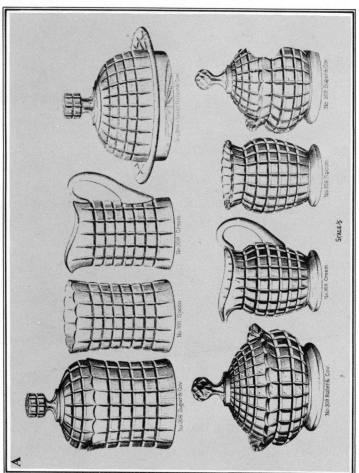

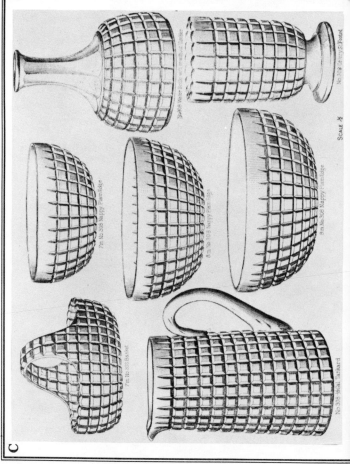

(**Plate A—D**) Wide assortment of *Duncan Block* pattern—note the four-piece table set comes with or without a base.

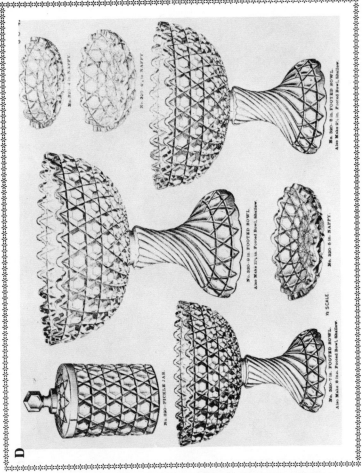

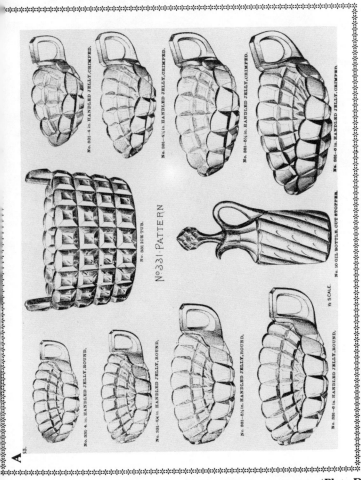

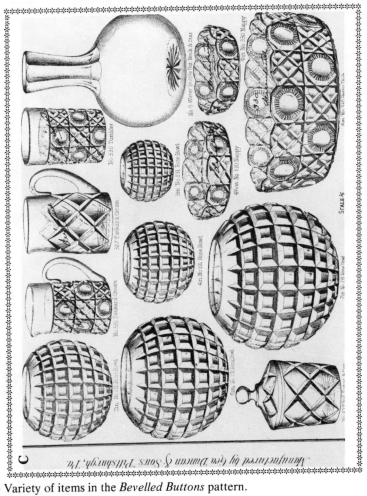

(Plates A—C) *Late Block* assortment; **(Plate D)** Variety of items in the *Bevelled Buttons* pattern.

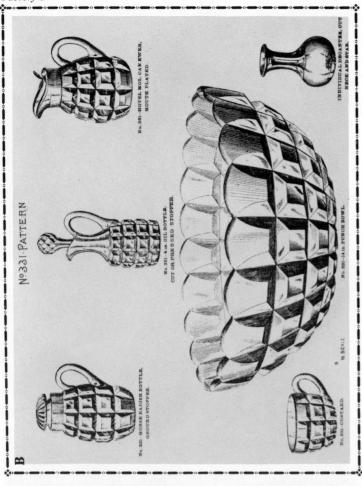

No. 331 PATTERN.

No. 331—Howl. Mol. Can Ewer, Mouth Plated.

No. 331—Individual Decanter, Cut Neck and Star.

No. 331—4 oz. Oil Bottle, Cut or Pressed Stopper.

No. 331—14 in. Punch Bowl. ½ Scale.

No. 331—Horse Radish Bottle, Ground Stopper.

No. 331—Custard.

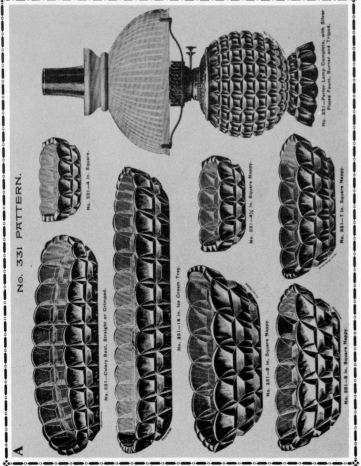

No. 331 PATTERN.

No. 331—4 in. Square.

No. 331—Parlor Lamp Complete, with Silver Plated Fount, Burner and Tripod.

No. 331—Celery Boat, Straight or Crimped.

No. 331—4½ in. Square Nappy.

No. 331—7 in. Square Nappy.

No. 331—14 in. Ice Cream Tray.

No. 331—9 in. Square Nappy.

No. 331—8 in. Square Nappy.

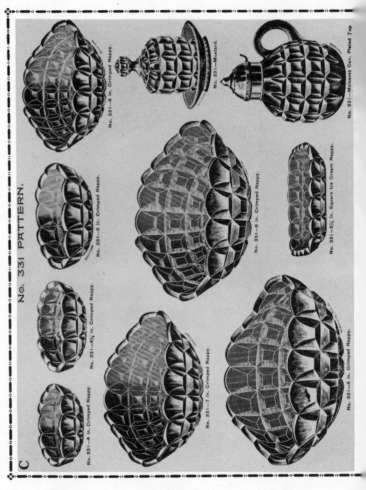

No. 331 PATTERN.

No. 331—6 in. Crimped Nappy.

No. 331—Mustard.

No. 331—Molasses Can, Plated Top.

No. 331—5 in. Crimped Nappy.

No. 331—8 in. Crimped Nappy.

No. 331—5½ in. Square Ice Cream Nappy.

No. 331—4½ in. Crimped Nappy.

No. 331—4 in. Crimped Nappy.

No. 331—7 in. Crimped Nappy.

No. 331—9 in. Crimped Nappy.

Plates A—C) Wide assortment of *Late Block* pattern, including a rare pattern glass lamp—note the horseradish bottle is a syrup without attached metal top.

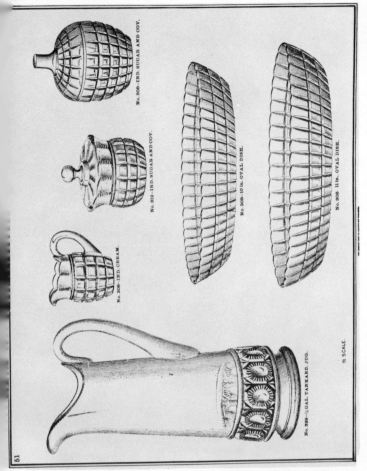

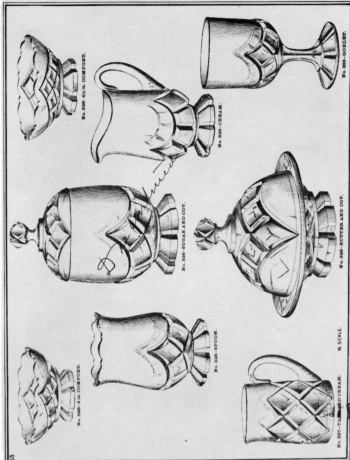

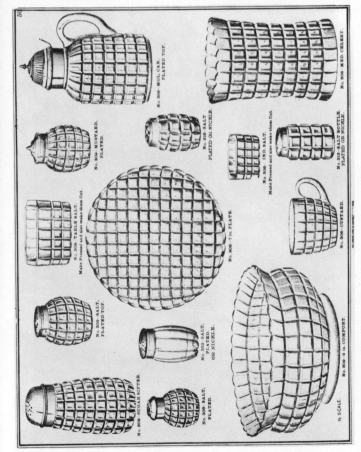

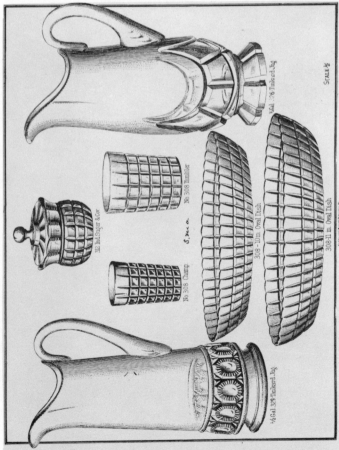

(Plates A—C) *Duncan Block* items—also tankard water pitchers in *Swag Block* and *Bracelet Band;* **(Plate D)** Assortment of Swag Block.

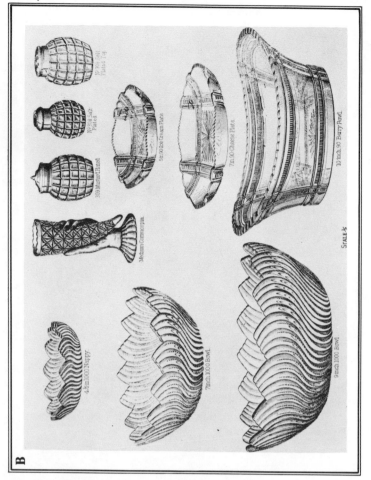

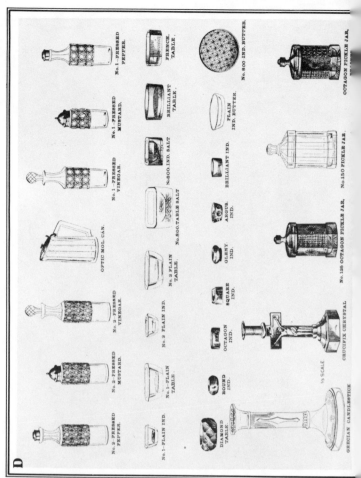

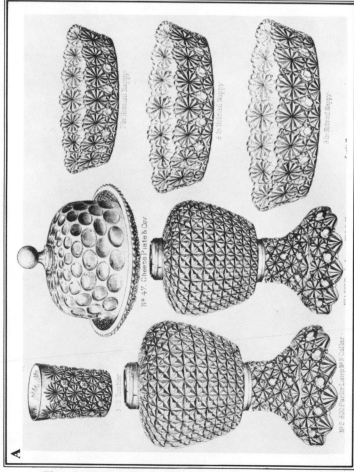

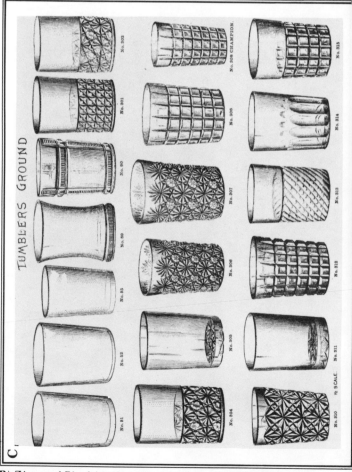

(**Plate A**) *Daisy & Button* items—also *Heavy Finecut* lamps; (**Plate B**) *Zippered Block* bowls, among other items; (**Plate C**) Variety of Duncan pattern glass tumblers; (**Plate D**) Novelty assortment.

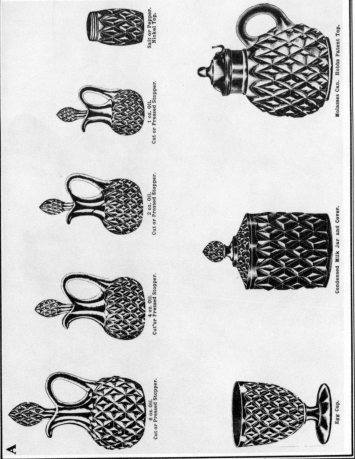

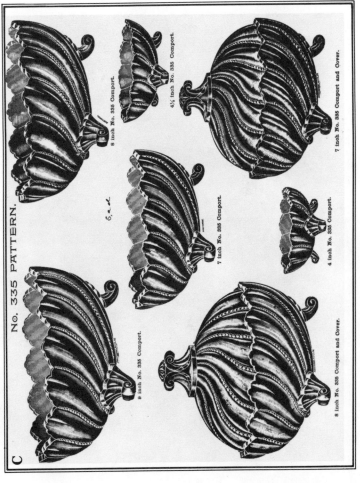

(Plate A & B) *Allover Diamond* pattern; **(Plate C)** *Beaded Swirl* items.

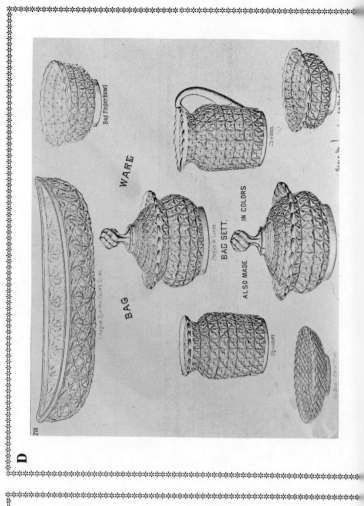

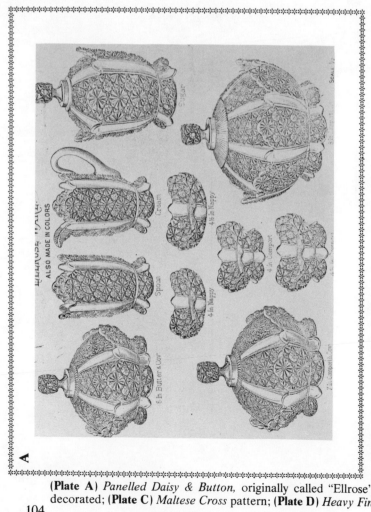

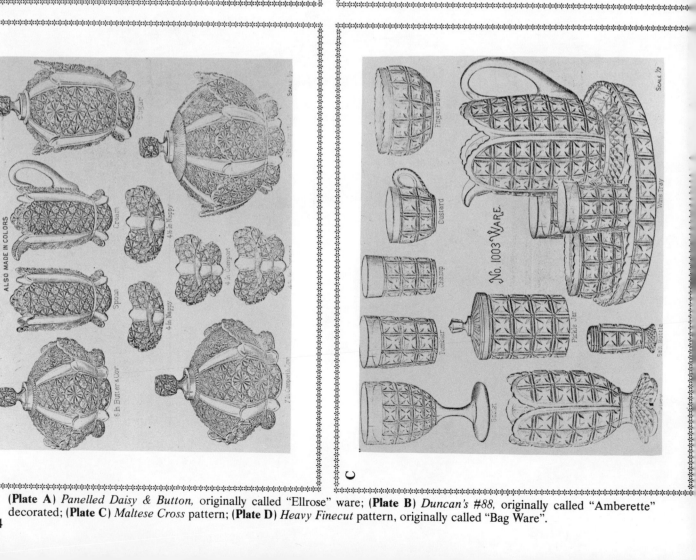

(**Plate A**) *Panelled Daisy & Button*, originally called "Ellrose" ware; (**Plate B**) *Duncan's #88*, originally called "Amberette" decorated; (**Plate C**) *Maltese Cross* pattern; (**Plate D**) *Heavy Finecut* pattern, originally called "Bag Ware".

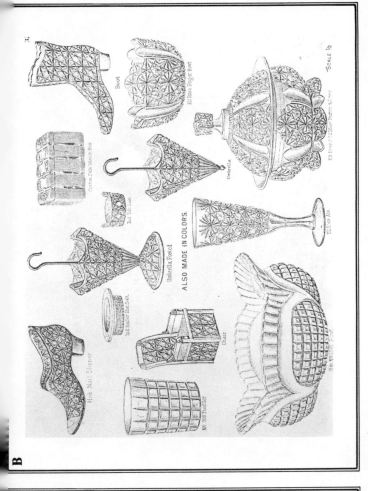

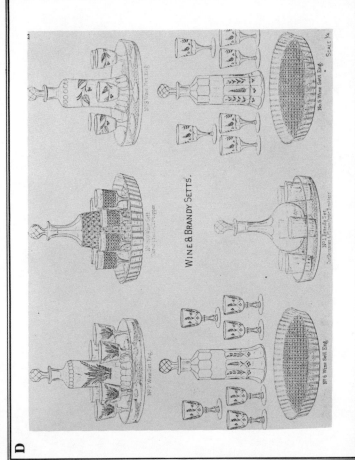

(Plate A) Assortment of Duncan tumblers; **(Plate B)** A variety of novelty and pattern glass items; **(Plate C)** Assortment of *Heavy Panelled Finecut* and *Heavy Finecut*; **(Plate D)** Several pattern and etched wine sets.

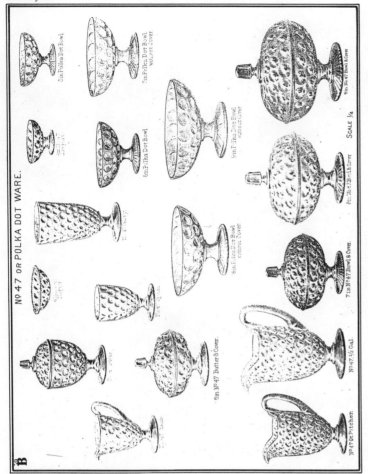

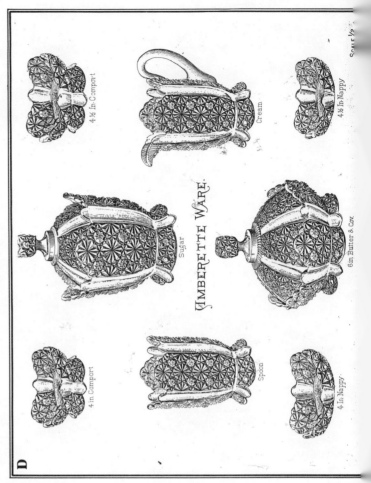

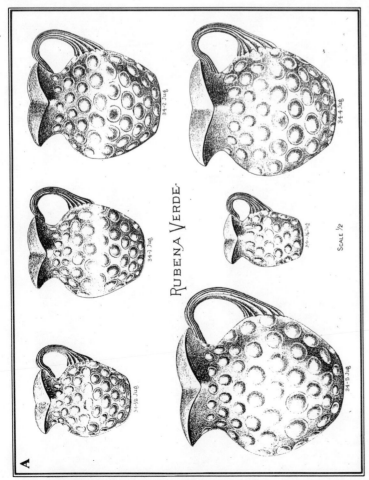

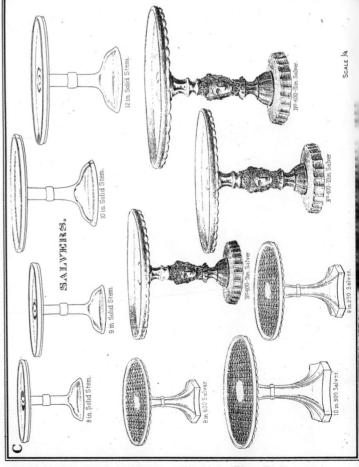

(**Plate A**) *Inverted Thumbprint* mold blown pitchers by Duncan, also made in crystal, cranberry and rubina; (**Plate B**) *Duncan's Dot* pressed glass pattern; (**Plate C**) Assorted cakestands—plain, *Heavy Finecut* and *Three Face*; (**Plate D**) Same as page 104, except this time called "Amberette."

Original Factory E title page from 1891 U.S.G.C. leather-bound catalogue.

Richards & Hartley

Tarentum, Pa.

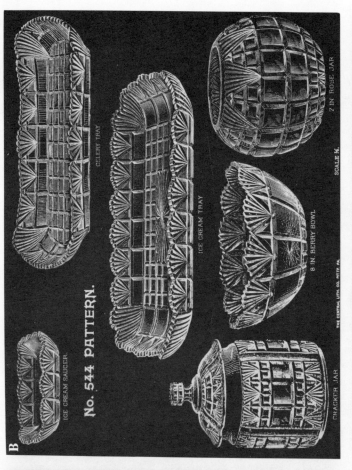

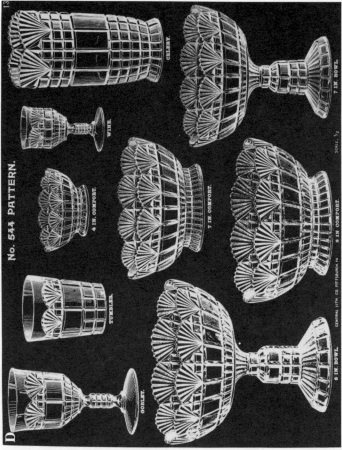

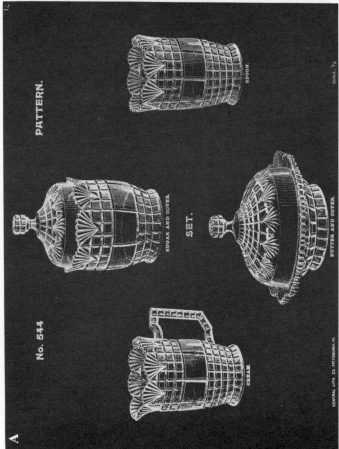

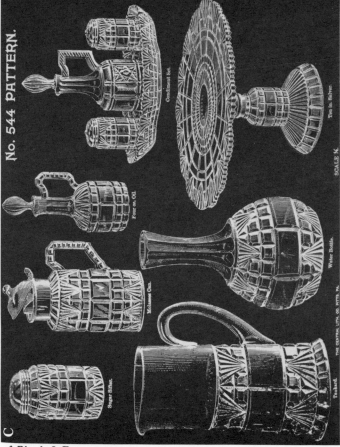

(Plates A—D) Wide assortment of *Block & Fan* pattern.

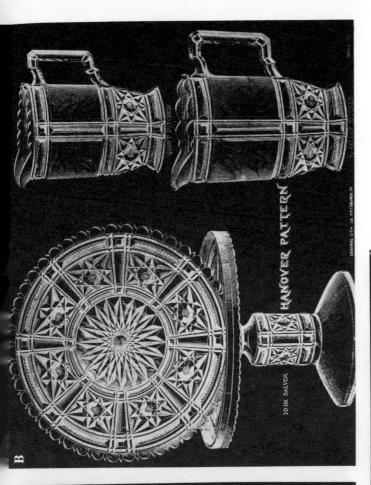

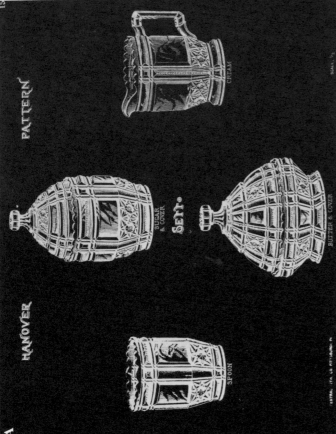

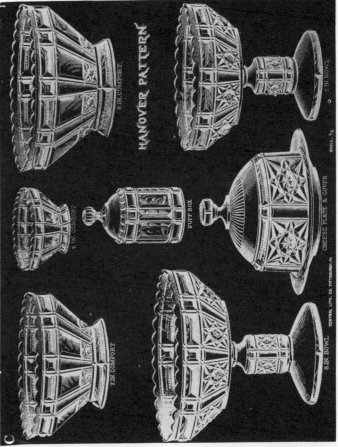

(**Plates A—C**) Variety of *Hanover* pieces, including an unusual puff box, which lacks many standard pattern characteristics.

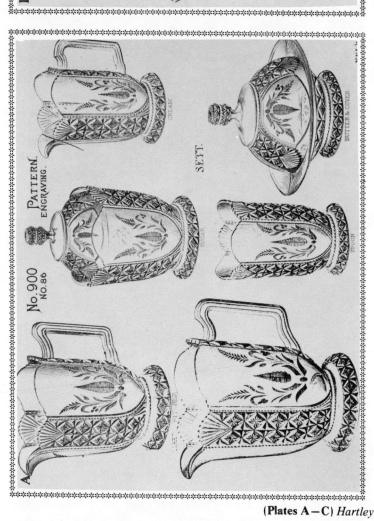

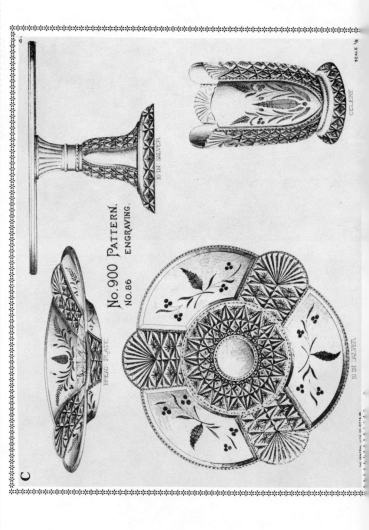

(Plates A–C) *Hartley* pattern assortment.

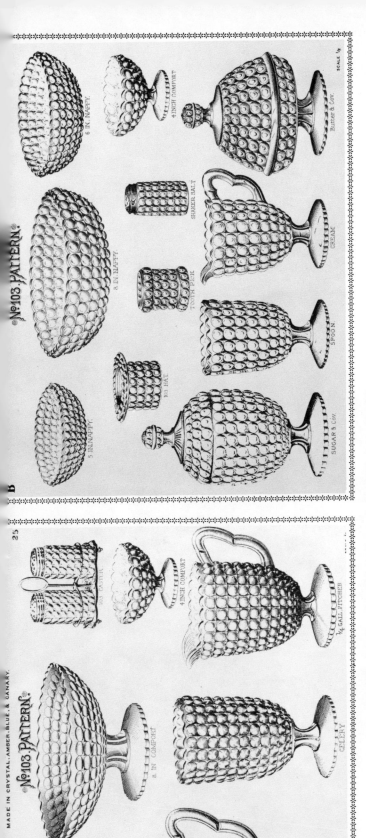

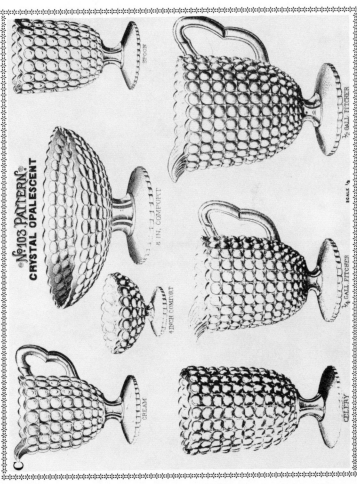

(Plates A—C) *Thousand Eye* pattern, including a rare twine holder—note the two toothpick holders.

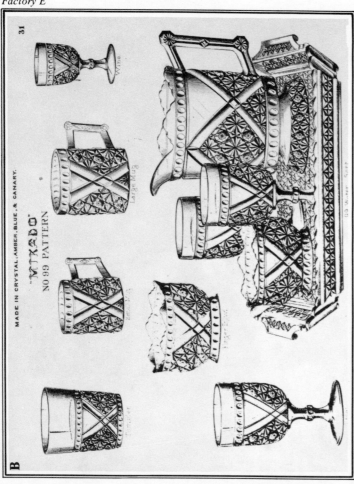

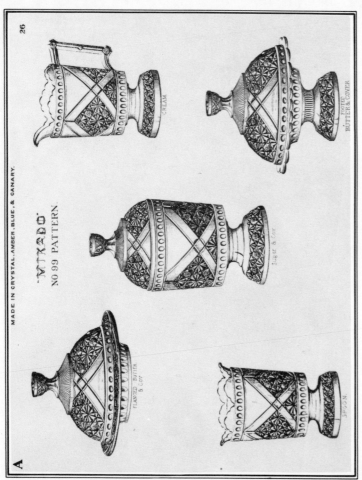

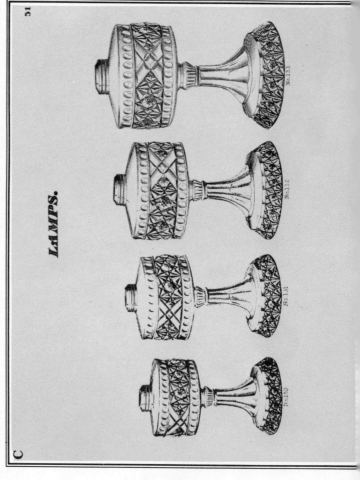

(Plates A—C) *Daisy & Button with Crossbars* assortment.

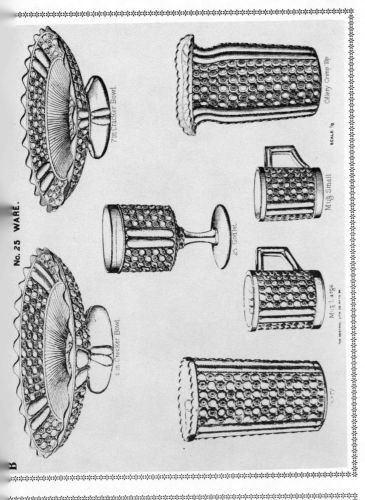

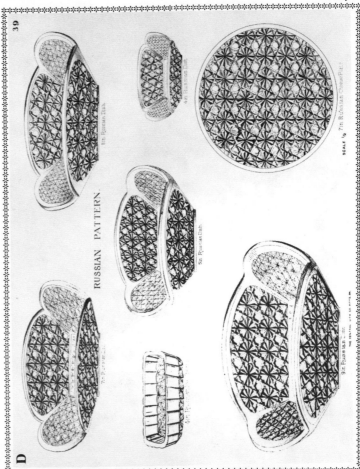

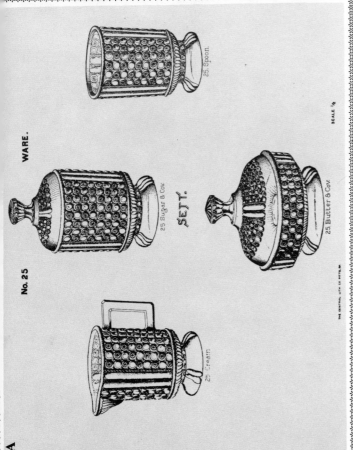

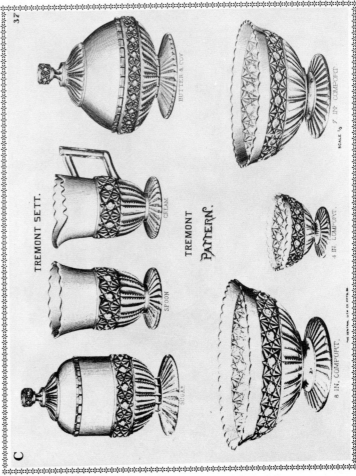

(**Plates A & B**) Several items in *Three Panel* pattern; (**Plate C**) *Tremont* pattern assortment; (**Plate D**) *Russian* pattern bowls and unusual plate.

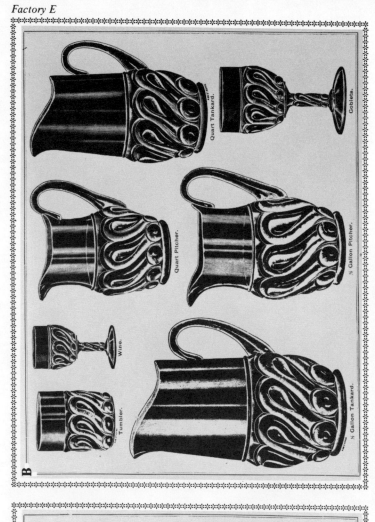

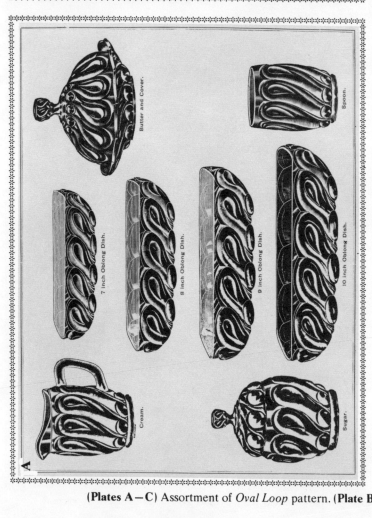

(**Plates A—C**) Assortment of *Oval Loop* pattern. (**Plate B**) Note loops on pitchers lean in two different directions.

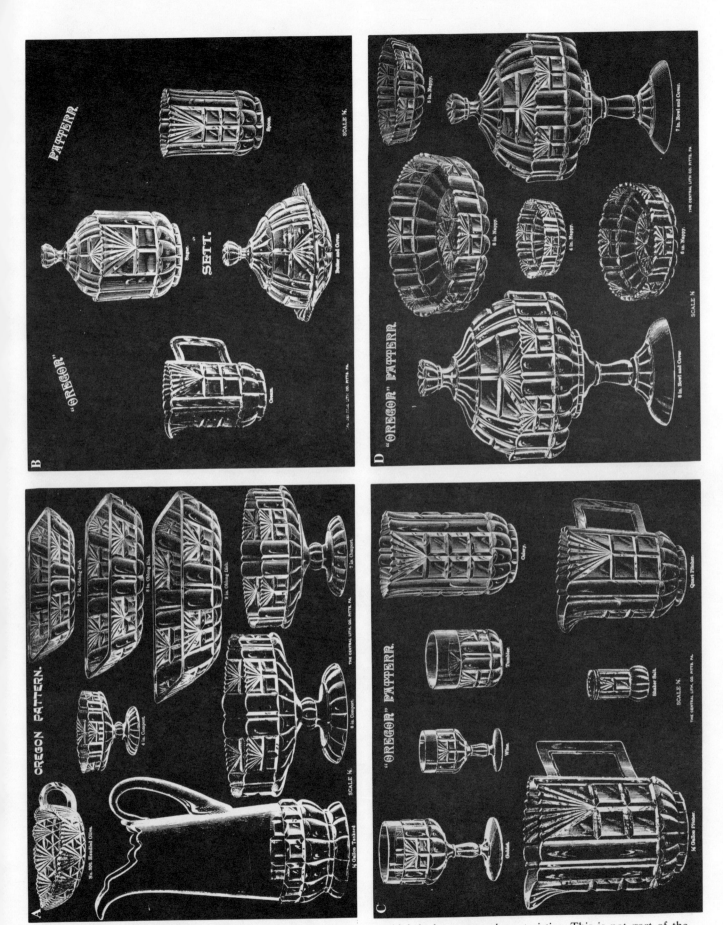

(**Plate A–D**) *Oregon* pattern, including unusual tankard pitcher which lacks pattern characteristics. This is not part of the "State" series.

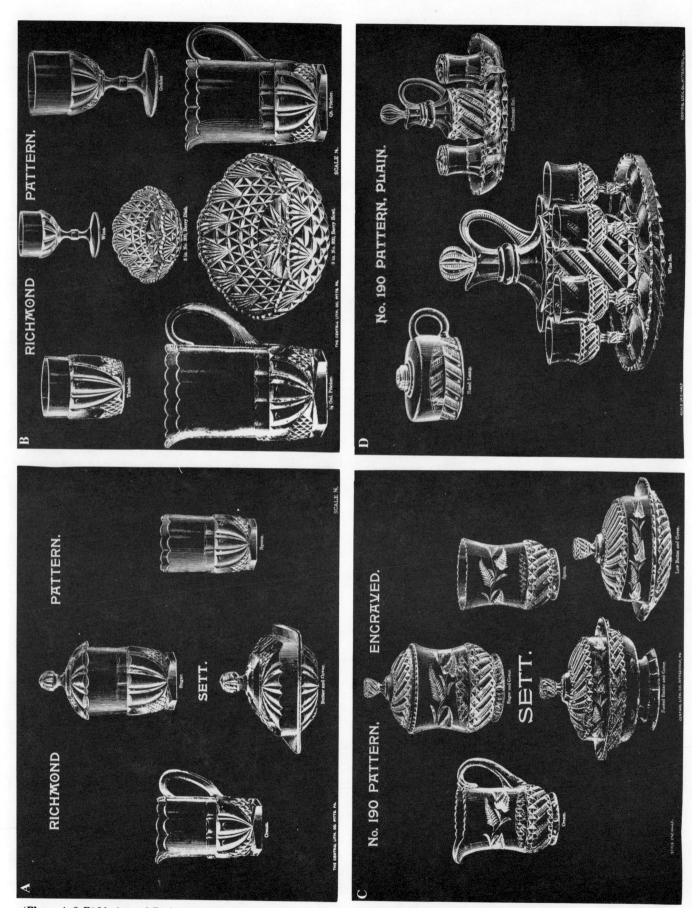

(**Plates A & B**) Variety of *Richmond* pattern items (do not confuse for "Nickel's Richmond"); (**Plates C & D**) Assortment of *Bar & Diamond* pattern.

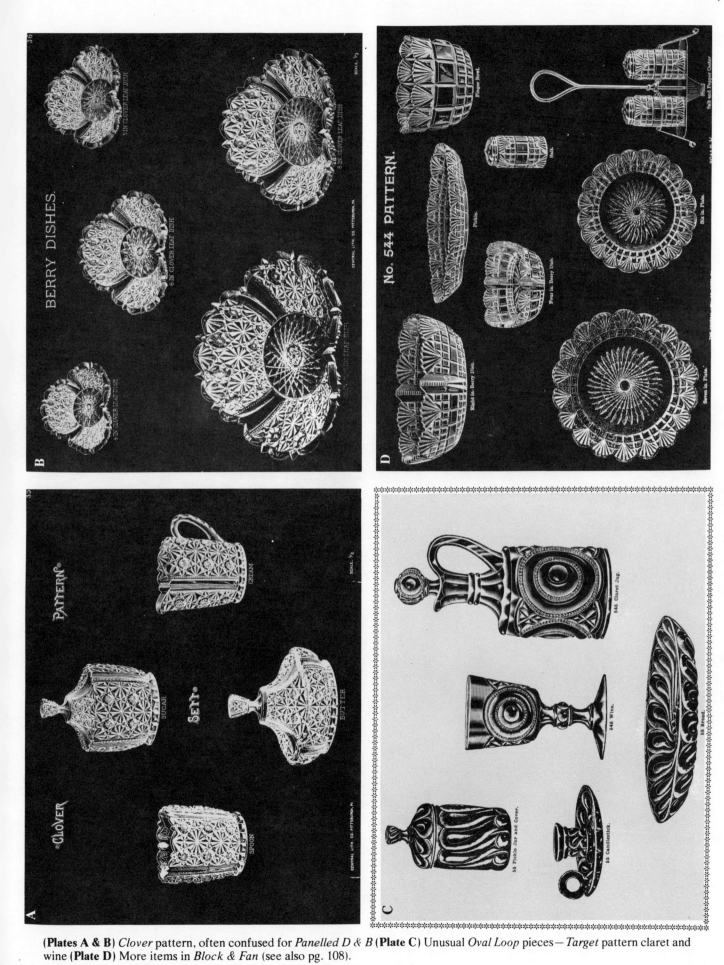

(Plates A & B) *Clover* pattern, often confused for *Panelled D & B* **(Plate C)** Unusual *Oval Loop* pieces—*Target* pattern claret and wine **(Plate D)** More items in *Block & Fan* (see also pg. 108).

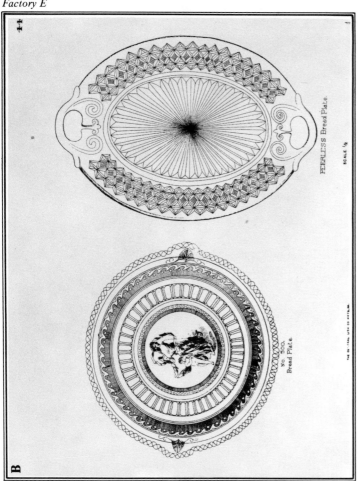

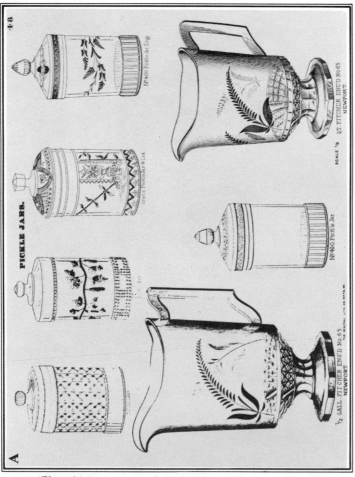

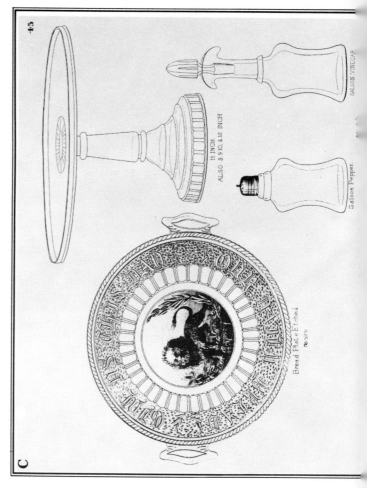

(**Plate A**) Assortment of pickle jars and *Newport* pattern pitchers (**Plate B**) Two unique bread plates (**Plate C**) Note the *Proud Lion* bread plate.

Factory F

Ripley & Company

Pittsburgh, Pa.

(Above) Three cake stands (salvers) in the popular Dakota pattern—note the cake cover which is rarely seen today. Also assorted engraved pitchers in several sizes.

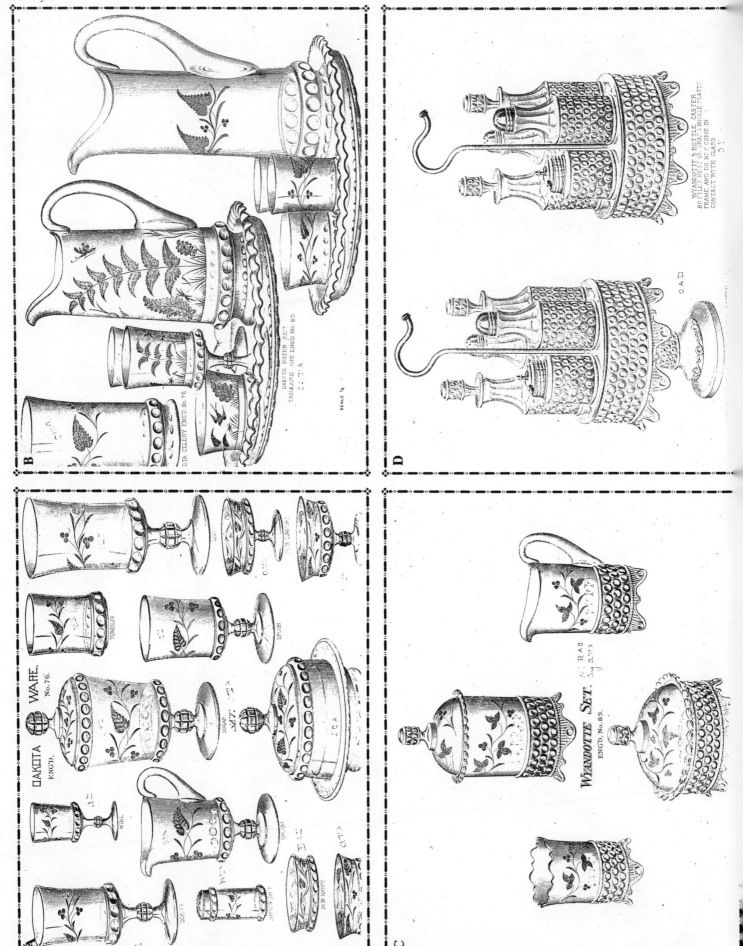

(**Plates A & B**) Assortment of popular *Dakota* pattern, shown here with etched decoration; (**Plates C & D**) *Wyandotte* pattern table and caster sets.

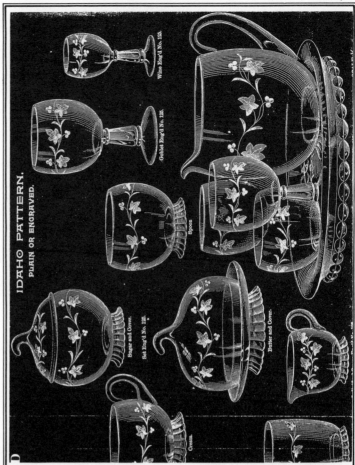

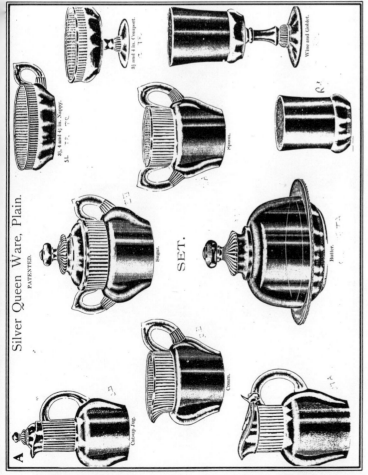

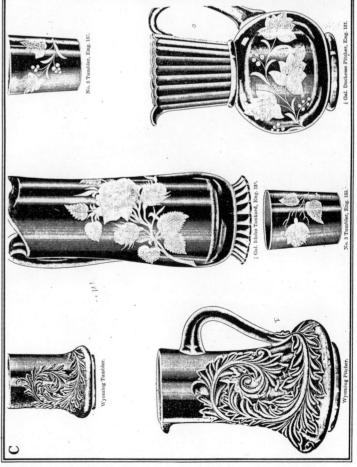

(**Plate A**) Assortment of *Silver Queen* pattern; (**Plate B**) More pieces of the popular *Nail* pattern—see also Book 3, pg. 71; (**Plate C**) Assortment of pitchers and tumblers, including *Wyoming* and *Idaho* patterns; (**Plate D**) *Idaho* pattern assortment.

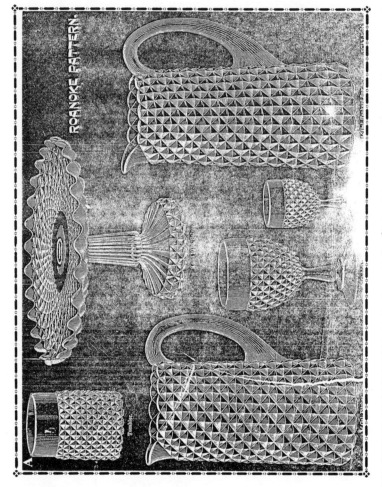

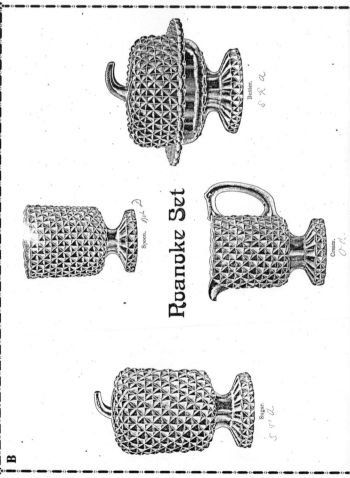

(**Plates A**) Assortment of *Roanoke* pattern; (**Plate B**) Table set in pedestalled variant of *Roanoke* pattern; (**Plate C**) Assortment of *Pavonia* pattern.

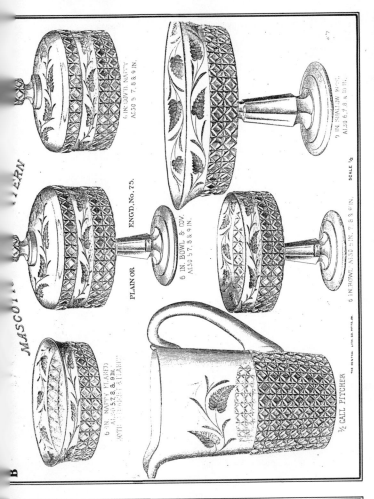

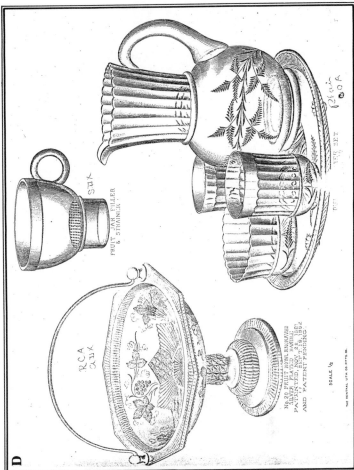

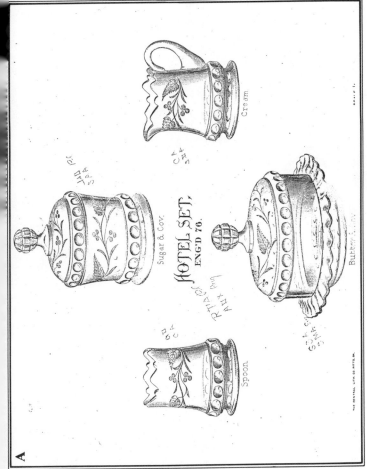

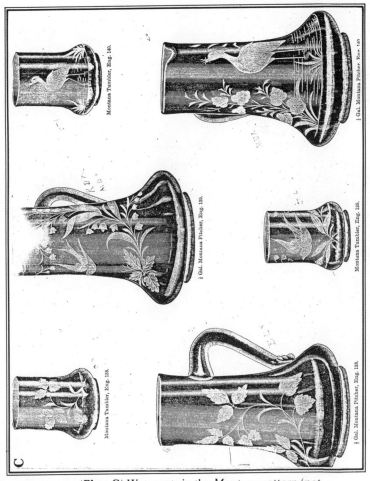

(Plate A) Table set in *Dakota* pattern; (Plate B) Assortment of *Mascotte* pattern (Plate C) Water sets in the *Montana* pattern (not part of the State series); (Plate D) Variety of Ripley items, including a *Dutchess* pattern water set (note spelling is different from Duchess pattern listed in my Books 2 and 3).

Previously unlisted Daisy & Button with Thin Bars water pitcher in vaseline color.

Gillinder & Sons
Pittsburgh, Pa.

PATTERNS

Ruffles
Diamond—variation of Sawtooth
Barred Star—#414 pattern
#419 Pattern—similar to Amazon
D & B With Thin Line
Daisy & Button—with reeded handles
#413 Daisy & Button—scalloped base with reeded handles
Leaf Platter—Diamond pattern interior edged with oak leaves
Leaf Pattern—5" & 6" footed and non-footed nappies
DAISY & BUTTON—master & individual tub-shaped salt dips
DAISY & BUTTON—cradle-shaped salt

NOVELTIES

Pluck Bread Plates
a. Boys in cart pulled by a dog chasing a rabbit
b. Boys falling over a log
ABC Plates:
a. "Sancho Panza & Dapple"
b. With a deer in the center
c. With Flower Bouquet in center
"Frolic" Toy Plate—Boy & Dog on steps
Frosted Figurals:
a. Lion Head ink stand
b. Lion Head paperweight
c. Reclining Lion paperweight
d. Boy & Dog
e. Shakespeare
f. "Just Out" Chick toothpick
g. Hand Bouquet small vase
h. Squatting peasant woman with a sheaf of wheat in arms

Listing of patterns & novelties shown in 1891 catalogue.

HOBBS GLASS COMPANY.

Manufacturers of

Fancy and Staple Table and Bar Glassware,

Pressed and Blown, Crystal and Colored.

Wheeling, W. Va. Sept 18" 1891

Original letterhead from Hobbs Glass Company invoice, September 18, 1891.

Factory H

Hobbs Glass Company

Wheeling, W. Va.

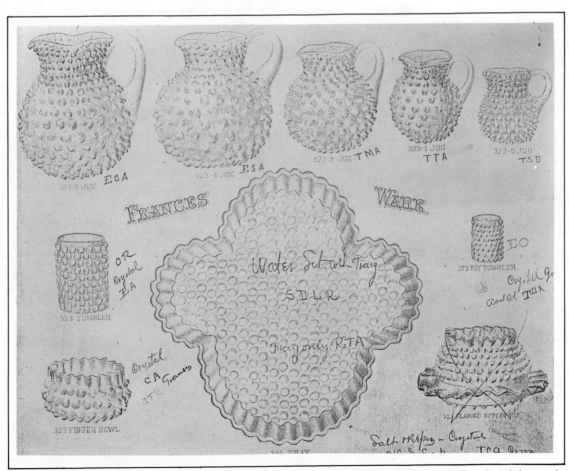

Reprint from original catalogue showing the many different sizes of *Hobnail* pitchers, including the miniature size made for the toy tumbler shown below it.

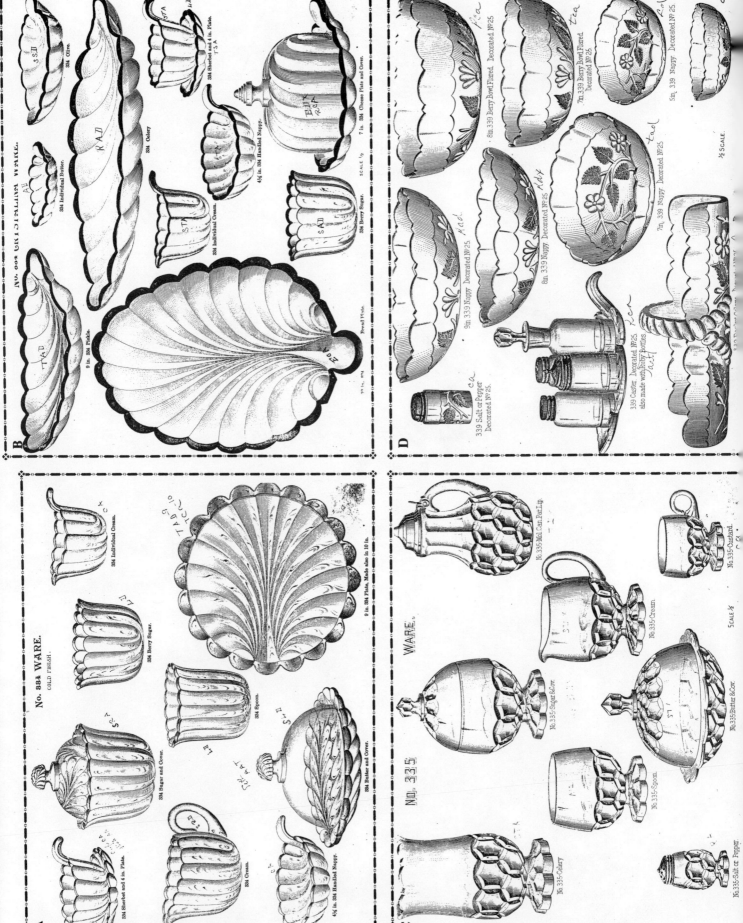

(Plates A & B) Variety of *Crystalina* pattern; **(Plate C)** *Hexagon Block* pattern, often confused for *Henrietta;* **(Plate D)** Assortment of *Leaf & Flower* pattern, including rare celery basket.

JENKINS, President.　　　　　　　　　　　　　　　WM. J. PATTERSON, Sec'y & Treas.

OFFICE OF

COLUMBIA GLASS CO.

Manufacturers of BLOWN & PRESSED

NOVELTIES, GLASS-WARE

Calvert Lith Co Detroit Mich.

FINDLAY, Ohio. Aug 18 1891

Original letterhead from Columbia Glass stationery, August 18, 1891.

Factory J

Columbia Glass Company

Findlay, Ohio

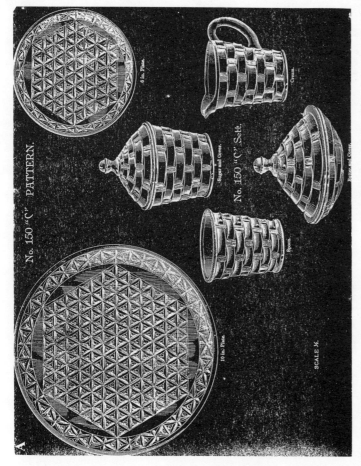

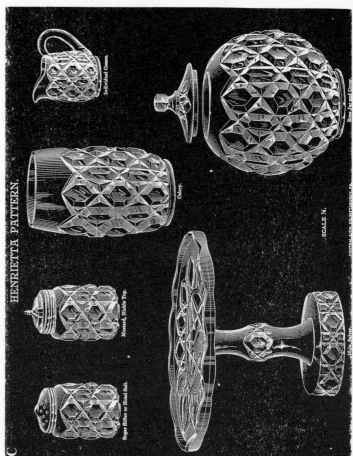

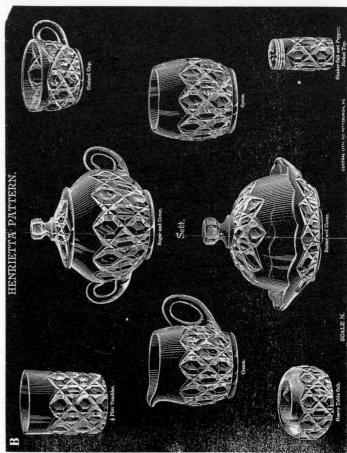

(Plate A) *Bamboo Beauty* table set, previously unlisted; note the plates do not appear to match the set; (Plate B & C) Wide assortment of the popular *Henrietta* pattern.

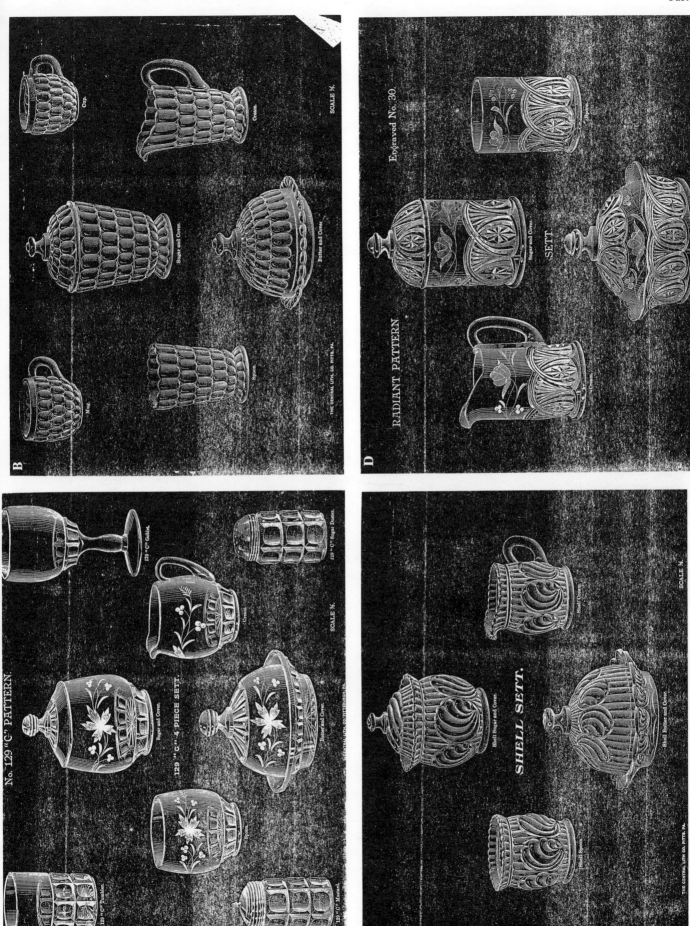

(**Plate A**) Assortment of *Thumbprint Block* pattern—a variant of the *Banquet* pattern shown on next page; (**Plate B**) Assortment of Columbia's *Tycoon* pattern; (**Plate C**) Table set in *Shell on Ribs* pattern, previously unlisted; (**Plate D**) Table set in *Radiant* pattern.

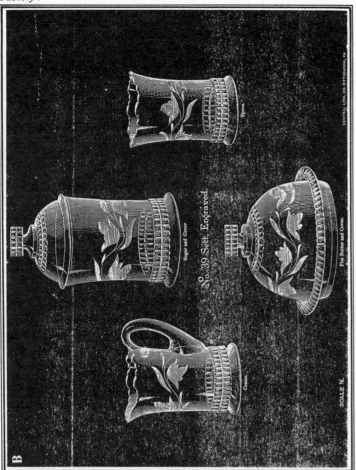

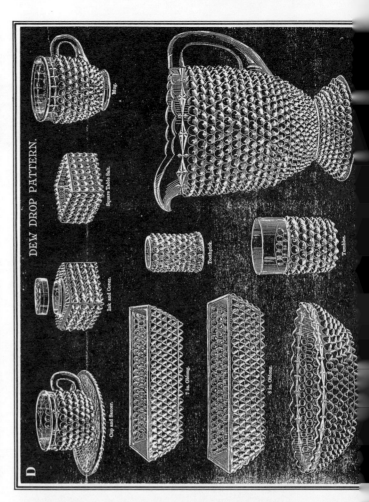

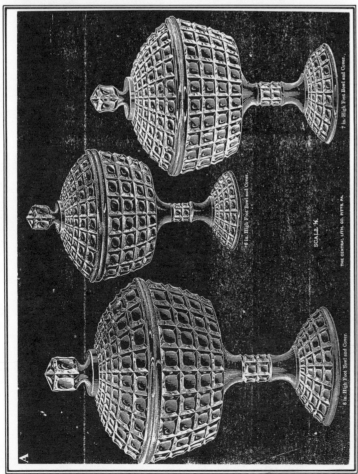

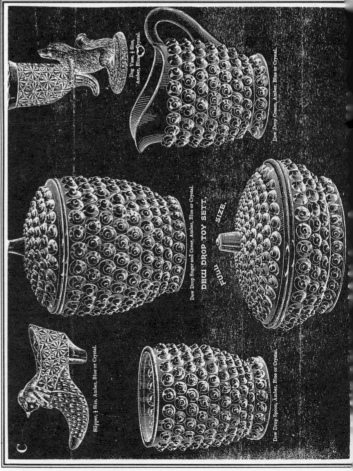

(**Plate A**) Assortment of *Banquet* pattern compotes; (**Plate B**) Assortment of *Climax* pattern, also called "Little Bullet Band"; (**Plate C**) Very rare Columbia "Dewdrop" *(Hobnail)* toy table set—also novelty "Dog Vase" and "Cat in Slipper"; (**Plate D**) Assortment of *Double Eye Hobnail* (see also Book 3, pg. 68 for other items).

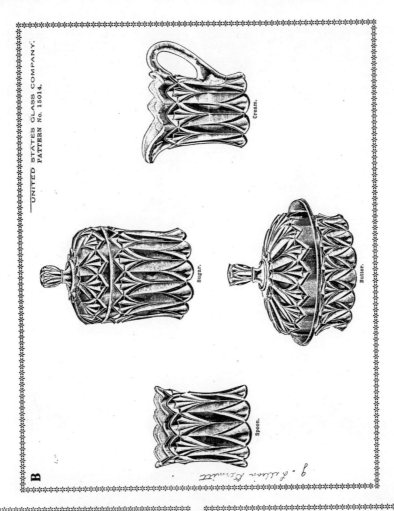

UNITED STATES GLASS COMPANY.
PATTERN No. 15014.

Cream.

Sugar.

Butter.

Spoon.

B

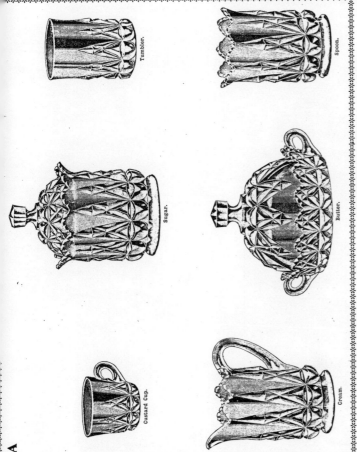

Tumbler.

Spoon.

Sugar.

Butter.

Custard Cup.

Cream.

A

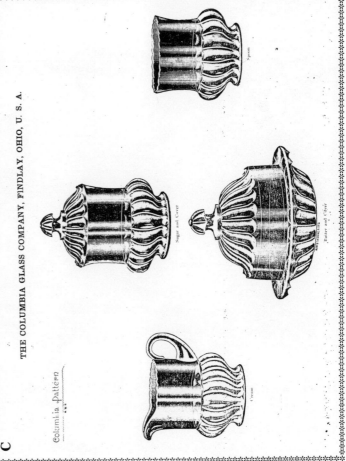

THE COLUMBIA GLASS COMPANY, FINDLAY, OHIO, U. S. A.

Spoon

Sugar and Cover

Butter and Cover

Columbia Pattern

Cream

C

(Plate A) Table set in *Pointed Jewel* pattern; **(Plate B)** *Heavy Gothic* pattern table set; **(Plate C)** Table set in *Old Columbia* pattern.

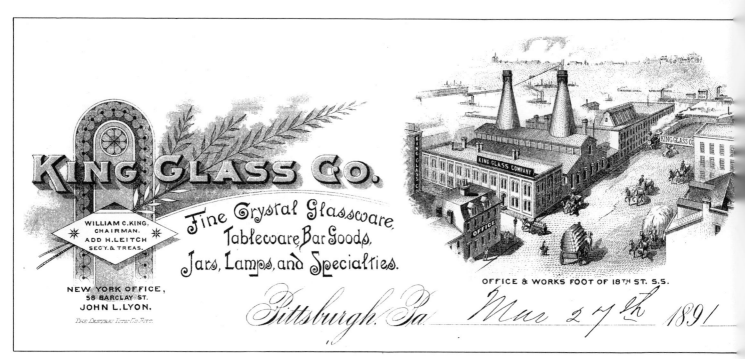

King Glass Co.

Fine Crystal Glassware, Tableware, Bar Goods, Jars, Lamps, and Specialties.

WILLIAM C. KING, CHAIRMAN.
ADD H. LEITCH SEC'Y. & TREAS.

NEW YORK OFFICE, 58 BARCLAY ST.
JOHN L. LYON.

OFFICE & WORKS FOOT OF 18TH ST. S.S.

Pittsburgh, Pa. Mar 27th 1891

Factory K

King Glass Company

Pittsburgh, Pa.

Oil cruet in previously unlisted *King's Block* pattern. This piece is in vaseline color and the stopper is missing (MMA Catalogue information).

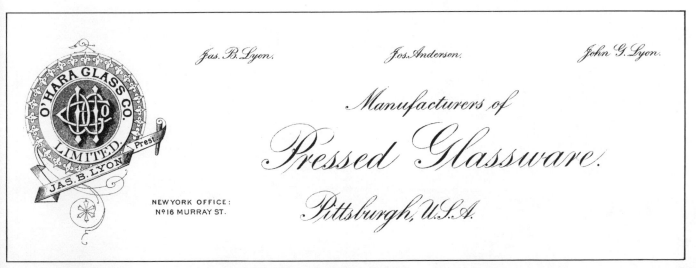

Original letterhead for O'Hara Glass Co., Pittsburgh, Pa.

Factory L

O'Hara Glass Company

Pittsburgh, Pa.

The Bellaire Goblet Co.
Findlay, Ohio, U.S.A.

M.L. Blackburn, Prest.
W.A. Gorby, Sec'y.

Original letterhead for Bellaire Goblet Co., Findlay, Ohio.

Factory M

Bellaire Goblet Company

Findlay, Ohio

Original letterhead from Nickel-Plate Glass Company stationery.

Factory N

Nickel-Plate Glass Company

Fostoria, Ohio

Opalescent Swirl lamps from 1891 U.S.G.C. catalogue—also made by Factory N in a water set, syrup, sugar shaker, barber bottle, cruet, toothpick and salt shaker.

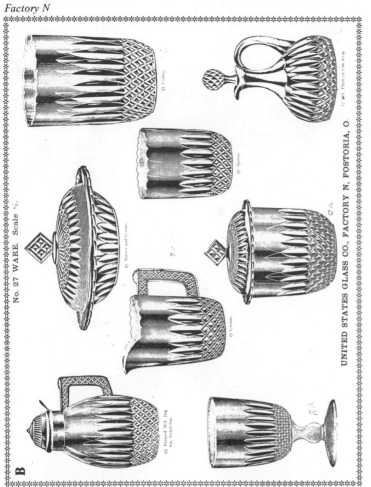

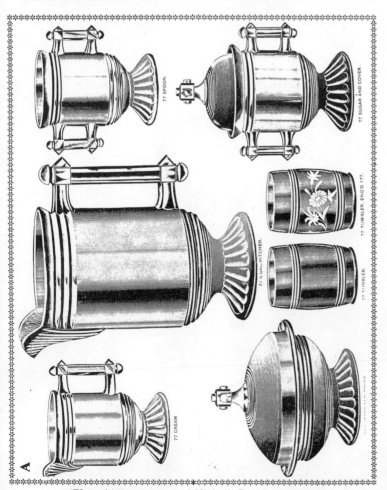

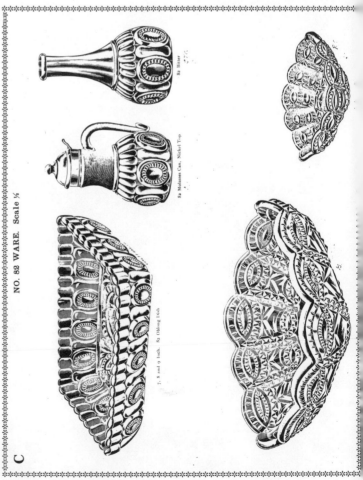

(Plate A) Assortment of *Nickel's Royal* pattern; **(Plate B)** Assortment of *Fostoria* pattern; **(Plate C)** Assortment of *Notched Oval* pattern, previously unlisted; **(Plate D)** Assortment of *Nickel's Richmond* pattern (do not confuse for pattern of same name by Richards & Hartley).

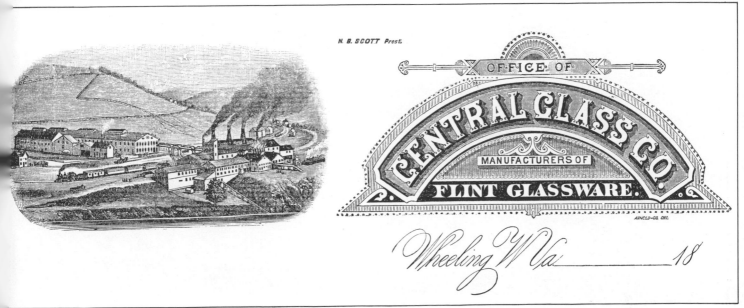

N. B. SCOTT Prest.

OFFICE OF

CENTRAL GLASS CO.

MANUFACTURERS OF

FLINT GLASSWARE

Wheeling W Va _____ 18

Original letterhead for Central Glass Co., undated.

Factory O

Central Glass Company

Wheeling, W. Va.

Original letterhead for Doyle & Co., dated November 17, 1891.

Factory P

Doyle & Company

Pittsburgh, Pa.

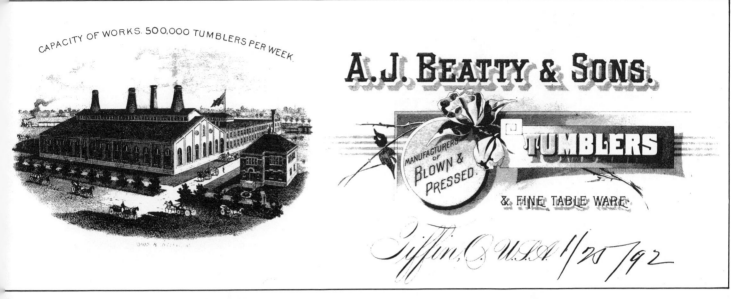

Original letterhead for A. J. Beatty & Sons stationery, January 25, 1892.

Factory R

A. J. Beatty & Sons

Tiffin, Ohio

Photograph from early postcard showing office building of Factory U—note the two factory smoke stacks appearing in the background.

Factory U

Gas City, Indiana

In June, 1892, the U.S.G.C. was offered free land and fuel if they would build a glassware factory in Gas City, Indiana. By September 14, 1892, the specifications for a new two-furnace factory were prepared and construction commenced.

By September, 1893, the new factory was producing a general line of pressed tableware, tumblers, bar goods and packer's glassware, suited to the bulk trade of the Western market.

The company was fortunate in selecting it's gas property, enjoying a bountiful supply for many years from it's wells. A gas compressor station was located only six miles from the factory. A sufficient amount of oil was derived from the gas wells—more than enough to pay for the costs of operating the pumping station.

Factory U was ideally located for taking advantage of cheaper freight deliveries to the growing Western states. It remained in full operation until it's closing in April 1932.

Glassport Factory

Glassport, Pennsylvania

A tract of 500 acres of land was purchased by the Glassport Land Company in 1893 for the proposed consolidation of the factories of the United States Glass Company which were located in Pennsylvania and West Virginia. This land development firm was actually a division of the U.S.G.C. The property was located on the Monongahela River, near the town of McKeesport. An early map revealed the ideal location of this property in relation to 438 nearby gas wells. This was the deciding factor in purchasing the property. By September of 1894 the company had completed the construction of a modern glassware factory with two 15-pot furnaces. The glassware would be produced by steam-powered presses whenever possible, and finished with the most modern equipment. A cooperage factory which would manufacture wooden barrels was also built, since glass was always shipped by barrel in those days.

The town and the factory both were named GLASSPORT. The U.S.G.C. actually founded a city, plotting the location of the industrial cites along the river front, grading the streets, and marking off residential areas. A paperweight appeared in a 1907 catalogue soliciting development with the words "BUY GLASSPORT LOTS". Also, a brochure pointed out the following advantages to the prospective industries wishing to locate in Glassport; "Coal delivered, .50 per ton, natural gas, .08 per thousand feet, and fuel oil delivered at $1.82 per 100 gallons." These prices are absolutely incredible when compared to today's energy-conservative rates.

After the turn of the century, the U.S.G.C. concentrated most of it's production to this new factory, as others were closed by fire, the Depression or efforts to cut costs. On August 3, 1963, a tornado destroyed the Glassport factory, as well as most of the town. There were over 1,300 insurance claims in the area, involving more than 400 insurance companies. This disaster left more than 200 employees of the U.S.G.C. without jobs, for it was management's decision, after receiving the estimates for reconstruction, not to rebuild.

1F106—Goblet — Decorated — Rub.,
Emerald and Gold,
$1.80 per dozen.

15119—Goblet—Decorated,
$2.50 per doz.

15119—Wine—Decorated,
$1.50 per dozen.

United States Glass Co.
1909-1910
Domestic Catalogue

15070 Wine.
Also make Wine
Flared.
50c Per doz.

15098 Wine.
70c Per doz.

15055 Wine.
60c Per doz.

15082 Wine, Flared.
Also make Straight
Shape.
64c Per doz.

15093 Wine.
70c Per doz.

15086 Wine.
64c Per doz.

15107 Wine.
Straight.
60c Per doz.

15099 Wine.
70c Per doz.

15110 Wine.
50c Per doz.
(Illustration ⅓ Size.)

15117 Wine.
70c Per doz.
(Illustration ½ Size.)

15121 Wine.
80c Per doz.
(Illustration ½ Size.)

15111 Wine.
60c Per doz.
(Illustration ½ Size.)

15104 Wine, Cupped.
60c Per doz.
Also make Flared Shape

15106 Wine.
60c Per doz.

▲ 15074 Large Goblet, 10 oz.
$1.00 per doz.

+ 15084 Goblet
86c per doz.

+ 15091 Goblet
Also make Optic
76c per doz.

+ 15059 Goblet
76c per doz.

+ 15095 Goblet
76c per doz.

+ 15084 Wine
60c per doz.

+ 15059 Wine
50c per doz.

▲ 15074 Wine, 2 oz.
74c per doz.

+ 15091 Wine
50c per doz.

A

Also make with Rose or Gold Decorations, $9.70 Per doz. Sets.   ILLUSTRATIONS SCALE HALF SIZE.

15110 Hotel Four Piece Set, $4.00 per dozen Sets.

Made to meet the demand for a lower priced set, the pieces are medium size, but in which the figure of the larger set is retained, the Sugar has three handles, the Cream and Butter are similar to those in the larger set, the Spoon is footed but without handles, and are all made from our best quality of clear crystal pot glass.

15110 Hotel Sugar and Cover, 3 Handles.
$1.20 Per doz.
Decorated Rose or Gold, $2.70 per doz.

15110 Hotel Cream, $1.00 Per doz.
Decorated Rose or Gold, $1.80 Per doz.

15110 Hotel Spoon, 60c Per doz.
Decorated Rose or Gold, $1.50 per doz.

15110 Hotel Butter and Cover, $1.20 per doz.
Decorated Rose or Gold, $3.50 Per doz.

B

Also make with Gold Decoration and Rose Decoration, $13.70 Per doz. Sets.   ILLUSTRATIONS SCALE HALF SIZE.

One of the most popular designs on the market. The pattern is Sunrise effect, with stars and diamonds in Crescent shape divisions. The articles are full size, medium weight, rich clear crystal pot glass, hand finished.

Cream Pitcher, $1.20 Per doz.
Decorated Rose or Gold, $2.20 Per doz.

15110 Sunshine Four Piece Set $6.60 per dozen sets.

Sugar Bowl and Cover, $1.80 Per doz.
Decorated Rose or Gold, $3.60 Per doz.

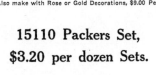

Spoon Holder, $1.20 Per doz.

Butter and Cover, $2.50 per doz.

C

Also make with Rose or Gold Decorations, $9.00 Per doz. Sets.   ILLUSTRATIONS SCALE HALF SIZE

15110 Packers Set, $3.20 per dozen Sets.

As an advertiser for the various lines of products for which this set can be used as containers, it stands in first place. The pattern is attractive, the different pieces constitute four of the most popular articles in glassware, on account of their utility for every day use.

Each article has an inside ledge for purpose of sealing the contents; and are made from our high grade clear pot glass.

15110 Packers Sugar and Cover, 84c Per doz.
Rose or Gold Decoration, $2.30 Per doz.

15110 Packers Cream, 80c Per doz.
Rose or Gold Decoration, $2.70 Per doz.

15110 Packers Spoon, 60c Per doz.
Rose or Gold Decoration, $1.50 Per doz.

15110 Packers Butter and Cover, $1.20 Per doz.
Rose or Gold Decoration, $3.50 Per doz.

(Plates A—C) Three different table sets in the popular *Rising Sun* pattern, originally called the "Sunshine" set—the differences were in size and the shape of the sugar bowl.

A

15041 Four Piece Sets $6.90 per dozen Sets
ILLUSTRATIONS ONE-THIRD SIZE.
One of the most popular patterns ever produced and which only time increases in popularity. Graceful shapes, handsome Strawberry and Fan Design, finished and polished to perfection.

Made from pot glass of rich brilliancy.

Sugar Bowl. $1.90 Per doz. Cream Pitcher. $1.50 Per doz. Spoon Holder. $1.10 Per doz. Butter Dish. $2.40 Per doz.

B

15047 Colonial Four Piece Set, $7.50 per dozen sets.
ILLUSTRATIONS ONE-THIRD SIZE.
Most glass dealers know this set and most of them buy it on account of its distinct individuality. The set is of medium weight, the glass is of pure crystal quality. The finish is the best that experts can produce, and the polish the best that is possible to obtain from the greatest degree of heat used in the manufacture of high grade glassware.

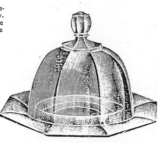

Sugar and Cover. $2.00 Per doz. Cream Pitcher. $1.70 Per doz. Spoon Holder. $1.10 Per doz. Butter Dish. $2.70 Per doz.

C

15048 Pennsylvania Four Piece Set $7.40 per dozen sets.
A popular cut pattern, well made and finished in every particular. Brilliant crystal pot glass. For a fast seller, buy this.

ILLUSTRATIONS ONE-THIRD SIZE.

Sugar Bowl. $2.00 Per doz. Cream Pitcher. $1.40 Per doz. Spoon Holder. $1.00 Per doz. Butter and Cover. $3.00 Per doz.

D

15048½ Four Piece Set $6.50 per dozen sets.
ILLUSTRATIONS ONE-THIRD SIZE.

Sugar and Cover. $2.00 Per doz. Cream Pitcher. $1.40 Per doz. Spoon Holder. $1.00 Per doz. Butter and Cover. $1.44 Per doz.

E

15052 Illinois Four Piece Set $8.50 per dozen sets.
The finest reproductions of heavy cut glass on the market. Massive design of eight point stars, in which are large and small diamond figures. The pieces are Squat shape, all handsomely finished and made of rich brilliant pot glass.

ILLUSTRATIONS ONE-THIRD SIZE.

Sugar and Cover. $2.00 Per doz. Cream Pitcher. $1.30 Per doz. Spoon Holder. $1.20 Per doz. Butter and Cover. $4.00 Per doz.

(**A**) *Pineapple & Fan* (**B**) *Plain Scalloped Panel* (**C**) *Pennsylvania* (**D**) *Pennsylvania* with odd butter (**E**) *Illinois.*

A — 15054 Massachusetts Four Piece Set Unfinished $5.80 per dozen sets.

Heavy cut pattern, Square Shapes, Sugar and Spoon each with two handles.   An extra large set for a small price.

ILLUSTRATIONS ONE-THIRD SIZE.

Sugar Bowl.
$1.60 Per doz.

Cream Pitcher.
$1.10 Per doz.

Spoon Holder.
90c Per doz.

Butter and Cover.
$2.20 Per doz.

B — 15055 MINNESOTA Four Piece Set $7.50 per dozen Sets

ILLUSTRATIONS ONE-THIRD SIZE.

A clear cut, well defined pattern, and a great favorite with the trade.   The pieces are large and shapely, finish and quality the best than can be produced by up-to-date methods.

Sugar Bowl.
$2.00 Per doz.

Cream Pitcher.
$1.40 Per doz.

Spoon Holder.
$1.20 Per doz.

Butter Dish.
$2.90 Per doz.

C — 15070 New Jersey Four Piece Set $7.10 per dozen sets.

Plain and figured Tear Drop Design.   Very bright, best finish, pure crystal pot glass.
ILLUSTRATIONS ONE-THIRD SIZE.

Sugar Bowl.
$2.00 Per doz.

Cream Pitcher.
$1.40 Per doz.

Spoon Holder.
$1.00 Per doz.

Butter and Cover.
$2.70 Per doz.

D — 15077 Michigan Four Piece Sets $7.50 per dozen Sets.

ILLUSTRATIONS ONE-THIRD SIZE.

A very desirable plain and figured pattern.   Mirror panels with lobe shape figures, harmoniously blended.   Rich clear crystal pot glass, elegantly finished and polished.

Sugar and Cover.
$2.10 Per doz.

Cream Pitcher.
$1.60 Per doz.

Spoon Holder.
$1.20 Per doz.

Butter and Cover.
$3.00 Per doz.

E — 15078 Manhattan Four Piece Set $7.80 per dozen Sets.

A shapely pattern with indent figured circles, picket flutes and plain bands, together making a very pretty and brilliant effect.   Handsomely made, highly fire polished, best quality pot crystal glass.

ILLUSTRATIONS ONE-THIRD SIZE.

Sugar and Cover.
$2.10 Per doz.

Cream Pitcher.
$1.70 Per doz.

Spoon Holder.
$1.20 Per doz.

Butter and Cover.
$3.00 Per doz.

(**A**) *Massachusetts* (**B**) *Minnesota* (**C**) *New Jersey* (**D**) *Michigan* (**E**) *Manhattan.*

A — 15082 Columbia Four Piece Set, $7.50 per dozen Sets.

ILLUSTRATIONS ONE-THIRD SIZE.

The Columbia Pattern is one of Touraine shape, with oval panels and heavy scolloped bottoms, and where something different is wanted in Colonial glassware, we recommend this set. The articles are large, finely finished, and the quality of the glass the best that it is possible to produce.

Sugar and Cover. $2.20 Per doz. Cream Pitcher. $1.70 Per doz. Spoon Holder. $1.40 Per doz. Butter and Cover. $2.70 Per doz.

B — 15086 Mirror Plate Hotel Four Piece Set $7.60 per dozen Sets.

ILLUSTRATIONS ONE-THIRD SIZE.

This set is preferred by many on account of the Squat shape, and while it costs us more to finish in this way, nothing is added to the price.
Handsomely made, highly polished, clear crystal pot glass.

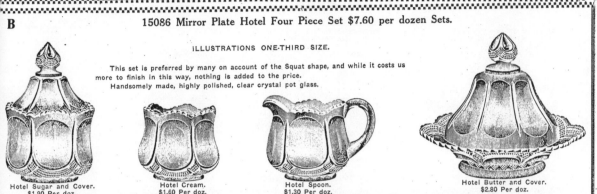

Hotel Sugar and Cover. $1.90 Per doz. Hotel Cream. $1.60 Per doz. Hotel Spoon. $1.30 Per doz. Hotel Butter and Cover. $2.80 Per doz.

C — 15086 Mirror Plate Four Piece Set, $7.60 per dozen Sets.

ILLUSTRATIONS ONE-THIRD SIZE.

Colonial effect with just enough figure to add to the attractiveness of the design. This is one of our largest and best selling patterns, and is classified by us as a Staple line. The quality of the glass and finish are up to our high standard of excellence.

Sugar and Cover. $1.90 Per doz. Cream Pitcher. $1.60 Per doz. Spoon Holder. $1.30 Per doz. Butter and Cover. $2.80 Per doz.

D — 15093 States Four Piece Set $7.50 per dozen sets.

ILLUSTRATIONS ONE-THIRD SIZE.

Sugar and Cover. $2.20 Per doz. Cream Pitcher. $1.60 Per doz. Spoon Holder. $1.20 Per doz. Butter and Cover. $3.00 Per doz.

E — 15098 REGAL Four Piece Set $8.00 per dozen Sets

ILLUSTRATIONS ONE-THIRD SIZE.

A beautiful cut pattern of rich rare brilliancy. The design is a combination of diamond figures, fourteen point stars and fans, together forming a most magnificent effect. The quality of the glass is of the highest grade, and the finish the best that experts can deliver.

Sugar and Cover. $2.30 Per doz. Cream Pitcher. $1.80 Per doz. Spoon Holder. $1.40 Per doz. Flanged Butter and Cover. $3.40 Per doz.

(A) *Church Windows,* originally "Columbia" **(B)** *Galloway* hotel set, originally called "Mirror Plate" **(C)** *Galloway* **(D)** *The States* **(E)** *U.S. Regal.*

A

15099 Royal Four Piece Set $8.00 per dozen sets.
ILLUSTRATIONS ONE-THIRD SIZE.

| Handled Sugar and Cover. $2.40 Per doz. | Cream Pitcher. $1.80 Per doz. | Spoon Holder. $1.40 Per doz. | Flanged Butter and Cover. $3.20 Per doz. |

B

15104 VICTORIA Four Piece Set $6.60 per dozen Sets
ILLUSTRATIONS ONE-THIRD SIZE.

A very attractive medium weight set. Whirling Star Design, surrounded by two crescents on either side of which are small diamonds and triangle figures, forming a pleasing and neat effect.

High standard pot glass, finished in the best manner possible.

| Sugar and Cover. $1.90 Per doz. | Cream Pitcher. $1.20 Per doz. | Spoon Holder. $1.10 Per doz. | Butter and Cover. $2.50 Per doz. |

C

15106 Buckingham Four Piece Set $7.00 per dozen sets.
ILLUSTRATIONS ONE-THIRD SIZE.

| Handled Sugar and Cover. $2.30 Per doz. | Cream Pitcher. $1.40 Per doz. | Spoon Holder. $1.00 Per doz. | Butter and Cover. $2.40 Per doz. |

D

15107 St. Regis Four Piece Set, $8.00 per dozen Sets—Ground Bottom.
ILLUSTRATIONS ONE-THIRD SIZE.

The design is of plain rich simplicity. The articles are made from the very best quality of pure crystal pot glass, and finished by the best workmen that it is possible to obtain. The Sugar, Cream and Spoon are made with cut bottoms, and the whole set is fire polished to the top notch of perfection.

| Sugar and Cover. $2.10 Per doz. | Cream Pitcher. $1.70 Per doz. | Spoon Holder. $1.40 Per doz. | Butter and Cover. $2.80 Per doz. |

E

Cafe Four Piece Set $7.10 per dozen Sets.

A new departure in glassware, made to stand the hard usage of Cafe and Restaurant kitchens. Sanitary, easy to clean and keep clean.

ILLUSTRATIONS ONE-THIRD SIZE.

| Sugar and Cover. $2.00 Per doz. | Cream Pitcher. $1.40 Per doz. | Spoon Holder. $1.10 Per doz. | Butter and Cover. $2.60 Per doz. |

(**A**) *Spinning Star,* originally "U.S. Royal" (**B**) *U.S. Victoria* (**C**) *Buckingham* (**D**) *Bevelled Windows,* originally called "St. Regis" (**E**) *Cafe Ware.*

5 in. Footed Jelly and Cover.

Toothpick.

Handled Mug.

Bread Plate.

9½ in. Salver. Also make 8½ and 10½ inch sizes.

9 in. Fruit Bowl. Also make 8 and 10 in. sizes.

Assorted items in Tenessee pattern, part of the state series.

Sugar and Cover.

Butter and Cover.

Spoon.

Cream.

Celery, Tall.

Mol. Can, T. T.

Goblet.

¼ Gal. Jug.

A

Celery Tray.

Toothpick.

Pickle Dish.

ILLUSTRATIONS ONE-THIRD ACTUAL SIZE.

8 in. Round Plate.

Small Syrup, Glass Lip.

8 in. Bowl. Also make 6 and 7 in. sizes.

(**Plate A**) Assorted items in *New Jersey* pattern, #15070; (**Plate B**) Several scarce items in *Delaware* are shown in this reprint, including the pomade box, and small open sugar and creamer.

B

Oil or Vinegar.

Puff Box and Cover.

Small Sugar. No Cover.

Small Cream.

Pomade Box and Cover.

Custard.

Celery, Tall.

9 in. Comport, Crimped, Gold Decorated.

Claret Jug, Gold Decorated.

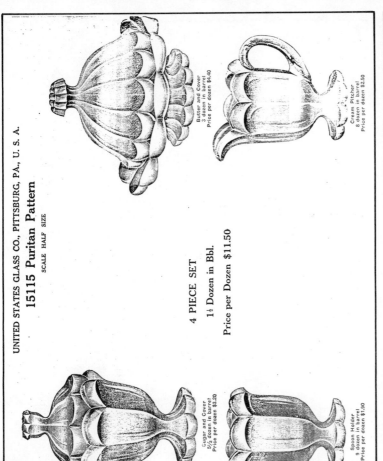

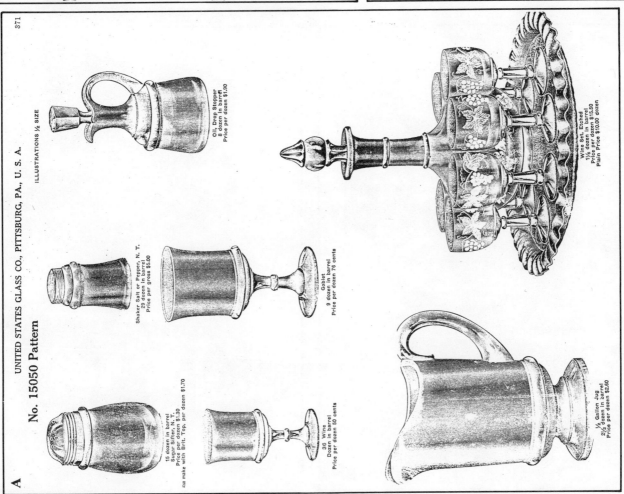

(Plate A) Wide assortment of the *Ohio* state pattern; **(Plate B)** Table set in *U.S. Puritan* pattern; **(Plate C)** Assortment of pieces in *Lacy Medallion,* originally called the Jewel pattern, primarily sold as souvenir ware. I believe the wines found without souvenir markings were meant to be part of the *Colorado* set.

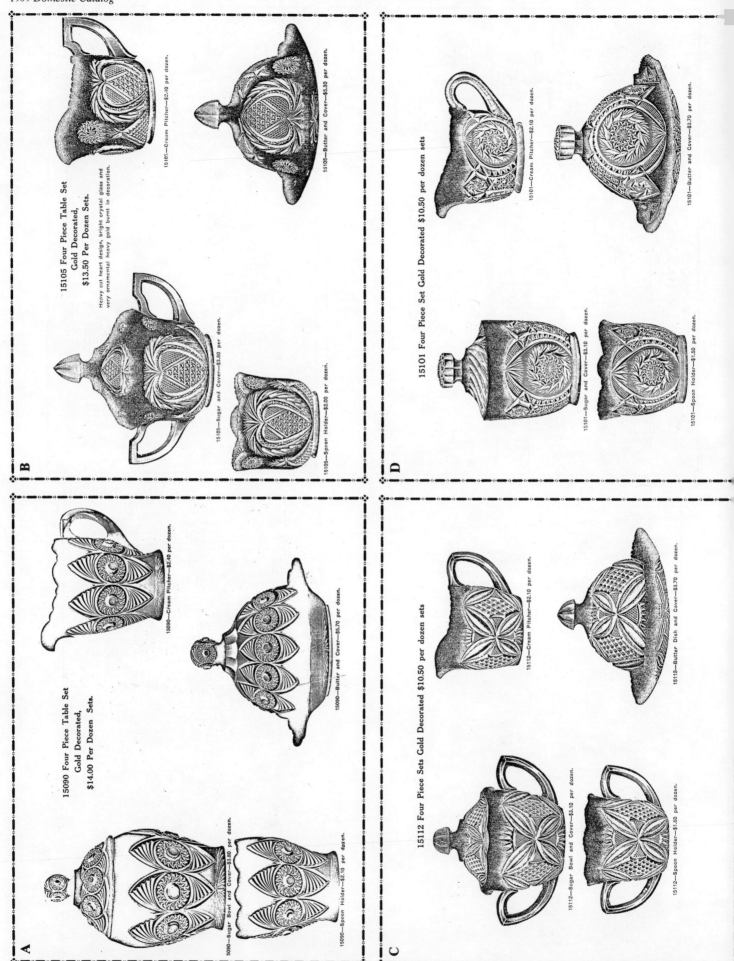

B

15105 Four Piece Table Set
Gold Decorated,
$13.50 Per Dozen Sets.

Heavy cut heart design, bright crystal glass and very ornamental heavy gold burnt in decoration.

15105—Cream Pitcher—$2.10 per dozen.

15105—Butter and Cover—$5.30 per dozen.

15105—Sugar and Cover—$3.80 per dozen.

15105—Spoon Holder—$2.00 per dozen.

D

15101 Four Piece Set Gold Decorated $10.50 per dozen sets

15101—Cream Pitcher—$2.10 per dozen.

15101—Butter and Cover—$3.70 per dozen.

15101—Sugar and Cover—$3.10 per dozen.

15101—Spoon Holder—$1.50 per dozen.

A

15090 Four Piece Table Set
Gold Decorated,
$14.00 Per Dozen Sets.

15090—Cream Pitcher—$2.40 per dozen.

15090—Butter and Cover—$5.70 per dozen.

15090—Sugar Bowl and Cover—$3.80 per dozen.

15090—Spoon Holder—$2.10 per dozen.

C

15112 Four Piece Sets Gold Decorated $10.50 per dozen sets

15112—Cream Pitcher—$2.10 per dozen.

15112—Butter Dish and Cover—$3.70 per dozen.

15112—Sugar Bowl and Cover—$3.10 per dozen.

15112—Spoon Holder—$1.60 per dozen.

(**Plate A**) Table set in *Bullseye & Fan* pattern; (**Plate B**) Table set in *Marlboro* pattern; (**Plate C**) Table set in *Pattee Cross* pattern; (**Plate D**) Table set in *Buzz-Star* pattern.

B

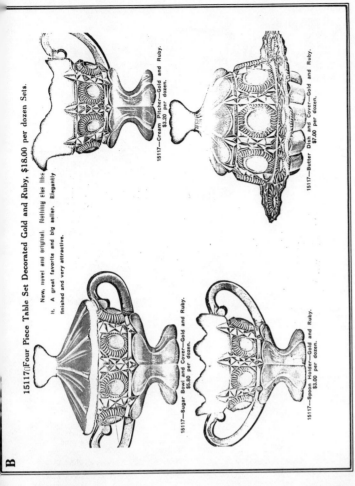

15117—Four Piece Table Set Decorated Gold and Ruby, $18.00 per dozen Sets.

New, novel and original. Nothing else like it. A great favorite and big seller. Elegantly finished and very attractive.

15117—Cream Pitcher—Gold and Ruby. $3.20 per dozen.

15117—Butter Dish and Cover—Gold and Ruby. $7.00 per dozen.

15117—Sugar Bowl and Cover—Gold and Ruby. $5.80 per dozen.

15117—Spoon Holder—Gold and Ruby. $3.00 per dozen.

D

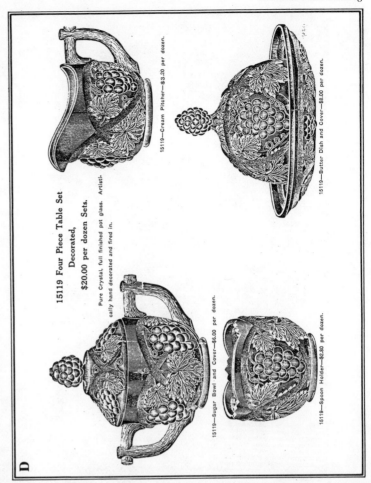

15119 Four Piece Table Set Decorated, $20.00 per dozen Sets.

Pure Crystal, full finished pot glass. Artistically hand decorated and fired in.

15119—Cream Pitcher—$3.20 per dozen.

15119—Butter Dish and Cover—$8.00 per dozen.

15119—Sugar Bowl and Cover—$6.00 per dozen.

15119—Spoon Holder—$2.80 per dozen.

A

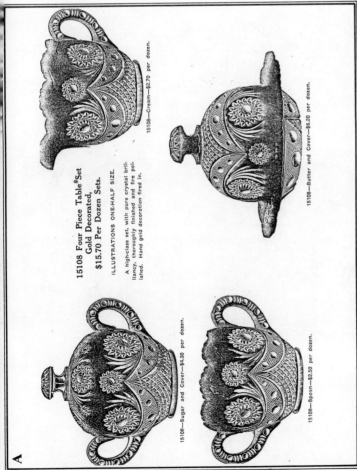

15108 Four Piece Table Set Gold Decorated, $15.70 Per Dozen Sets.

ILLUSTRATIONS ONE-HALF SIZE.

A high-class set, with pure crystal brilliancy, thoroughly finished and fire polished. Hand gold decoration fired in.

15108—Cream—$2.70 per dozen.

15108—Butter and Cover—$6.20 per dozen.

15108—Sugar and Cover—$4.30 per dozen.

15108—Spoon—$2.50 per dozen.

C

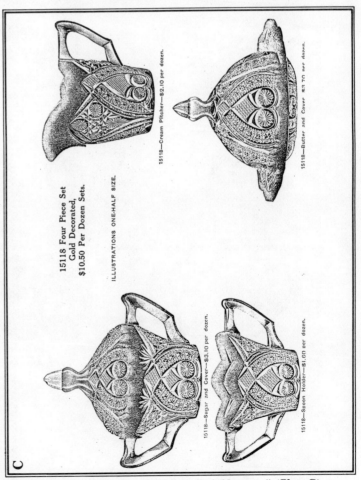

15118 Four Piece Table Set Gold Decorated, $10.50 Per Dozen Sets.

ILLUSTRATIONS ONE-HALF SIZE.

15118—Cream Pitcher—$2.10 per dozen.

15118—Butter and Cover—$3.70 per dozen.

15118—Sugar and Cover—$3.10 per dozen.

15118—Spoon Holder—$1.60 per dozen.

(**Plate A**) Table set in *Star & Crescent* pattern; (**Plate B**) Table set in *Bullseye & Daisy* pattern, originally called "Newport"; (**Plate C**) Table set in *Cane Horseshoe* pattern; (**Plate D**) Table set in *Palm Beach* pattern, very popular in opalescent and carnival glass colors.

A ILLUSTRATIONS ONE-THIRD SIZE.

15099 Medium Cream.
$1.50 Per doz.

15103 Individual Cream.
70c Per doz.

Cafe Individual Cream.
72c Per doz.

15106 Jersey Cream.
80c Per doz.

15055 Jersey Cream.
80c Per doz.

15098 Small Cream.
$1.20 Per doz.

15077 6 oz. Tankard Cream.
80c Per doz.

15055 Lemonade Cup.
80c Per doz.

15033 Lemonade Cup.
86c Per doz.

15093 Custard Cup.
86c Per doz.

15106 Lemonade Cup.
86c Per doz.

15061 Custard or
Lemonade Cup.
86c Per doz.

15039 Custard Cup.
86c Per doz.

15077 Lemonade Cup.
86c Per doz.

15098 Custard Cup.
86c Per doz.

15082 Custard Cup.
86c Per doz.

15041 Custard Cup.
86c Per doz.

15055 Mug.
80c Per doz.

15077 Handled Lemonade.
80c Per doz.

15106 Small Mug.
70c Per doz.

15106 Large Mug.
80c Per doz.

15041 Mug.
56c Per doz.

3475 Mug.
30c Per doz.

15098 Footed Mug.
80c Per doz.

B

15106 Medium Sugar.
$1.20 Per doz.

15106 Medium Cream.
$1.00 Per doz.

15061 Individual Sugar.
90c Per doz.

15061 Individual Cream.
80c Per doz.

15041 Individual Sugar and Cover.
$1.76 Per doz.

15041 Individual Cream.
$1.44 Per doz.

15093 Individual Sugar.
90c Per doz.

15093 Individual Cream.
80c Per doz.

15093 Medium Sugar.
$1.50 Per doz.

15093 Medium Cream.
$1.40 Per doz.

15086 Toy Water Set, $3.50 Per doz. sets.

15077 Toy Stein Set, $3.50 Per doz. sets.

15077 Toy Water Set. Finished Tumblers, $3.20 Per doz. sets.
" " " Unfinished " 2.60 " "

(Plate A) Assorted creamers and mugs in a wide variety of patterns by U.S. Glass in 1909 (and earlier); **(Plate B)** Assortment of
toy sets, including the previously unlisted "stein set" in *Michigan*, and a variety of individual creamers and open sugars.

United States Glass Co.

Export Catalogue

1919

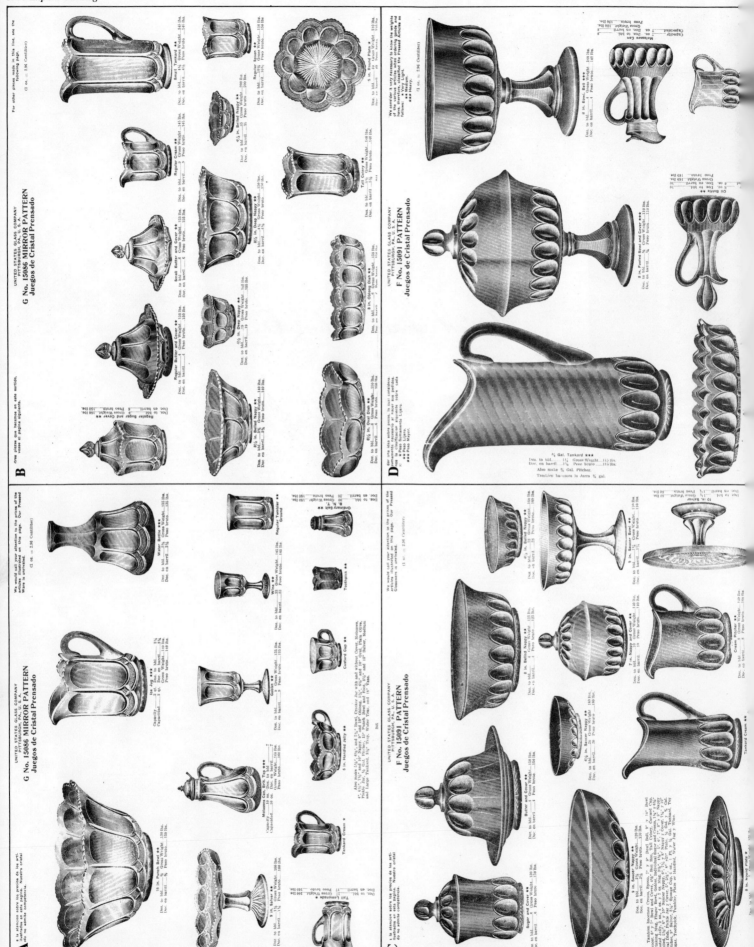

(Plates A & B) Assortment of *Galloway* pattern, originally called "Mirror"; **(Plates C & D)** Assortment of *Arched Ovals* pattern.

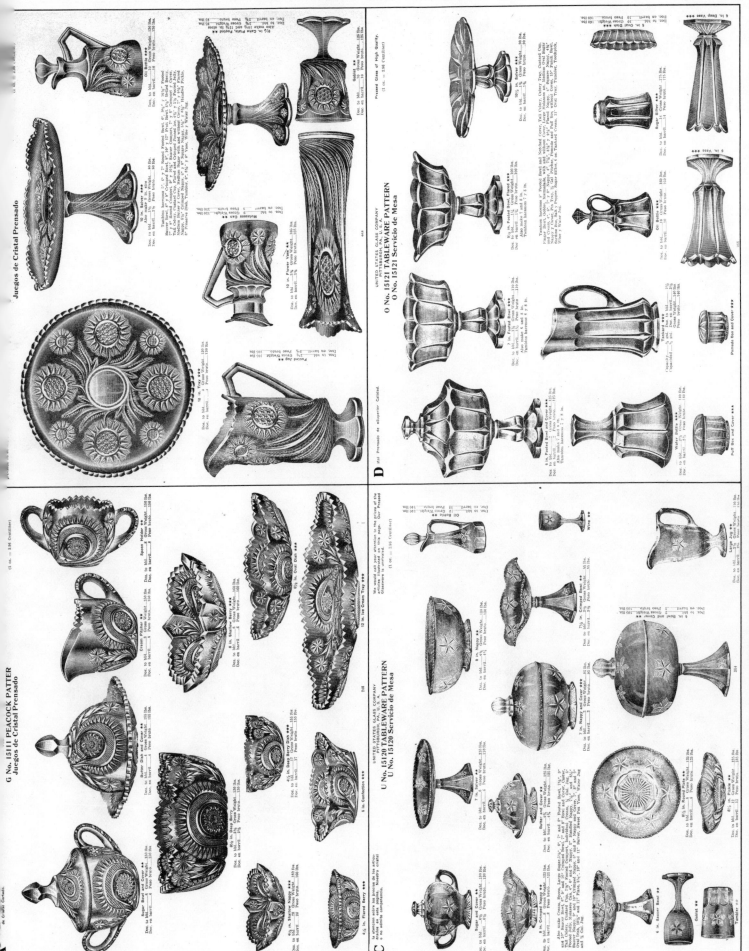

(Plate A) Assortment of *U.S. Peacock* pattern; **(Plate B)** Interesting items in *Solar* pattern; **(Plate C)** Assortment of *Starglow* pattern, not to be confused with the similar "Cut Sunburst" pattern which has eight-pointed stars; **(Plate D)** A number of pieces of *Portland* pattern.

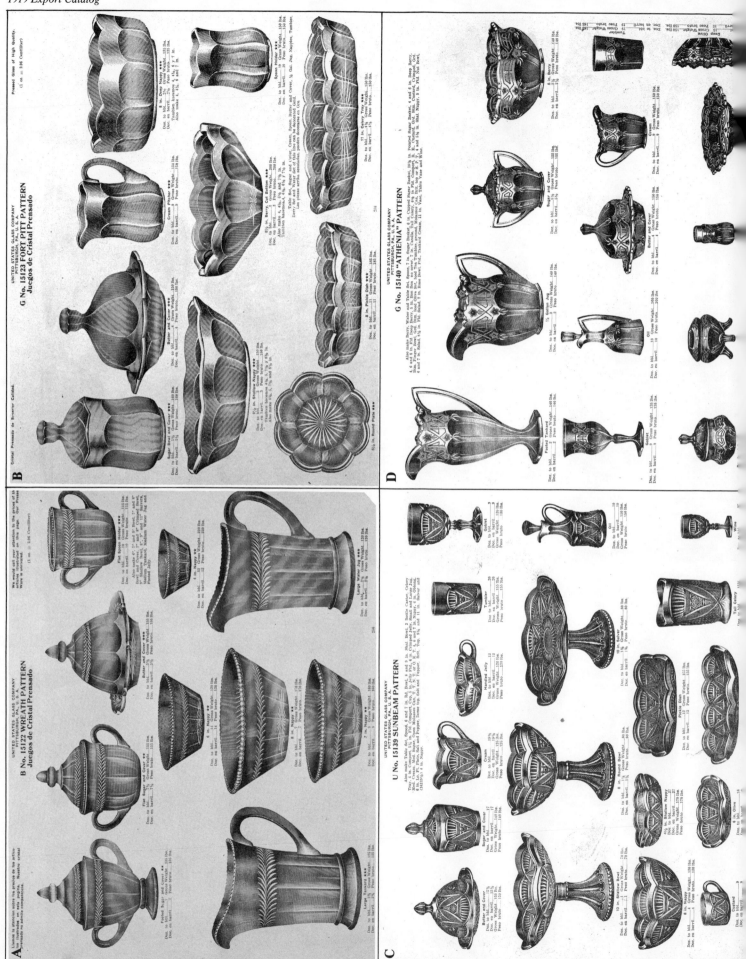

(Plate A) Assortment of *Feather Band* pattern, orig. called "Wreath"; (Plate B) Assortment of *Fort Pitt* pattern; (Plate C) Wide varietry of *Twin Stowshoes* pattern, originally called *Sunbeam* by U.S.G.C.; (Plate D) Assortment of *Panelled 44* pattern, originally called "Athenia".

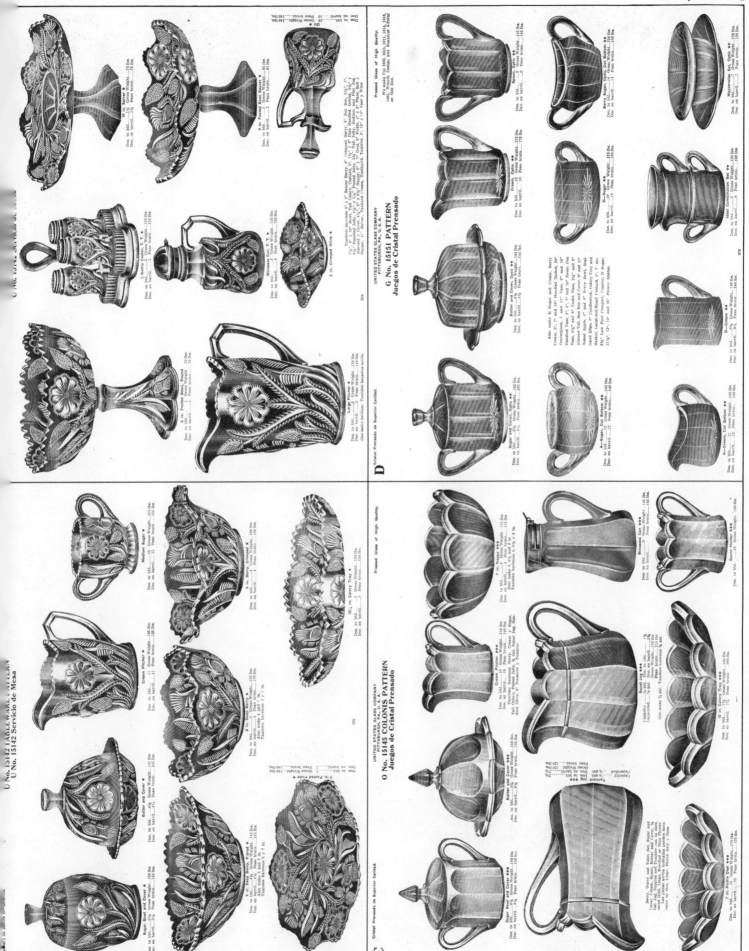

(Plate A & B) Wide assortment of *Field Thistle* pattern; **(Plate C)** Assortment of *Colonis* pattern; **(Plate D)** Setting of the simple *Pompeian* pattern.

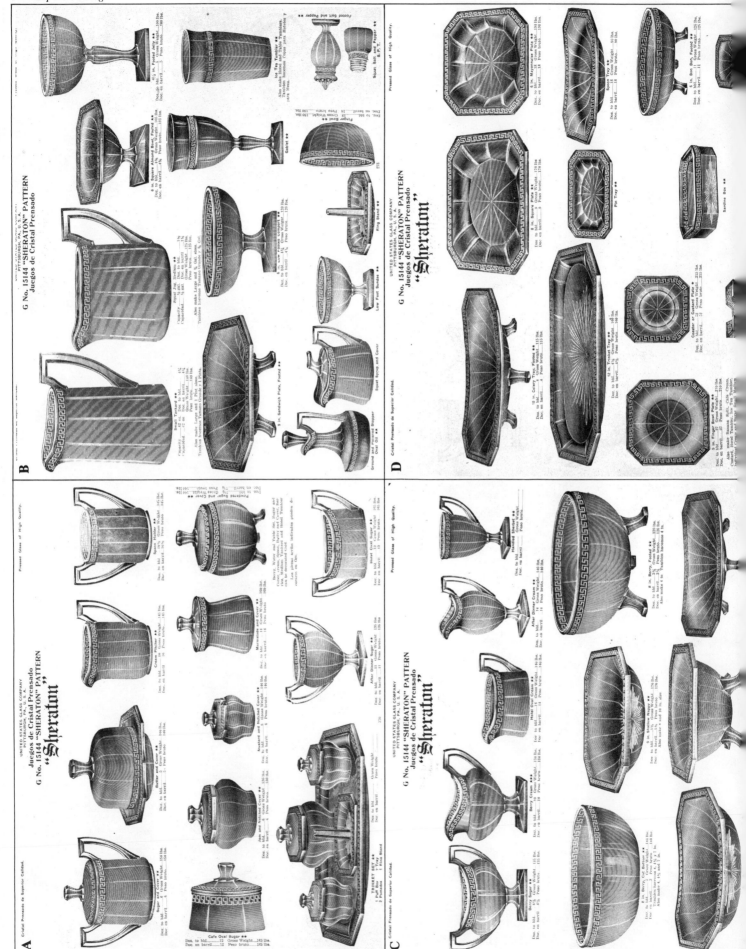

(Plates A—D) Wide assortment of *U.S. Sheraton* pattern; also made in lamps.

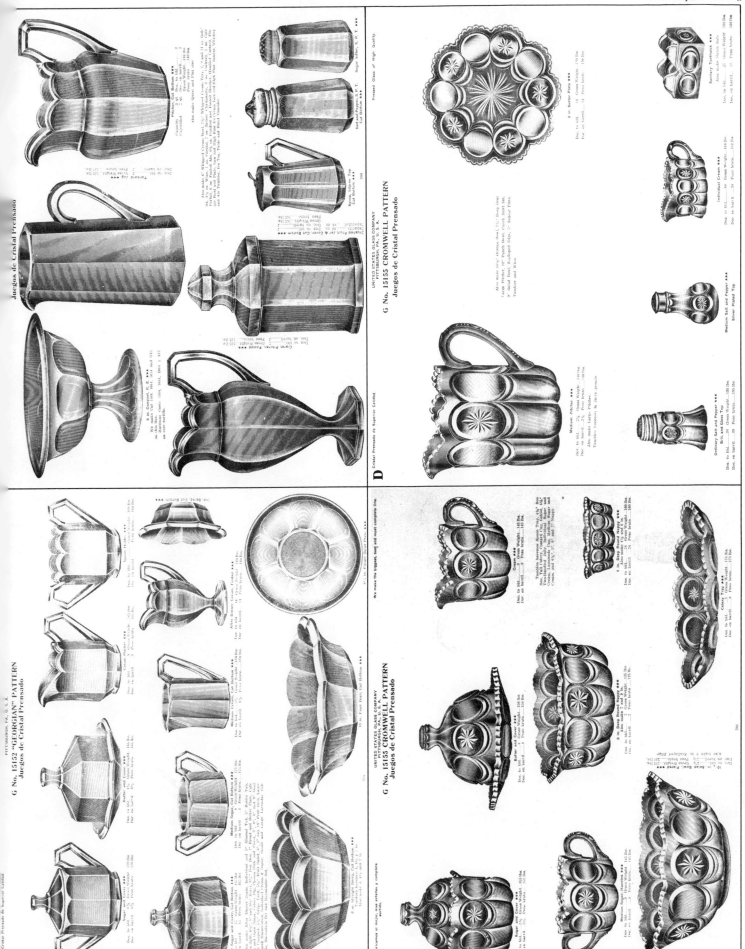

G No. 15152 "GEORGIAN" PATTERN
Juegos de Cristal Prensado

UNITED STATES GLASS COMPANY
PITTSBURGH, PA., U.S.A.
G No. 15155 CROMWELL PATTERN
Juegos de Cristal Prensado

UNITED STATES GLASS COMPANY
PITTSBURGH, PA., U.S.A.
G No. 15155 CROMWELL PATTERN
Juegos de Cristal Prensado

(**Plate A & B**) Assortment of *U.S. Georgian* pattern, not to be confused with the *Georgia* state pattern; (**Plates C & D**) Assortment of *Cromwell* pattern, also known as *Knobby Bulls Eye.*

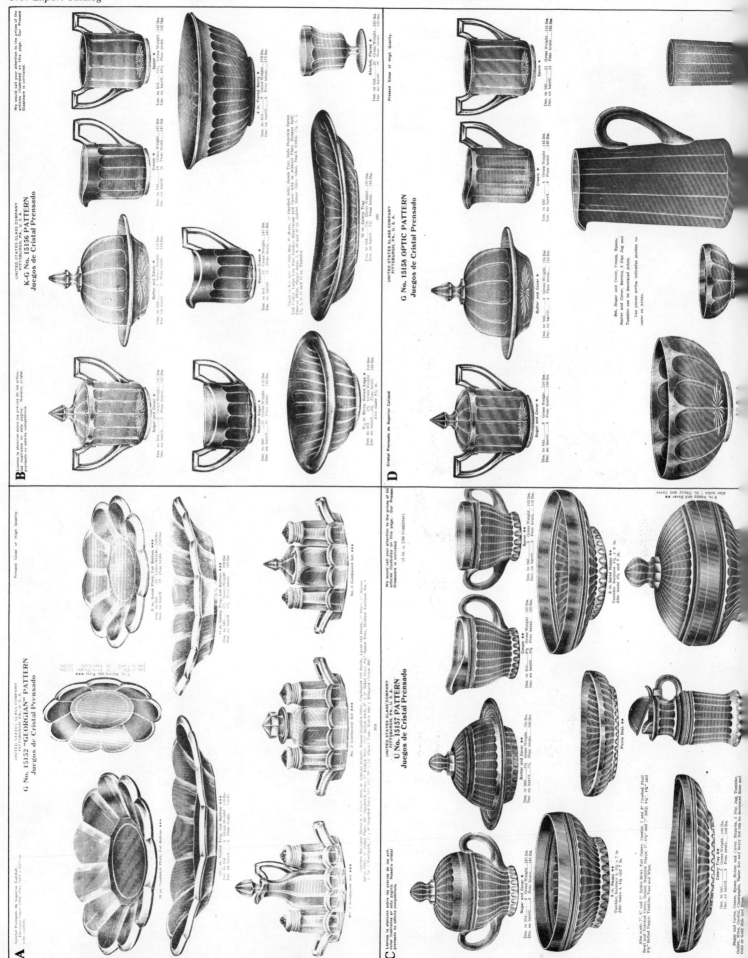

(Plate A) More items in the *U.S. Georgian* pattern; **(Plate B)** Assortment of pieces in the *Alpha* pattern; **(Plate C)** Assortment of *Beta* pattern; **(Plate D)** Assortment of *U.S. Optic* pattern, almost identical to the *Alpha* pattern, except for differences in creamer, bowls, and weight of other items.

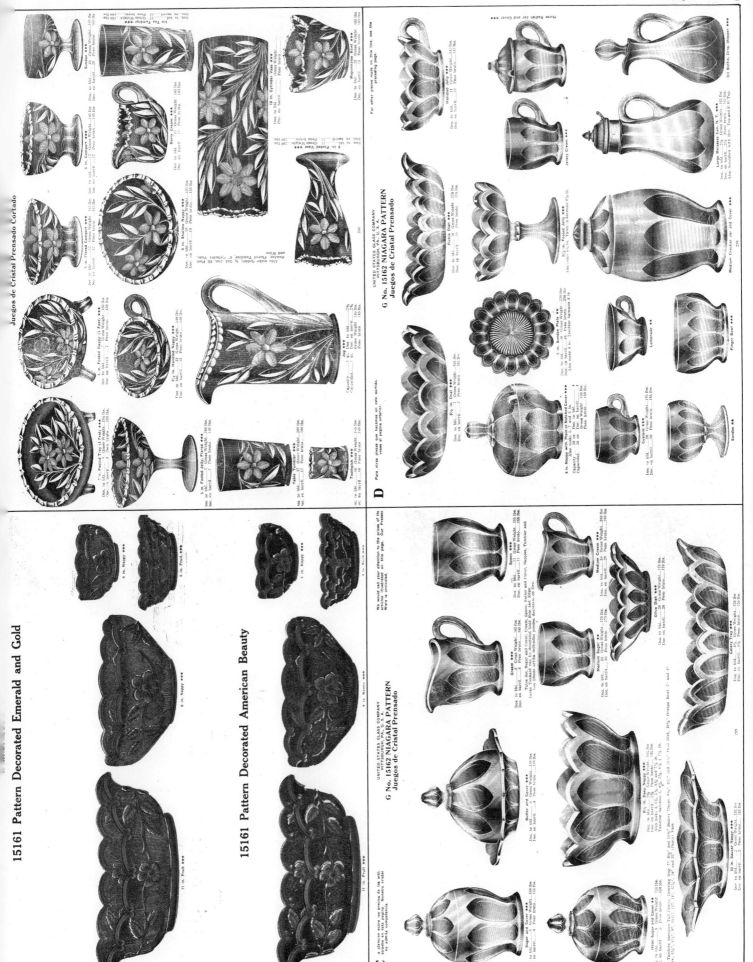

(Plate A) Assortment of bowls in *Panelled Dogwood;* **(Plate B)** Assortment of *Floricut* pattern; **(Plates C & D)** Wide variety of items in *Niagara* pattern.

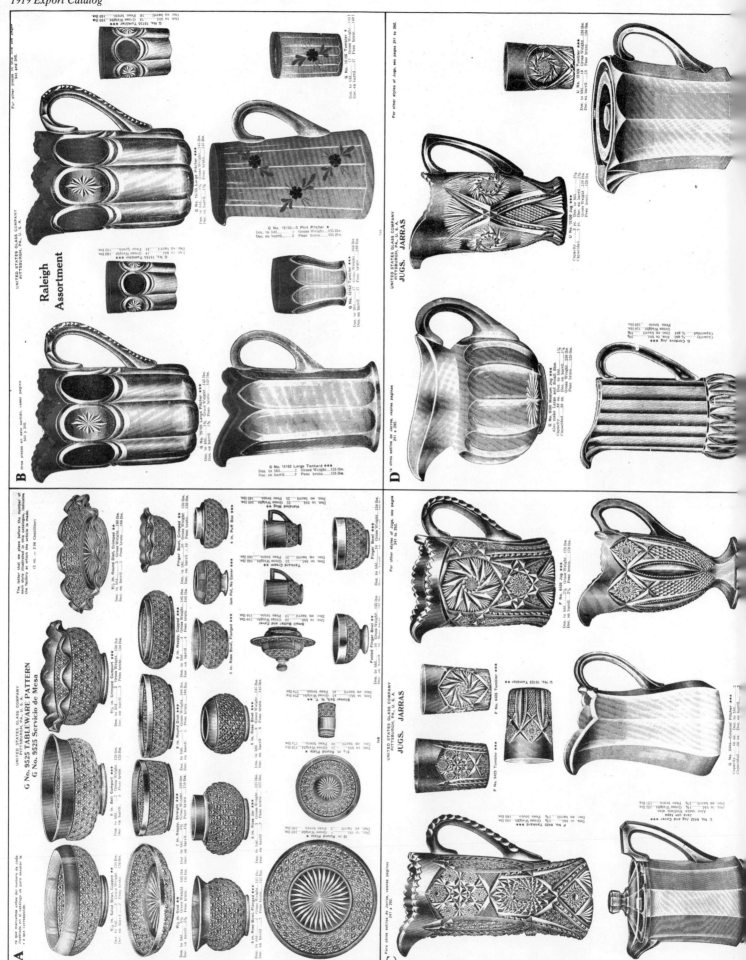

(Plate A) Assortment of *Lacy Daisy* pattern; **(Plate B)** Assortment of decorated water pitchers, called "Raleigh" for ordering identification only; **(Plate C & D)** Assorted pitchers and tumblers, including *Stellar, Cordova* and *Diamond Whirl.*

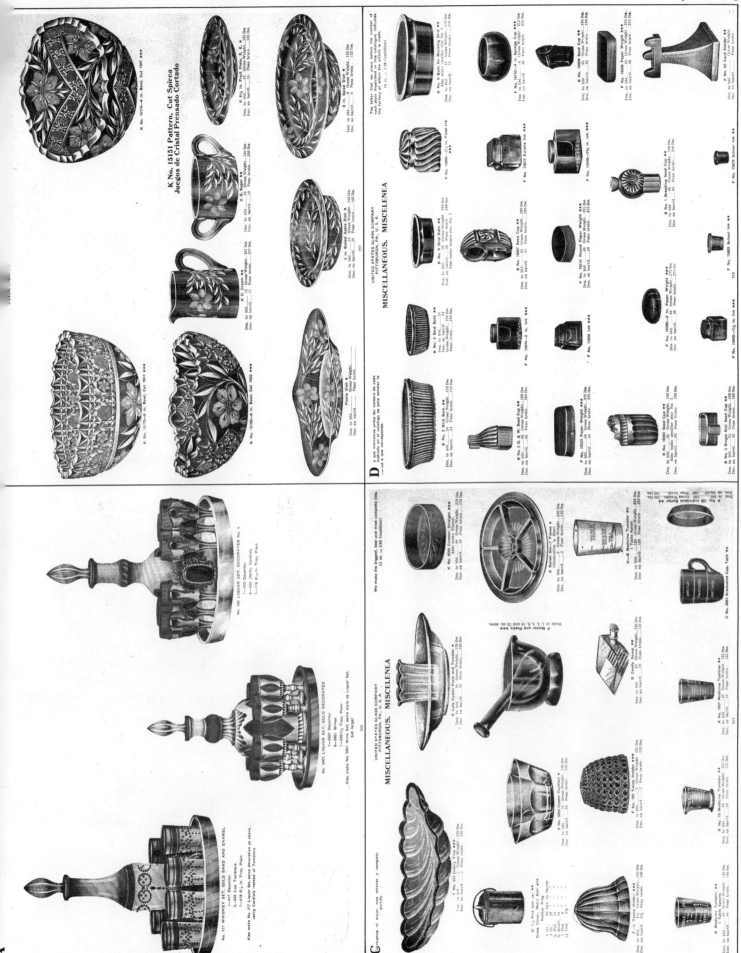

(Plate A) Assorted Liquer and whiskey sets, including late *Mirror & Fan* and *Pendant*; **(Plate B – D)** Miscellaneous whimseys.

No. 15053 4-inch Nappy, Notched Cover.

No. 15085 4-inch Nappy.

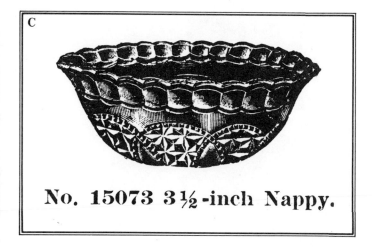

No. 15073 3½-inch Nappy.

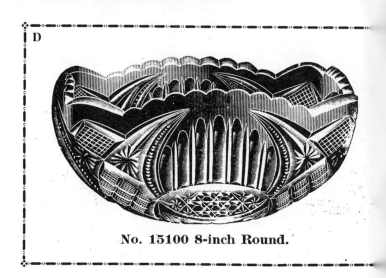

No. 15100 8-inch Round.

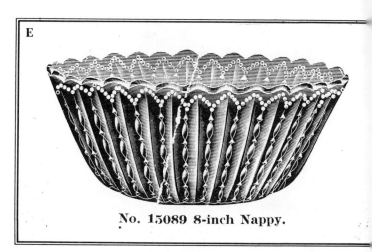

No. 15089 8-inch Nappy.

No. 1901 4-in Nappy, Square

No. 15141 Custard.

(**Figure A**) Louisiana covered nappy; (**Figure B**) Beaded Swirl with Disc nappy; (**Figure C**) Oregon (state) tiny nappy; (**Figure D**) Gloved Hand bowl, sometimes called "Coat of Arms"; (**Figure E**) Serrated Panels bowl; (**Figure F**) Diamond & Sunburst, Variant pattern square nappy; (**Figure G**) Flower with Cane custard cup.

United States Glass Co.

Mexican - South American Catalogue

1915

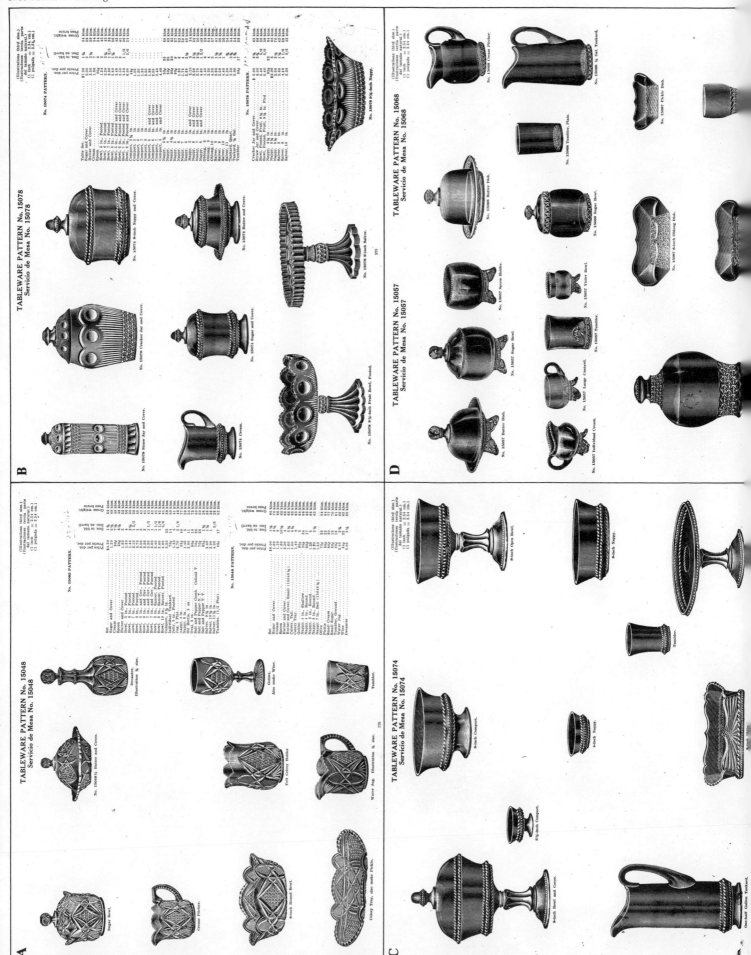

(Plate A) Assortment of *Pennsylvania* pattern; **(Plate B)** Assortment of items in *Manhattan* and *Washington* patterns; **(Plate C)** More pieces of *Washington* pattern; **(Plate D)** Variety of pieces in *Colorado* (15057), *Connecticut* (15068) and *Frazier* (15087) patterns.

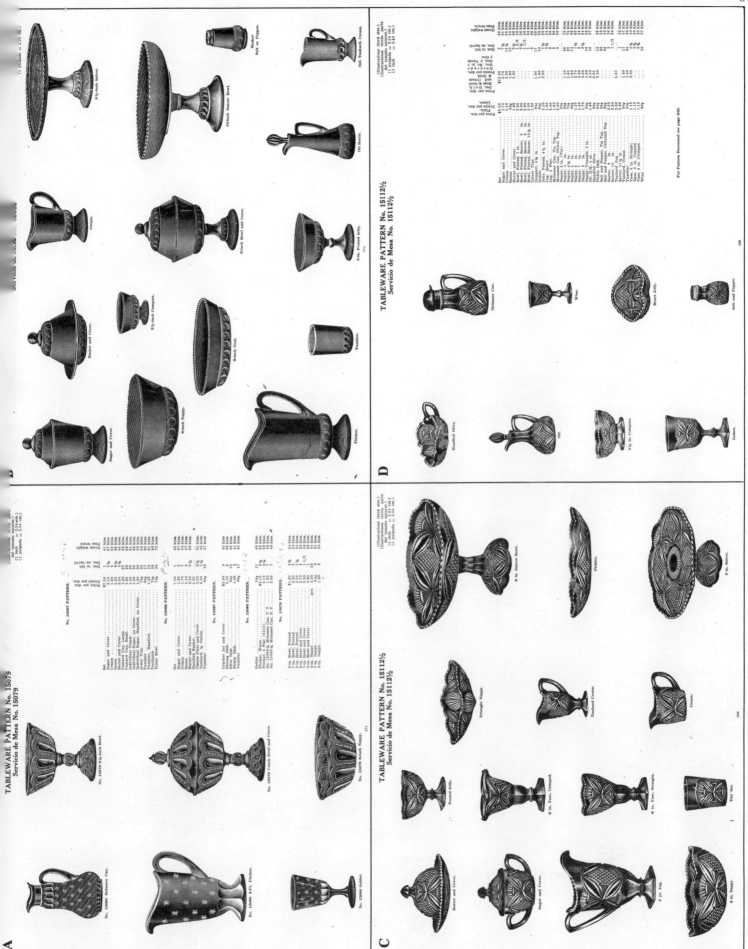

(Plate A) Pieces of *Utah* (15080) and *Wisconsin* (15079) patterns; **(Plate B)** Assortment of *Carolina* pattern, originally made in 1903; **(Plate C & D)** Wide assortment of *Pattee Cross* pattern, including a tankard-shape creamer which also served as a toy water pitcher to a child's water set.

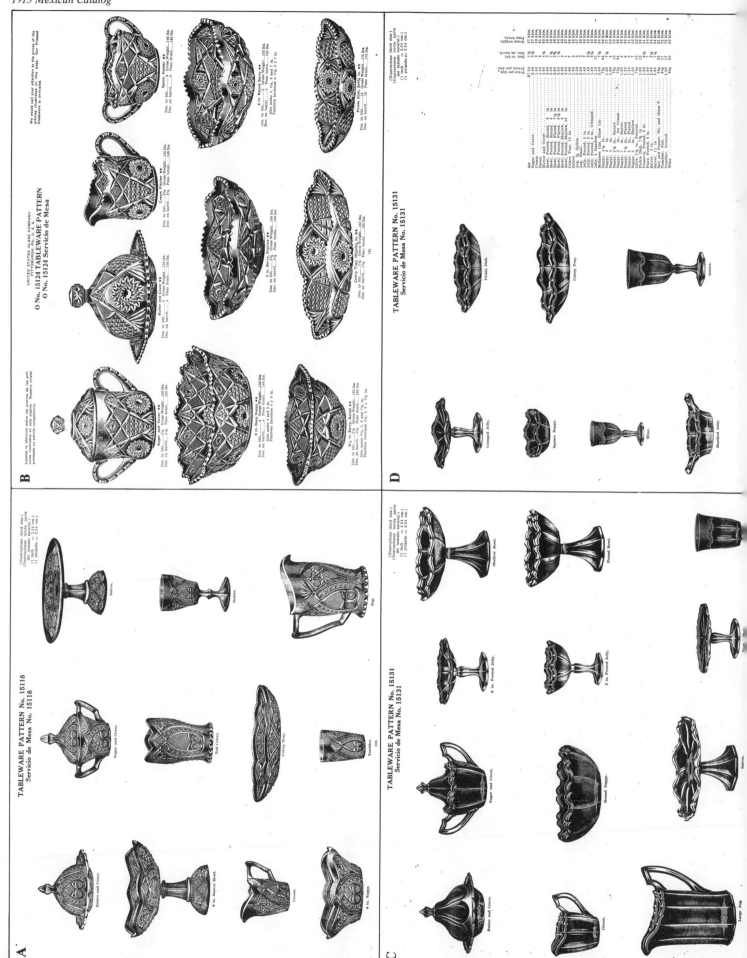

(Plate A) Assortment of *Cane Horseshoe* pattern; (Plate B) Assortment of imitation-cut pattern which I have named *Omnibus;* (Plate C & D) Wide assortment of *Evangeline* pattern.

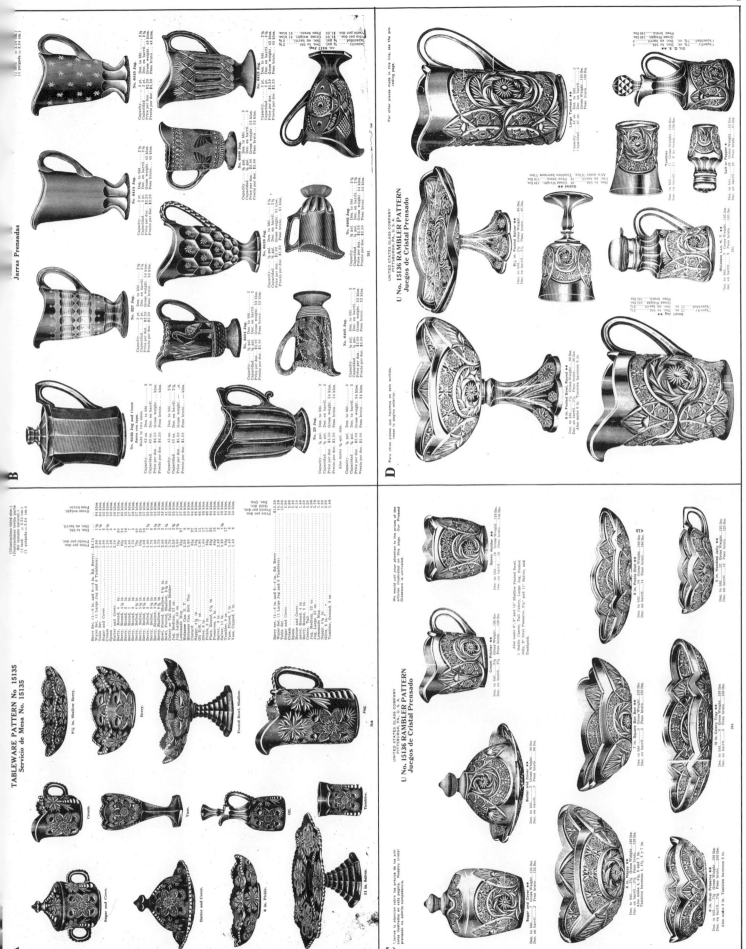

(Plate A) Assortment of *Snowflower* pattern; **(Plate B)** Variety of water pitchers available, including *Utah*, *Butterfly* and the popular *Aquarium*; **(Plate C & D)** Assortment of *Rambler* pattern.

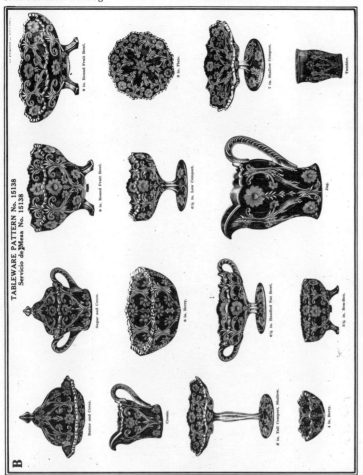

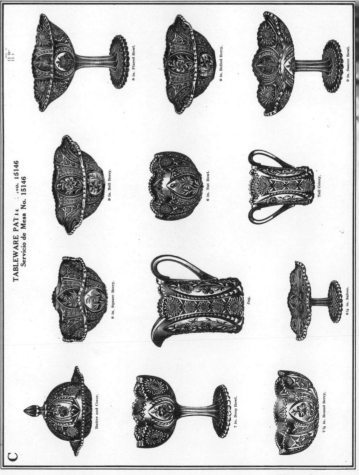

(Plate A) Assortment of *Intaglio Daisy* pattern; **(Plate B)** Assortment of *Two Flower* pattern, previously unlisted; **(Plate C)** Assortment of *Panelled Sunburst & Daisy* pattern, previously unlisted; **(Plate D)** Assortment of *Flower and Diamond* pattern, also previously unlisted.

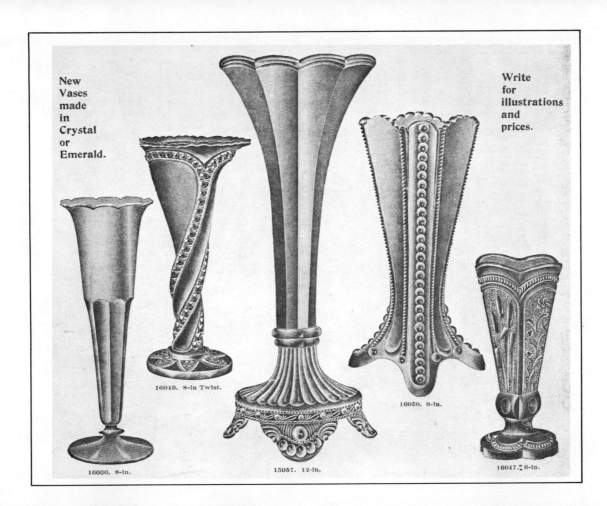

New Vases made in Crystal or Emerald.

Write for illustrations and prices.

16049. 8-In Twist.

16050. 9-In.

16080. 8-In.

15057. 12-In.

16047. 6-In.

Miscellaneous Ad & Catalogue Reprints

16045. 6-In.

16048. 6-In.

16046. 6-In.

UNITED STATES GLASS CO.
PITTSBURG, PA.

16046. 7½-In.

16049. 8-In.

BRANCH OFFICES:

NEW YORK: 29 Murray Street.
PHILADELPHIA: N. E. cor. 9th and Market Sts.
BALTIMORE: 16 So. Charles Street.

BOSTON: 146 Franklin Street.
CHICAGO: Room 109 Atlas Block.
SAN FRANCISCO: 18 Sutter Street.

May, 1898, advertisement featuring a number of vases made by U.S. Glass.

1896 ads featuring "Superior" (top) and "Leafy Scroll" (bottom) patterns.

172

Florida Pattern.

Jan. 1898 ad featuring the "Florida" pattern, which incorrectly includes a "Louisiana" pattern butter dish.

SAMPLES OF ➤ TWO OF OUR TEN NEW LINES

......OUR

Texas,

......OR

No. 15067 Pattern

Made also with

Rose Decoration

......OUR

Iowa,

......OR

No. 15069 Pattern

Made also in

Crystal, Crystal with Rose Decoration, and Crystal with Gold Decoration.

BE SURE to see all of our new patterns before ordering. If you cannot visit us—write.

UNITED STATES GLASS COMPANY
PITTSBURGH, PA., U.S.A.

1900 ad featuring "Texas" and "Iowa" states patterns.

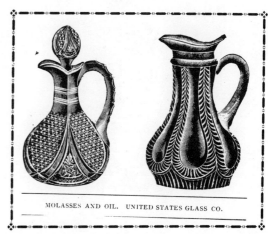

MOLASSES AND OIL. UNITED STATES GLASS CO.

Feb. 1901 ad featuring "Massachusetts" cruet and "Loop Herringbone" syrup.

The illustrations show the set in our 15103 Stellar Pattern made in Plain Crystal also with a very attractive decoration.

Circa 1907 ad featuring #15103 "Stellar" pattern.

No. 15101 Tankard with 6 Tumblers to match makes a very attractive, inexpensive Water Set.

Circa 1907 ad showing a #15101 "Buzz-Star" water pitcher.

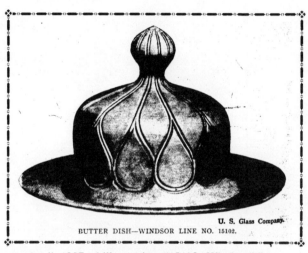

BUTTER DISH—WINDSOR LINE NO. 15102.

April, 1907 ad illustrating #15102 "Windsor" line.

May, 1916 ad illustrating their "Rubenia Cut Flowers" trinket set, from the English "Pottery Gazette".

United States Glass Company

PITTSBURGH, PA.
THE WORLD'S ONE BIG GLASS CONCERN

3989 COLONIAL PATTERN

Straw Jar.   Crushed Fruit Bowl with Ledge.   High Foot Sundae.

Have you received our 16 page catalogue illustrating our most recent productions of

Beautiful Colonial Patterns for High Class Hotel, Bar and Soda Fountain Trade

If not, a postal card request will bring it to you post haste together with prices.

SAMPLES ARE NOW ON EXHIBITION AT OUR VARIOUS SHOWROOMS, TOGETHER WITH MORE THAN TWENTY THOUSAND DIFFERENT ARTICLES OF GLASSWARE COMPRISING Pressed Tableware, Lead Blown Stemware, Lead Blown Tumblers, Show Jars, Soda Fountain Supplies, Decorated Ware (gold etched, enameled, engraved and sand blast), Lamps plain and decorated. Pressed Stemware, Pressed Tumblers, Pressed Beer Mugs, Confectioners' Supplies, Druggists' Ware, Packers' Ware, Novelties, Photographers' Goods, Wine Sets, FANCY CUT GOODS, Etc. Separate catalogues of the different branches of our business furnished on request.

THE TRADE IS CORDIALLY INVITED TO INSPECT SAMPLES AT THE
GENERAL OFFICES AND SHOW ROOMS, South Ninth and Bingham Streets, Pittsburgh, Pa.

OR AT THE FOLLOWING BRANCH SHOW-ROOMS

NEW YORK, 29 Murray Street
BOSTON, 127 Federal St., Arco Building
PHILADELPHIA, Ninth and Market Sts.
MEXICO CITY, 2 A de Platernos No. 9
SIDNEY, N. S. W., Commerce Building, Martin Lane

BALTIMORE, 110 Hopkins Place
ST. LOUIS, 627 Granite Bldg., 4th & Market Sts.
SAN FRANCISCO, 271 Stevenson Street

CHICAGO, 409 Atlas Block, 35 Randolph St.
DENVER, 1430 Arapahoe Street
SALT LAKE CITY, 127 East South Third St.
LONDON, 55 Farrington Street, E. C.
HAVANA, CUBA, 70 San Rafael Apartato 948

April, 1908 ad featuring the "3989 Colonial" pattern—not to be confused with the earlier #15047 "Colonial" line, better known today as "Plain Scalloped Panel".

September, 1905
GLASS AND POTTERY WORLD.

Crystal Rock Pattern
Made Plain and Decorated

PITCHER

TUMBLER

5½-IN. BERRY

10-IN. BERRY

United States Glass Co.

PITTSBURG, - PA.

New Patterns in Up-to-date Effects will be on Exhibition January 1st

20,000 DIFFERENT ARTICLES IN GLASSWARE

INCLUDING

Pressed Tableware, Lead Blown Stemware, Lead Blown Tumblers, Show Jars, Soda Fountain Supplies, Decorated Ware; Gold, Etched, Enameled, Engraved and Sand Blast Lamps, Plain and Decorated; Pressed Stemware, Pressed Tumblers, Pressed Beer Mugs, Confectioners' Supplies, Druggists' Ware, Packers' Ware, Novelties, Photographers' Goods, Wine Sets, FANCY CUT GOODS, etc., etc., etc.

BRANCH SHOWROOMS

NEW YORK, - - - 29 Murray Street
BOSTON, - - - 144 High Street
PHILADELPHIA, - 9th and Market Streets
BALTIMORE, - - 110 Hopkins Place
CHICAGO, - - - 409 Atlas Block
SAN FRANCISCO, - 18 Sutter Street
ST. LOUIS, - - - 411 Granite Building
4th and Market Streets

Dec., 1905 ad featuring their "Crystal Rock" pattern.

United States Glass Company

PITTSBURG, PA.

Cut Sunburst Pattern

SUNBURST SUGAR

SUNBURST CREAM

Our Celebrated Lead Blown Cut Sunburst Pattern contains over Sixty different articles in large variety—Pitchers, Tumblers, Berry Sets, Stemware, Water Bottles, Decanters, Finger Bowls, Custard Cups, Sundaes, Cruet and Oil Bottles, Etc.

We have by far the most complete and popular design of this character on the market; its beautiful brilliancy attracts the admiration at first glance of lovers of artistically cut glassware.

Prices and Illustrations on request.

Sept., 1908 ad illustrating their "Cut Sunburst" pattern.

175

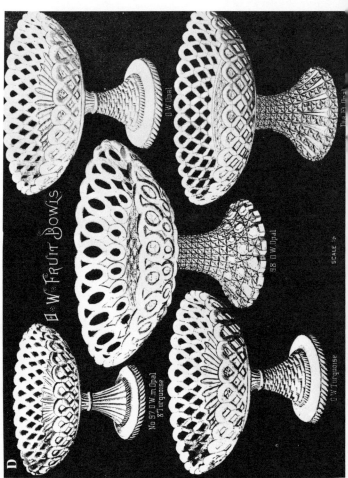

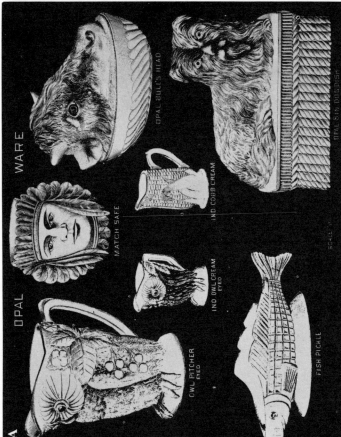

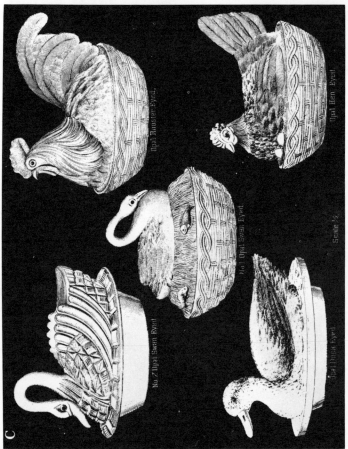

Miscellaneous items shown in the 1891 Factory C catalogue: (**Plate A**) Variety of opal ware, including an *Owl Pitcher* and creamer, two rare animal-covered dishes, etc.; (**Plate B**) Assorted lattice-edge bowls and plates and religious candlestick; (**Plate C**) A variety of fowl-covered dishes; (**Plate D**) Assorted lattice-edge fruit compotes.

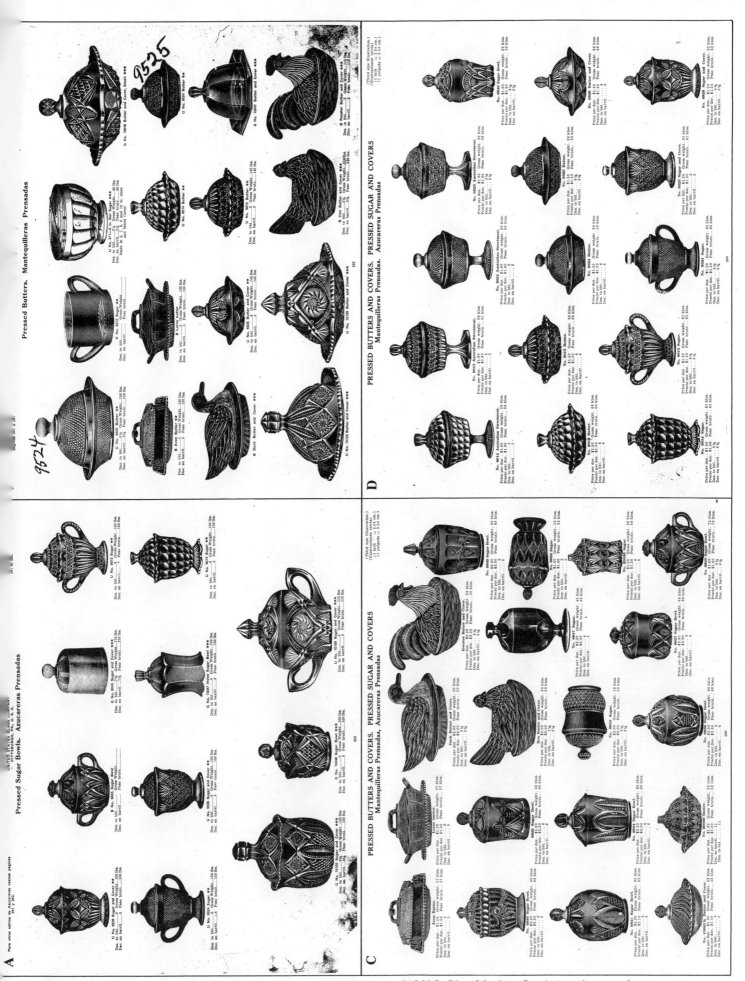

(Plates A—D) Assorted butters, sugar bowls, compotes, etc., shown in 1915 U.S. Glass Mexican-South American catalogue—note the items in *Stellar* (15103), *Diamond Whirl* (15109), and *Beaded Swirl and Disc* (15085).

UNITED STATES GLASS COMPANY

World's Largest Makers of Household Glassware.

PITTSBURGH, PA.

Sales Offices in All Principal Cities.

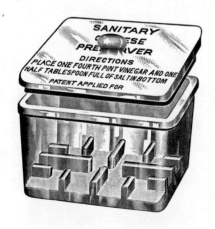     

Assorted reprints from advertising woodcuts found at Tiffin, Ohio factory—these items date circa 1930-1935.

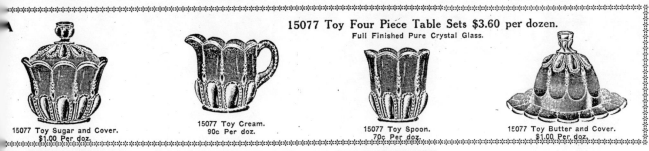

A

15077 Toy Four Piece Table Sets $3.60 per dozen.
Full Finished Pure Crystal Glass.

15077 Toy Sugar and Cover.
$1.00 Per doz.

15077 Toy Cream.
90c Per doz.

15077 Toy Spoon.
70c Per doz.

15077 Toy Butter and Cover.
$1.00 Per doz.

B

15048 Toy Sugar

15048 Toy Cream

15048 Toy Spoon

15048 Toy Butter

No. 15048 Toy Table Set
Price per dozen $3.00

Also make Gold Decorated $6.50 per dozen

C

THE UNITED STATES GLASS CO., PITTSBURG, PA.

D

B No. 9945 Night Lamp Complete ★★★
Doz. to bbl..............8   Gross Weight... 100 lbs.
Doc. en barril 8   Peso bruto....... 100 lbs.

E

No. 15125—Straw Jar and Cover
2 dozen in barrel. Price per dozen $8.00

F

Nº 175 TOY CUP & SAUCER.

G

PLANTERS

PLANTERS

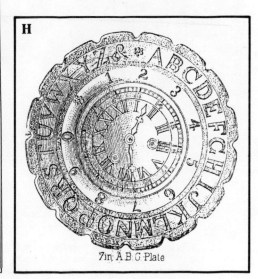

H

7 in. A B C Plate

(**Figure A**) Toy table set in *Michigan* pattern, circa 1908; (**Figure B**) Toy table set in *Pennsylvania* pattern; (**Figure C**) *Panama* pattern water pitcher, circa 1904; (**Figure D**) *U.S. Sheraton* night lamp, circa 1915; (**Figure E**) Straw jar in *Intaglio Sunflower* pattern, circa 1911; (**Figure F**) *Cat on a Cushion* toy cup and saucer, Factory F, circa 1891; (**Figure G**) *Planters Peanut* covered jar, lifted from woodcuts found at Tiffin factory site (circa 1930); (**Figure H**) *Clock* patterned 7" ABC plate, Factory F, circa 1891.

Venetian Wine Set, Crystal.

Parisian Wine Set.

No. 5601 Wine Set.

National Bread Plate.

7 IN. COMPORT BELLED. CONNECTICUT PATTERN.   5½ IN. FOOTED JELLY. CONNECTICUT PATTERN.

8 IN. COMPORT BELLED. CONNECTICUT PATTERN.

(Figure A-C) Assorted wine sets appearing in 1915 Mexican catalogue, including Figure B *Tiny Finecut* pattern, which was also made much earlier; (Figure D) Reprint from Factory E, circa 1891, which includes *Cube and Block* water pitcher; (Figure E) Assorted items from 1900 ad featuring the **Iowa** and **Connecticut** patterns; (Figure F) Bread plate from 1891 Factory F catalogue—this plate is very rare today; (Figure G) Assorted items from 1900 ad featuring the *Connecticut* pattern.

(Continued from page 11)

of the factories that were not in operation or where production costs were too high. Factory "L" was sold to Park Bros. Company, Ltd. They also were wanting to sell Factories E, H, M, N, O, and J, as well as the land upon which Factory "C" formerly stood before the fire.

At the time of consolidation in 1891, the company's records showed a stock of glassware on hand amounting to $715,000. Much of this was found to be old, discontinued stock. Owing to the general depression of all trades, and the policy to carry in stock only those items that were of staple character, it was not deemed advisable to add to this large stock. It was decided to market the glassware on hand and change the item of manufactured goods to cash in the bank. By January 1, 1894, they had sold over $400,000 of this stock at full list price.

At Glassport, Pa., Monongahela Avenue was being grated, the new electric street railway was being constructed, and a handsome passenger station of Roman brick and cut stone was being erected. Two new fifteen pot furnaces were being completed at the glass works, together with the accompanying buildings. It was intended that this new plant was to be the most modern, up-to-date glassware manufacturing plant in the U.S.A. It was to have the newest and most productive machinery for saving labor in the manufacture of glassware. Steam power presses were to be utilized and the glassware was to be finished by machinery whenever possible.

It was also the policy of the company to encourage new glassware designs and labor saving machinery from its employees. Mr. William H. Barr, an employee of Factory "R" at Tiffin Ohio, was issued a patent in 1894 for finishing tumblers and glassware. He offered to sell these to the United States Glass Co. for $7,500, but the management thought this was too much to pay, especially when they were still in the throes of a strike. He sold the patents to the Rochester Tumbler Co. for an undisclosed amount. Even so, the company used this and many other inventions of its employees which were to be introduced with beneficial results into nearly all departments of the company.

The organizers of the United States Glass Co. brought into the firm a number of patents from which the company would receive royalties for a number of years. Licenses were issued to other glassware manufacturers and thinking that the U.S.G.C. would be too preoccupied with strike difficulties, simply forgot to pay for them. One party was issued licenses for fifteen of the company's patented machines, and no effort was expended to pay a single dollar for their use until such time as it became apparent to them that the U.S.G.C. intended to take steps to protect its interests. It was necessary to enter suits against some of these in order to collect. Others were settled amicably.

On March 18, 1895, President Ralph Baggaley resigned after serving about one and one-half years. His job of reorganization having been completed, Mr. Daniel Ripley was once again elected to the presidency at a time when the company was still on strike with the union glass workers.

One of Mr. D. C. Ripley's first official duties was to start rehiring some of his old employees whose skill in producing quality glassware was well known but had been following other occupations since the big strike. These men were being employed again now in order to bring the quality of the glassware manufactured up to its old rating. In dealing with Mr. Ripley, the men felt they had one man who was sympathetic with the traditions of the glass trade, and who was able to intelligently discuss issues connected with it.

The cut glass trade at this time was beginning to work towards non-union factories and outside independent shops. Union rules and restrictions drove this fine art entirely out of the union control. It was impossible for union factories to successfully compete with non-union cutting shops using imported blanks, with the one exception of Libbey at Toledo. The number of independent shops using imported blanks, rough unfinished glass purchased at a low rate of duty, had more than tripled. In this country, the major manufacturers of cut glass had decreased to three.

In February, 1896, the periodical "China, Glass & Lamps" noted the following:

> *"The Glassport works of the United States Glass Co. which has been operating one 15 pot furnace for the past year, has been enjoying such a large run on their new patterns since the first of the year, that the second furnace will be put into operation in order to satisfy the demand."*

Two months later, the following was also reported:

> *"The United States Glass Co. is doing a fine business, the present year having thus far shown a gain of more than 50% over last year. Their general line of fine lead blown bar goods, stemware, etched and decorated in the variety of which they exceed all competitors, are having a large and steady increasing sale."*

Concerning sales, the year 1896 was one of the best for the U.S.G.C., exceeding that of any previous year since their consolidation. They were gradually increasing their output even more. An additional furnace was being rebuilt at Tiffin, Ohio to meet this output. In 1896 the company placed seven new sets of tableware on the market, embracing between 450 and 500 separate articles at a cost of over $50,000 for tooling.

The U.S.G.C. during this time also brought out a new all-glass lamp with a threaded ferrule blown into the bowl. This improvement enabled closer packing of the bowls and feet, which were fitted together by the customer at the point of destination.

During the Presidential campaign of 1896, the U.S.G.C. brought out tumblers, decorated with white enameled etched portraits of the principal candidates, McKinley & Hobart and Bryan & Sewall. For the campaign of 1900 a number of tumblers and goblets was also produced. Busts of McKinley and Roosevelt were shown side by side, surmounted by the American Eagle, and heads of Bryan and Stevenson appear together. Other designs were issued with McKinley or Bryan on one side and a crowing rooster on the other. There were also large milk glass plates bearing black printing or white relief portraits of the nominees. All of these are avidly hunted by collectors today.

It was not until Jan. 1, 1897 that the officers of the American Flint Glass Workers Union publicly admitted defeat in the fight with the United States Glass Co.

"From this time on, it will be no longer possible to say boastfully, that the great A.F.G.W.U. has ever been defeated, for the record now shows that no American labor union ever suffered a more humiliating defeat than their own deligates and officers have acknowledged during the past week. Not only have they been forced to consent to a removal of the move limit on jellies and common tumblers, but the turn has been encreased from 4½ to 4¾ hours, while a voluntary reduction of from two to eight percent has been accepted by pressers, finishers and gatherers."

"This is practically conceding everything demanded of the flint workers union by the United States Glass Co. three and a half years ago, except withdrawal from the union, and as one of the flints said to the writer: "There is nothing whatever in the strike that we can look back upon with any satisfaction. We have lost three and a half years work, and gained nothing. We have underfed and underdressed our families, physically and intellectually starved our children, nearly every one of us has gone desperately into debt, and many of us have sacrificed nearly four years wages at a time of life when we have no hope of ever making it up again, and here we are, after all these years, forced to swallow the bitterest pill ever offered a lot of strikers in the world."

As strong and frank as this language is, it fails to present the whole picture. The strike against the United States Glass Co. proved a most disastrous one to the flint workers union. As far as Pittsburgh was concerned, several glass factories were built as a direct result of the strike, which would otherwise not have been built. The factory of George Duncan's Sons & Co., Washington, Pa., Bryce Bros., Mount Pleasant, Pa., and the A. H. Heisey & Co., Newark, Ohio all took workmen and their families out of Pittsburgh. Bryce Bros. and Rochester Tumbler Co. both had become non-union, since it was well known that these companies, composed of members of some of the oldest glass manufacturing families in the city, were forced to break away from union control. They found it impossible to compete with punch tumblers and blown ware factories enjoying unlimited production, unhampered by the restrictions of union rules and petty interferences of the factory committees. It was futile for even the most powerful flint glass workers union to set themselves against improved machinery, increased efficiency of labor and the reduction of the cost of production. Basically, the American Flint Glass Workers Union lacked the power to hold back permanently the industrial development of this country.

In July of 1897, the United States Glass Co. transferred twenty three of its presses from the Tiffin, Ohio plant to the Gas City plant because it controlled cheaper, and had a more abundant supply of natural gas. The first class workmen were also sent to Gas City, while the strikers were still loafing about town, wondering when they would be going back to work.

It was at this time, the different plants were being changed to manufacture only certain types of glass. The Tiffin, Ohio plant would eventually become a blown ware factory, making lead-blown tumblers, stemware, and fancy cut glass. Gas City, Indiana became a pressed ware factory for tumblers, beer mugs, jellies and tablewares, of which whole train loads would be shipped to their customers.

Outbreak of hostilities with Spain was brought on by the sinking of the American battleship MAINE in Havana harbor on February 15, 1898. The American public sentiment accused Spanish agents and war became inevitable. We mention this in order to fix the period in which the States patterns were produced. Prior to this outbreak with Spain, the States patterns Pennsylvania, Maryland, Ohio, Kentucky and Illinois were being produced in crystal with gold, and emerald with gold decoration. After this time, Dewey blue with gold was added to honor Admiral Dewey and the battle of Manila Bay.

The States patterns produced in Dewey blue with gold were not popular and the production in this color was short lived. This is why blue pieces in any of the States patterns are rare today and difficult to find.

To show the versatility of the U.S.G.C., we note two paragraphs in the March and May issues of "Glass & Pottery World," 1898:

"The United States Glass Co. has done a remarkably good trade the past month. The Massachusetts, Minnesota and Colorado patterns, the last named in emerald green, as well as cyrstal, have been the leaders. In their other departments, such as tumblers, steinware, druggist and stationers goods, cut glass and a variety of sundries, they have been quite busy. The United States Glass Co. factory at Glassport, Pa. is working on a very large rush contract for the government. The order is for deck globes, signal light glasses and reflectors for war vessels."

By July of 1898, the company was exhibiting 218 different styles and decorations of glass lamps, with their #9851 in emerald green one of their better sellers. The States patterns, Colorado, Massachusetts and Minnesota were first produced in 1898, of which a four piece table set was advertised for the first time in the January, 1898 issue of "Glass and Pottery World." These were worthy successors to the Ohio, Indiana, Kentucky, Maryland and Illinois patterns introduced in 1897. Ten new novelty vases in crystal and emerald, with gold decorations, were also brought out in 1898. Business was remarkably good, enough to keep eight of the United States Glass Co. factories working two shifts without accumulating any pieces for stock; all being shipped directly to the customer.

In January 1899, the blown and pressed glass tableware business was at a depressed state. The concerned stockholders of the United States Glass Co. held a number of meetings pertaining to this situation and gave permission to President Daniel C. Ripley to enter into the formation of the National Glass Co. The 12 plants of the company were appraised in preparation for the consolidation. When it became known to the other prospective incorporators that the Glassport, Pa. property of the U.S.G.C. was appraised at over a million dollars alone, they objected, and asked the company to separate this property from the others. Their objection was not that the amount of appraisal was not correct, but the one million dollars would have equaled a large portion of the capital stock, thus giving the U.S.G.C. control. As this was one of the most modern glassware plants in the United States at the time, the U.S.G.C. decided it would be impractical to join and notified the others to go ahead with the consolidation of the National Glass Co. As a result of a meeting held during the week of September 4, 1899 in Pittsburgh, Pa., the following glassware manufacturers agreed to the condition of consolidation and the National Glass Company was formed:

> Rochester Tumbler Co., Rochester, Pa.
> McKee Brothers, Pittsburgh, Pa.
> Crystal Glass Co., Bridgeport, Ohio
> Indiana Goblet & Tumbler, Greentown, Ind.
> Model Flint Glass Co., Albany, Ind.
> Cumberland Glass Co., Cumberland, Md.
> Greensburg Glass Co., Greensburg, Pa.
> Riverside Glass Co., Wellsville, W. Va.
> Robinson Glass Co., Zanesville, Oh.
> Royal Glass Co., Marietta, Oh.
> Central Glass Co., Summitsville, Ind.

After the formation of this new conglomerate, it's President, H. C. Fry, and the President of the U.S.G.C., Daniel C. Ripley, worked very closely in controlling the prices of blown and pressed glass tableware in the United States. These two large corporations produced about 85% of glass tableware at the turn of the century.

By November, 1899, the following companies had also joined with the National Glass Company, making a total of nineteen factories:

> Northwood Company, Indiana, Pa.
> Keystone Tumbler Co., Rochester, Pa.
> Dalzell, Gilmore & Leighton Co., Findlay, O.
> Ohio Flint Glass Co., Lancaster, Oh.
> West Virginia Glass Co., Martin's Ferry, Oh.
> Canton Glass Co., Marion, Ind.
> Beatty-Brady Glass Co., Dunkirk, Ind.
> Fairmont Glass Co., Cumberland, Md.

U.S.G.C. sales for the year 1899 amounted to $1,297,651.96 or 4½% more than the previous year. The surplus earnings were $28,401.77, but no dividend was declared. In his circular to the stockholders, President Ripley blamed this on the fact that the general rise in prices had not reached the flint glass industry. However, he pointed out the success in enlarging the export trade of the company with large orders coming from South America, South Africa and Australia.

Effective January 1, 1900, the U.S.G.C. announced an advance in wages to its employees of 5% in Pittsburgh, and 6% in Tiffin, Ohio. Ever since the Beatty factory at Tiffin became part of the U.S.G.C., it had shown a higher percentage of profit, with fewer labor problems than any other plant.

The following States patterns were first produced in 1900; *Texas, Connecticut, Iowa,* and *New Jersey.*

A "Pineapple and Fan" pattern wine set was brought out also in 1900 which was in demand for many years to come. This set was produced in crystal with gold decoration and emerald green with gold decoration.

In the President's report to the stockholders in August of 1900. Mr. Ripley gave an encouraging report in which he intimated that the period of ruinous competition in prices had been effectively checked since the formation of the National Glass Co. Sales had increased more than 20% amounting to $1,568,177.68. Net profit was shown to be $85,993.91.

On September 6, 1900 Captain Joseph Anderson, Vice President and General Manager of the United States Glass Co. died at Lake Chautauqua. His death was unexpected, although he had been in poor health for a couple of years. The announcement was a great shock to his many friends. Captain Anderson was born in Pittsburgh, Pa. in 1840 and began his business life as a clerk. He made a name for himself as a volunteer in the Civil War and returned to take up his labors in the glass industry. He was General Manager of the O'Hara Glass Co. when it became a part of the United States Glass Co. He left a widow and one son, William M. Anderson, who was Assistant General Manager of the United States Glass Co.

Four new lines of lamps in six new decorations were brought out in 1901. The #9911 was an antique design in plain crystal and also American Beauty decoration. The #9872 glass lamps came with pictures of the American Girl historically represented from the aboriginal period to the present day, having on the four sides the Indian, Colonial, Revolutionary, and the Twentieth Century girls. This was the start of the Art Nouveau period, and the designs of much of the glass were reflective of it.

The Pennsylvania Glass Industry reports for this period that unskilled boys received a daily wage of $1.95, women $.84, and children $.60 per day.

One cannot write about the Pittsburgh glass era without mentioning the Monongahela House, the city's finest hotel. Originally built in 1840 overlooking the Monongahela River, it was destroyed by the great fire of 1845, in which one third of Pittsburgh was destroyed. A new and finer hotel was built on the same site. In the past it had been a meeting house for both presidents and peddlers. The rise of the custom of holding an annual exhibit of glassware originated with the Co-Operative Flint Glass Co. in 1888. A veteran salesman, W. T. Ranney, held the show alone twice a year for a couple of years, until other glass firms began to follow suit. During the Depression of 1892, the twice-a-year exhibits were cut to once a year, held in January of each following year. The exhibits of virtually all glassware manufacturers would then be held during the months of January and February, allowing all the buyers from the U.S. and foreign countries ample time to make the journey to see firstland the glassmakers' latest lines.

Around the turn of the century, there was a movement started in the U.S. to restrict the employment of children in industry, but by 1901 it had not gained enough support to make such employment illegal.

The gradual failure of the natural gas supply in the Indiana gas belt was a serious concern to many manufacturers of glass. However, the management of the U.S.G.C. had foreseen this possibility had previously installed gas producers fueled with coal.

In 1901 the public demand for thin blown glassware with needle etchings had increased to the point where the company found it necessary to add several furnaces to those which were already producing this variety of glassware. In general, every department of the industry was showing a uniform increase in business and all the factoies of the U.S.G.C. were running at their full capacity.

A paragraph in the April 15, 1902 issue of "Illustrated Glass & Pottery World" advises how the newer patterns were being accepted by the public:

"The Chicago office of the U.S.G.C. reports good business on their new #15077 Michigan pattern. This is certainly one of the neatest designs shown in town and with the Sunrise decoration it makes a quick seller. The quality of the material used in this line is exceptionally clear and the workmanship good. The #15078 Manhattan pattern, plain and with Sunrise decoration is also proving a winner. The #15075 Nevada pattern is also a new pattern produced in both plain and with enamel decoration. They are also putting out fine new designs in lamps with burned in decorations."

In January of 1903, there was a bill before the Pennsylvania Legislature prohibiting the employment of persons under the age of eighteen in factories at night and those under sixteen in the daytime. The glass manufacturers were very concerned. Previously the minimum age was thirteen and even then it was often difficult to get enough juvenile help. Boys were considered an absolute necessity in glass factories and when a proposition would be made to establish a new plant in any locality, the question of the availability of young boys was foremost in the mind of management.

A meeting of the glass manufacturers was held in Pittsburgh in February, 1903, and strong resolutions were adopted against the proposed bill. A committee of three, consisting of President Ripley, John Ralston of Cunningham & Co., and James Morrison of the Fidelity Glass Co. were appointed to go to Harrisburg and use their influence to prevent passage of the bill. At the Pennsylvania Legislature, Mr. Ripley argued that the adoption of the bill would place manufacturers of Pennsylvania at a serious disadvantage in competing with those states where no such restrictions were imposed. It was also pointed out that many families were dependent upon their boys for an income, and that these boys should not be deprived of the opportunity to learn a good trade. Mr. Ripley and his associates must have been convincing as the bill was defeated.

In July, 1903, however, a law was passed in Pennsylvania raising the age limit for compulsory school attendance from fifteen to sixteen years of age. The old law was in many cases evaded, but the new one called for a fine against the manufacturer if caught hiring youths to work during school hours. Where one proposed bill on child labor had failed, the end result was the same with the new law on compulsory school attendance.

As a result of more widely distributed prosperity of the past few years, parents were not compelled to put their children to work at as early an age as they used to and this also helped to make the available supply of youthful labor more scarce.

During the year 1903 insects were the fad when it came to glass and pottery design. Katydids and grasshoppers were used the most, and the cutters of the U.S.G.C. cut these designs into thousands of pieces of thin blown ware which were shipped to all points of the globe.

Five new patterns were added to the States series during 1903 and as in the past found instant customer acceptance.

An article in the Feb. 1904 issue of "Glass and Potter World" gives us some information on the National Glass Co. which was one of the more aggressive competitors of the U.S.G.C. "The American Flint Glass Workers Union has ordered a general strike against the factories operated by the National Glass Co," No reason was given as to the difficulty between the management of this large glass combine and the AFGW Union.

The glass periodical February, 1904 "China Glass & Pottery Review" advises us of further problems of the National Glass Co. "The National Glass Co. of Pittsburgh known as the "Glass Trust" has dissolved. Each factory will hereafter be operated separately." Originally this combine consisted of twenty-one factories, but at the time of dissolution, there were only 8 members. The National Glass Co. had also been organized with too many top management, over paid executives, but unlike the USG Co., failed to reduce this financial burden. This was the chief contributing factor to the failure of this combine.

The new wave of prosperity which had been passing over the United States during the early 1900's found the customers demanding more expensive products. Fancy cut glass, art glass, and the more expensive decorations in pressed glass were finding favor with the woman of the house, and there appeared to be money abundant to gratify this demand for luxuries.

Again we note a paragraph in the glass periodical, Sept. 1904 issue of "Glass & Pottery World."

"The annual report of the U.S.G.C. recently made public was an excellent showing. No concern was ever more liberal with its employees. Numerous instances of financial aid to salesmen under special circumstances have filtered into the trade gossip, and the loyalty among the force is proverbial. There is a touch of human interest prevailing every root and branch of this big corporation."

In Feb., 1904, the company brought out a new pattern #15088 *Panama,* in recognition of the new independent republic. The United States immediately recognized the new government and concluded with it a treaty for the construction of the Panama Canal.

Pressed glass baskets were among the latest acquisitions to the U.S.G.C. output for 1905. They were made in six sizes from five to twelve inches and were in the long popular *Illinois* pattern, which was first produced in 1897. While most of the pieces possessed handles, others were left without them, being designed for the use of wire frames.

The winter of 1905-1906 was a very severe one, closing roads and rail traffic. Heavy snow and rains occasioned by floods kept the salesmen of the U.S.G.C. from visiting the larger cities. The weather also kept the buyers, especially from the Mid-Western and the Western states, from attending the annual exhibition of glassware at the Monongahela House, Pittsburgh, Pa. Because of cold weather, factory production was also cut to a minimum, which caused additional hardships on the workers.

The demand for ruby stained ware for 1907 did not diminish, and new patterns brought out by the company decorated in that manner gained new prestige with new and old customers alike.

In June, 1907 another novelty was added to the 20,000 or more different glassware articles produced by the company. It was the Teddy Bear plate. President Theodore (Teddy) Roosevelt's portrait occupied the center of the plate and around the border were pictured smaller Teddy bears. They were depicted in golf attire, the battlefield, the tennis court and other equally strenuous surroundings. The plate measured 7¾" by 10⅜" and was in great demand at that time. This novelty is in even greater demand today.

Since the early 1900's the master cutters of the U.S.G.C. Tiffin, Ohio factory had been producing brilliant cut glass and rich lead crystal with a silvery ringing tone. The employees at Tiffin objected to a statement made in the January 1907 issue of "Glass & Pottery World", saying that they cut a short line of cut glass. At that time they were running twenty-four cutting frames and could not keep up with the demand for their wares, which was chiefly for table use. The cuttings were refreshingly different from anything that was being shown by the exclusive cut glass factories. A trade note advises that the prices were popular, yet there was no slighting of work or finish down to the minutest detail. The cut glass bowl illustrated on page 25 demonstrates the merit of the deep cuttings and the handsome design.

At the Conference between the American Flint Glass Workers Union and the National Association of Manufacturers of Pressed and Blown Glassware held in March, 1908 at Pittsburgh, the former arbitrary summer shutdown was eliminated. This closing down of glass factories had lasted from six to eight weeks in the past and had always been a bone of contention between the owners and the workmen. The depression in the glassware business had thrown nearly 50% of the glass workers out of work, so that when business did revive the AFGW did not stand on old precedents. The U.S.G.C. was not affected by this decision as they had expressed the desire to eliminate the summer shutdown in 1893, and this was one of the items of dispute that brought on the strike of three and one-half years duration. The remaining pressed and blown glassware factories had accomplished in 1908 what the U.S.G.C. had resolved in 1893.

The depressed conditions of the table glassware business had been partly the result of the closing of several National Glass Co. factories which had large amounts of finished stock which was cast on the market by this bankrupt concern. Instructions to sell regardless of value had a demoralizing effect on the market. As a result of these conditions the U.S.G.C. turned its attention to another branch of the glass business, thus catching their competitors "off guard." This was indicated by a paragraph in the "Glass & Pottery World," August, 1908:

"Either the soda drinking habit has increased this summer or the U.S.G.C. has encroached upon some other fellows trade. The company sale of glassware adaptable for sundaes, ice cream, sodas, phosphates and the like has never been so heavy."

The spread of the prohibition movement in 1908-1909 had a disastrous effect on the bar glassware business, and the U.S.G.C. was greatly affected by the reduction of income from this trade.

Being a diversified company, they turned their attention to a new line of pressed glass. Pattee Cross, Puritan, Solar, Bullseye & Daisy, and Palm Beach, shown vividly decorated in their 1909 catalogue, all found favorable customer acceptance.

At the eighteenth annual board meeting of the U.S.G.C. on August 19, 1909, President Daniel C. Ripley was succeeded by Joseph A. Knox, of the Fidelity Title & Trust Co. of Pittsburgh. A year before, Mr. William McKelvey, the largest holder of U.S.G.C. stock, died and his heirs were not pleased with the management of the company. The McKelvey estate had been placed in the hands of the trust company, of which Mr. Knox was one of the directors.

It was shortly thereafter that Mr. Ripley resigned from the company. He established a new glassware factory at Connellsville, Pa., which produced a fine grade of pressed and blown glass including all kinds of tableware and specialties. His son, D. A. Ripley, superintendent of Factory "F", also resigned so that he could take charge of his father's new plant at Connellsville.

In 1910, the U.S.G.C. brought out many new patterns which they arranged into assortments. These were known as "Glorious", "Four Beauties", "Four Charmers", and "Big Success", the latter consisting of plain ware. There were also three new etched patterns, known as the "Baroness", "Duchess", and "Empress", each comprising of a long line of stemware and tumblers.

In this year, the U.S.G.C. was operating the following factories:

FACTORY A — Lead Blown Tumblers
FACTORY B — Lamps & Tableware
FACTORY C — Decorating Plant
FACTORY D — Gold Decorating Plant
FACTORY E — Common Tumblers & Jellies
FACTORY F — Jars & Specialties
FACTORY G — High Grade Tableware (Glassport)
FACTORY H — Fancy Deep Etched Ware
FACTORY K — Pressed Tumblers, Mugs & Stemware
FACTORY R — Lead-Blown Tumblers, Stemware, Cut Glass
FACTORY U — Pressed Tumblers, Beer Mugs, Jellies, Tableware

During 1910 a brand new factory was being built at the Glassport complex which was known as Factory "O" and a decorating shop which was known as factory "N". Not to confuse our readers we have underlined the factories that were operating in 1910 which were *added* by the U.S.G.C. These were not the same ones that originated the company in 1891.

The U.S.G.C. would continue to be in business for another 63 years and produced many of the collectable glassware patterns of today. Marble glass, carnival, irridescent, and stretch glass were all produced in later years, and the company would experiment with glass equaling that of Tiffany. The cut and etched glass of the Tiffin factory and the hand painted lamps with the reverse paintings on the shades are all sought by collectors today.

The United States Glass Company

1891 Catalogue, Metropolitan Museum of Art

FACTORY F—Ripley & Co., Pittsburgh, Pa.

PAVONIA
ROANOKE
WYANDOTTE
MASCOTTE
GREEK PATTERN ("Diagonal Band & Fan")
DAKOTA

FACTORY H—Hobbs Glass Co., Wheeling, W. Va.

TREE OF LIFE—lampshades & fingerbowls
WINDOWS—#333 in six colors
CRYSTALINA—#334
BULBOUS BASE OPTIC—#346, also engraved
SEAWEED—#346, 2 sizes of celery vases, (regular and smaller hotel), water bottle

FACTORY J—Columbia Glass Co., Findlay, Ohio

POINTED JEWELS—"Long Diamond" toy set
DOUBLE EYE HOBNAIL
RADIANT

FACTORY K—King Glass Co., Pittsburgh, Pa.

KING'S #500—goblet is plain in the bowl, with pattern in the stem, also wine; a **complete** service is shown
FINE CUT & BLOCK—only stemware is shown; #25 pattern cordial, wine, claret, champagne, goblet
ABC PLATE—tiny size with an elephant

FACTORY L—O'Hara Glass Co., Pittsburgh, Pa.

COLUMN BLOCK—#500 pattern
DAISY IN DIAMOND—#725 pattern
CORDOVA—including an ink well
CHANDELIER—originally called "Crown Jewel"
LENS & STAR—#870 pattern; berries are oddities
DAISY & BUTTON—originally called "Florentine" or "Tycoon"
RETICULATED CORD—#600 pattern, shown in a bowl
STRAIGHT HUBER—#9 pattern, complete set
NOVELTIES:
    a. "Finecut" slipper
    b. Toboggan shaped salts, celery & olive dish

FACTORY M—Bellaire Goblet Co., Findlay, Ohio

QUEEN'S NECKLACE—#101 pattern, in all shapes, including a cruet, pickle jar & colognes (8 or 12 oz. bottles)
BELLAIRE—#91 pattern
STARS & BARS—#373 pattern, 3½ oz. cologne, 5½ oz. cruet, 8 oz. catsup, spice set, covered mustard, 4 sizes of mugs
LOG & STAR—#600 pattern, shown in rare 6 oz. oil cruet, bitter bottle, covered pickle jar, and very rare "pickle and olive" caster set
WINES AND GOBLETS:
    a. Panelled Jewels—#259 pattern
    b. Diagonal Block Band—#410 pattern

FACTORY O—Central Glass Co., Wheeling, W. Va.

RECLINING HORSE Ink Well
Mostly shows etched and plain blown stemware, bar ware, and tumblers; Cruets in "PRESSED DIAMOND" & "PRESSED SWIRL"

FACTORY P—DOYLE & CO., Pittsburgh, Pa.

TRIPLE TRIANGLE—#76 pattern
RED BLOCK—#250 pattern
HOBNAIL WITH THUMBPRINT—#150 pattern
HOBNAIL WITH FAN TOP—also #150 pattern
#65 PATTERN—Previously unlisted pattern

FACTORY R—Beatty & Sons, Tiffin, O.

DAISY & BUTTON WITH V-BAND
Mostly Bar Ware, including:
    a. "Grover Cleveland" etched tumbler
    b. "Garfield" etched tumbler
    c. "Blaine" etched tumbler

BIBLIOGRAPHY REFERENCES

B — Barrett, Richard C.   "Popular American Ruby-Stained Pattern Glass"   Forward's Color Productions, Inc., Manchester, Vt.

H1 — Heacock, William
H2
H3
H4   "Encyclopedia of Victorian Colored Pattern Glass" Volumes 1, 2, 3 & 4   Antique Publications Marietta, Ohio 45750

HTP — Heacock, William   "1000 Toothpick Holders"   Antique Publications Marietta, O. 45750

K — Kamm, Minnie W.   Series of 8 books on Pattern Glass   Kamm Publications, Grosse Pt., Mich.

LPG — Lee, Ruth Webb   "Early American Pressed Glass"   Lee Publications, Wellesley Hills, Mass.

LVG — Lee, Ruth Webb   "Victorian Glass"

M1 — Metz, Alice H.   "Early American Pattern Glass"   Author

M2 — Metz, Alice H.   "Much More Early American Pattern Glass"

MD1 — Millard, S.T.
MD2   "Goblets 1" and "Goblets 2"   Wallace-Homestead Des Moines, Iowa

PS — Peterson, Arthur   "Glass Salt Shakers 1,000 Patterns"   Wallace-Homestead Co., Des Moines, Iowa

PP — Peterson, Arthur   "Glass Patents and Patterns"   Celery City Printing, Sanford, Fla.

R — Revi, Albert C.   "American Pressed Glass & Figure Bottles"   Thomas Nelson, Inc. New York, N.Y.

S — Smith, Don E.   "Findlay Pattern Glass"   Gray Printing Co., Fostoria, Ohio

U1 — Unitt, Doris & Peter
U2   "American & Canadian Goblets" "American & Canadian Goblets," Volume II   Clock House Petersborough, Ont., Can.

MORE CORRECTIONS AND ADDITIONS TO BOOK II

PATTERN	NOTES	PAGE
PALM BEACH	An opalescent jelly compote was made also	22
SUNBURST-ON-SHIELD	A water set can now be confirmed	23
WIDE STRIPE	See notes below	46

MORE ADDITIONS AND CORRECTIONS TO BOOK III

PATTERN	NOTES	PAGE
ALBA	Also made in a berry set	14
AZTEC MEDALLION	Also made in sapphire blue and in opalescent white; reported in a miniature lamp and salt shaker (Peterson called this *Stippled Acanthus)*	15
BULGING MIDRIFF	Can be confirmed in blue now	17
CURRIER & IVES	Also made in milk glass	22
DAISY & BUTTON WITH THUMBPRINT	Also made in vaseline	22
FAMOUS	Rare in blue	23
FERN, INVERTED	Also made in a salt shaker	24
GARGOYLE	Reported in green slag	25
GUTTATE	Am investigating reports of reproductions in the cranberry and cranberry cased colors (shiny and satin finih)	27
PRESSED OCTAGON	Also made in milk glass	36
SCROLL AND NET	Also made in red satin	40
STRIPE, WIDE	Figures 295 and 296 were made by Nickel Plate Glass, at Fostoria, Ohio; also made in several shape water pitchers, creamer & open sugar, mustard, barber bottle, bottle, pomade and finger bowl	42
ESTHER	A rare syrup pitcher was also made	55
MISSOURI	A syrup was indeed also made	56
CATHERINE ANN	Syrup at top left of page 84 is this pattern (#387)	84

ADDITIONS AND CORRECTIONS TO BOOK 4

PATTERN	NOTES	PAGE
LOUIS XV	This pattern also made in a toothpick holder, which is very, very rare (see 1000 TH)	30
SPOOL	This is not Northwood—actually made by Atterbury & Company, circa 1885, originally called "Reeded"	35
FLUTE	This is not the "Flute" pattern, but the "Fenton Blackberry" compote	35
PUNTY BAND	Also made in a custard tumbler, usually souvenired	41
GEORGIA GEM	Rare in ruby-stained crystal	44
TARENTUM'S VICTORIA	Also made in green with gold and in crystal	45
CANE INSERT	Also made in a very rare celery vase—no toothpick holder or salt shakers known	46
HONEYCOMB (393)	No longer believe this to be McKee—it is most likely a U.S. Glass pattern	52
DELAWARE	A butter dish in "ivory" can now be confirmed (shown in this Book 5)	54
HARVARD	I failed to mention this pattern was made by Tarentum Glass Co., circa 1900—also made in open sugar & creamer	54
SERENADE MUG	See "1000 TH" for another example of Greentown glass in custard color, "Wild Rose with Bowknot"	55
RINGS & BEADS	Also made in a water set (pitcher is plain)	55
LOUIS XV	Also made with garish brown staining (see 1000 TH)	57
BLUEBIRDS	This is Fenton glass—has "Bearded Berry" pattern on reverse side of bowl	57
PRAYER RUG	This is Fenton, not Imperial	57
CHRYSANTHEMUM	Believe this was made by Fostoria Glass, not Fenton—at least the molds came from Fostoria originally	58
BULGING TEARDROP	The text should read "the holder . . . is **not** original"	58
GRAPE & GOTHIC ARCHES	Also made in green with gold and in carnival glass; Custard also found with fired-on staining of purple grapes and green leaves	33

INDEX

*N.I. — Not illustrated

—have you missed *any* of these books on **Victorian Colored Pattern Glass** by William Heacock?

SAME BIG 8-1/2" x 11" FORMAT

4 MORE GREAT VOLUMES OF FASCINATING READING!

(with additional volumes forthcoming)

ENCYCLOPEDIA OF VICTORIAN COLORED PATTERN GLASS, Book I — Toothpick Holders from A to Z (Edition 2)

67 pgs., 38 full color plates in vivid detail, comprehensive research data, complete information on patterns and their makers, line drawings, information on reproductions and how to avoid them, early ad & catalogue reprints, bibliography, index, no repetition of any toothpicks shown in **"1000 Toothpick Holders."** $9.95
Accompanying price guide $1.00

ENCYCLOPEDIA OF VICTORIAN COLORED PATTERN GLASS, BOOK II — Opalescent Glass from A to Z (Edition 2)

119 pgs., 44 in brilliant color, detailed research findings on hundreds of opalescent glass patterns, comprehensive historical data, line drawings, early ad reprints, illustrations of opalescent glass reproductions, bibliography, listing of corrections & additions to text of Book I, complete index, much much more $12.95
Accompanying price guide . . . . $ 1.00

ENCYCLOPEDIA OF VICTORIAN COLORED PATTERN GLASS, Book III — Syrups, Sugar Shakers & Cruets from A to Z

96 pgs., 51 in glorious color, detailed research data on same page as accompanying illustrations, bibliography, historical data, dozens of catalogue and ad reprints (some in their original color), listing of corrections and additions to texts of Books I & II, index to first three volumes $12.95
Accompanying price guide . . . . $ 1.00

ENCYCLOPEDIA OF VICTORIAN COLORED PATTERN GLASS, Book IV — Custard Glass from A to Z (over 500 items pictured in detail)

68 pgs., 48 in vivid color, in-depth research into early custard glass production, text on same page as illustrations, featured information on Northwood's production — including color close-ups of glass shards unearthed at his Indiana, Pa. factory site, catalogue and ad reprints (some in color), listing of further corrections and additions to earlier volumes $12.95
Accompanying price guide . . . . $ 1.00

How about our handy pocket guide?
VICTORIAN COLORED GLASS — PATTERNS AND PRICES —

136 pgs., in full color, an abridged version of Books 1, 2 and 3 of the "Encyclopedia of Victorian Colored Pattern Glass" in a handy pocket size, easy to carry in pocket or purse for carrying to auctions and flea markets, updated prices yearly, no separate price guide, prices on same page as illustration, index $8.95

Another Great Toothpick Holder Book!
1000 TOOTHPICK HOLDERS —

112 pgs., 6" x 9" format, over 1,000 toothpick holders listed, mostly in beautiful closeup color, this superb publication not only illustrates and identifies colored pattern glass, but also art glass, fine china, figurals, pressed crystal, cut glass, silverplate and bisque, sponsored by National Toothpick Holder Collectors' Society $10.95
Accompanying price guide . . . . $ 1.00

ORDER THESE PRICELESS FULL-SIZE VOLUMES
FROM YOUR FAVORITE BOOK DEALER
Or send the handy order blank on the back of this
page with check or money order to:

ANTIQUE PUBLICATIONS
P.O. Box 655   Marietta, Ohio 45750

Encyclopedia of Victorian Colored Pattern Glass

by William Heacock

- -

PLEASE RUSH ME THE FOLLOWING BOOKS!
—with my satisfaction guaranteed

ENCYCLOPEDIA OF VICTORIAN COLORED PATTERN GLASS
Book 1 (Toothpicks) @ 9.95 (Hardbound—$13.95)................_____
Book 2 (Opalescent Glass) @ 12.95 (Hardbound—$16.95).........._____
Book 3 (Syrups, etc.) @ 12.95 (Hardbound—$16.95).............._____
Book 4 (Custard Glass) @ 12.95 (Hardbound—$16.95)............_____
Book 5 (U.S. Glass) @ 14.95 (Hardbound—$18.95)..............._____
1000 TOOTHPICK HOLDERS (A Collectors Guide) @ $10.95....._____
Updated Price Guides for each of the above ($1 each)..............._____
VICTORIAN COLORED GLASS I (Patterns & Prices)@ $8.95....._____

TOTAL AMOUNT ENCLOSED.................................

Name_____

Address_____

City/State_____

_____

Zip Code_____

ANTIQUE PUBLICATIONS, P.O. Box 655, Marietta, Ohio 45750